Great American Events on Stage

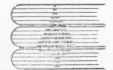

Great American Events on Stage

15 Plays to Celebrate America's Past

Edited by
Sylvia E. Kamerman

Publishers   PLAYS, INC.   Boston

Great American events on stage : 15 plays to celebrate America's past / edited by Sylvia E. Kamerman.
   p. cm.
   Summary: Dramatic adaptations of fifteen events in American history, including the American Revolution, the Civil War, and immigration.
   ISBN 0-8238-0305-8 (pbk.)
   1.   United States–History–Juvenile drama.   2. Children's plays, American.   3. One-act plays, American. [1. United States–History–Drama. 2. Plays.]   I. Kamerman, Sylvia E.
PS627.H55G74   1996
812.008'0358–dc20   96-32197
                                    CIP
                                      AC

Manufactured in Canada

CONTENTS

Great American
Events on Stage

Cornerstone of Civil Rights

by Julian E. Miranda

Colonists at Jamestown speak out for freedom . . . .

Characters

TWO NARRATORS
TOM KENT, *Chairman of the House of Burgesses*
JOHN FLETCHER ⎫
JAMES BAKER ⎬ *Burgesses*
OTHER BURGESSES, *extras*
THREE SOLDIERS
JAN ⎫
STEFAN ⎪
THEODORE ⎬ *Polish colonists*
HEDI ⎪
PETER ⎪
NINA ⎭
ANNA ⎫ *German colonists*
FRANZ ⎭
MARCO ⎫ *Venetian colonists*
STELLA ⎭
OTHER COLONISTS, *extras*
SIR GEORGE YEARDLEY, *Governor of Virginia*

3

SCENE 1

BEFORE RISE: TWO NARRATORS *enter in front of curtain and speak to audience.*

1ST NARRATOR: We all know that the settlement of Jamestown in 1607 was a most meaningful event in American history—it was the first permanent English settlement in what is now the United States. But it was important for other reasons, too, which we might not all be aware of.

2ND NARRATOR: Most textbooks describe Jamestown as a completely English settlement. Actually, that was not the case. From its very start, Jamestown was a tiny "nation of immigrants." Among the racial and ethnic groups living in Jamestown at the time were Englishmen and Native Americans, Africans, Swiss, Italians, Germans, and others.

1ST NARRATOR: That makes Jamestown a lot like a modern American city. Had you been on its streets in 1619, you could have heard many languages and accents. Have you ever thought of Jamestown as that kind of place—a place like New York or Cleveland or San Francisco?

2ND NARRATOR: Do you know that Jamestown experienced the first civil rights demonstration ever to take place in America? It was a demonstration conducted mostly by Polish workers and soldiers, some of whom had come from Europe to Virginia in the very first ships and all of whom had contributed greatly to the life of the colony at every level.

1ST NARRATOR: We do not know the exact details of the demonstration, but we know that it actually happened. Let us try to imagine what it may have been like. (*Curtains open.*)

* * *

TIME: *1619.*

SETTING: *Meeting room of the Virginia House of Burgesses, in Jamestown. A lectern is up right and chairs for the Burgesses face it at an angle down left.*

AT RISE: TOM KENT *is standing at lectern, addressing assembly.* JOHN FLETCHER *and* JAMES BAKER *sit in front row,*

with OTHER BURGESSES *filling in chairs behind them.*
THREE SOLDIERS *guard the door.*

2ND NARRATOR: We are in a meeting room of the Virginia
House of Burgesses, the first representative assembly in
America. Let's watch and listen. (TWO NARRATORS *join*
BURGESSES.)

TOM KENT: Well, gentlemen, English law and liberty have
come to Jamestown. The London company has issued instruc-
tions to our new Governor, Sir George Yeardley, that we shall
have a voice in our own governance.

JOHN FLETCHER: What does that mean?

KENT: It means that the rights of men under English law in the
Mother Country will now be available to Englishmen here. It
also means that we may elect a representative assembly to
make laws.

JAMES BAKER: Who will elect this assembly? Who will be
allowed to vote?

KENT: All free Englishmen, seventeen years of age and up-
ward. Those are the requirements—to be English and a man.

ALL (*Ad lib*): Hurrah! Long live King James! Long live freedom
for all Englishmen! (*Etc.* KENT *bangs gavel for silence.*)

KENT: Well, gentlemen, it is my suggestion that we adjourn for
today and celebrate our new freedom. (*There is a commotion
offstage. Shouting is heard. Then* JAN, STEFAN, *and* PETER
appear in doorway.)

JAN: What about us?

STEFAN: We, too, wish to have a voice in government!

1ST SOLDIER (*Stepping forward and barring their way*): You
cannot come in. This is a closed session.

PETER: We must have a say in the laws that govern us!

2ND SOLDIER (*Firmly*): You are not Englishmen—and only
Englishmen have the right to participate in this assembly.
You must leave. (SOLDIERS *push* JAN, STEFAN, *and* PE-
TER *out.*)

FLETCHER (*Shaking his head*): Those troublesome foreigners
again—those colonists from Poland, Italy, and Germany.

BAKER (*Incensed*): Are they not satisfied to be allowed to come and live here and work with us? This is an *English* settlement!

FLETCHER: This is a great piece of insolence.

BURGESSES (*Ad lib*): Yes, such insolence! What are they thinking? So unreasonable. (*Etc. Suddenly*, JAN, STEFAN, THEODORE, PETER, ANNA, FRANZ, MARCO, HEDI, NINA, STELLA *and* OTHER COLONISTS *burst into room, carrying tools.* SOLDIERS *try to restrain them.*)

3RD SOLDIER: Stand back! Disperse!

KENT (*Loudly, to crowd*): What right have you to break into this meeting? (JAN *steps forward and crowd grows quiet.*)

JAN (*Proudly*): I have the same right as any other man in Jamestown. Indeed, my rights are greater—for I have worked harder and have been here longer than most of you. I came from Poland on one of the first ships.

HEDI: We are not Englishmen, but we work hard. We are shipbuilders, carpenters, sailmakers. We are an important part of this settlement.

STEFAN: Captain John Smith himself told me he would rather have a few such as we than a hundred lazy, indolent gentlemen who make nothing but trouble. Yet any idler may have rights I do not possess because he is from England and I am from Poland.

KENT (*Hotly*): How dare you come here and make demands upon us and criticize those who are better than you!

THEODORE (*Loudly*): We make demands because we do the work of the colony.

PETER: Our contributions to this settlement are great, and we should have a say in how it is run.

FLETCHER (*Sarcastically*): The next thing you know, the Germans and the Italians and the indentured servants will be looking for a vote.

FRANZ (*Proudly*): Yes! I am Franz, a German, and I am here with my Polish and Italian friends. The Swiss are with us, too. We all work and struggle here. It is not just Englishmen who have built Jamestown. The Venetians who are here make glass; those who make tar and pitch, those who build houses, have rights. A man should be judged for himself and his gift to this settlement, not by his nation.

ANNA: I am Anna, Franz's wife. I did not come to Jamestown to be the wife of a man who will be ruled by others merely because he is from a different country than they.

KENT (*Matter-of-factly*): The London merchants and the King have agreed that only Englishmen shall have the right to vote in Jamestown. No others!

MARCO (*Angrily*): I am a glassmaker from Venice. It was because of John and Sebastian Cabot, Italians like me, that King James has some claim to this land. Did not we Venetians plant our own flag together with the English flag on these shores? Without other Italians—Columbus, the Cabots and Amerigo Vespucci—would any of you be here?

KENT (*Annoyed*): Soldiers, get these men out!

BAKER: Yes, call up the militia and get these men out! (*There is movement and angry shouting among* BURGESSES. SOLDIERS *advance on* COLONISTS.)

STEFAN (*Hotly*): Very well, then! Very well! If we cannot vote, we will not work. From this time forth we will lay down our tools! Let us see how well you do with only men of your own nationality. No vote—no work!

BURGESSES (*Ad lib*): Vote, indeed! How dare they! Foreigners! (SOLDIERS *try to crowd* COLONISTS *out.*)

THEODORE (*Shouting over noise*): Build your own ships and make your own tar!

MARCO: Make your own glass!

FRANZ: *Ja! Ja!* Build your own houses.

COLONISTS (*Ad lib*): No vote, no work! Freedom now! (*Etc. They exit, muttering angrily.* BURGESSES *speak together in groups excitedly.* YEARDLEY *enters.*)

FLETCHER (*Seeing him; relieved*): Thank heavens! Here comes Governor Yeardley. (*Others quiet down. Bowing*) Welcome, Your Excellency.

YEARDLEY: Thank you. (*Going to lectern; seriously*) I have heard what has been going on.

BAKER: Those impudent and ungrateful foreigners!

KENT: We'll soon have them on their knees!

YEARDLEY (*Holding up his hands for quiet*): Wait a moment. Let us think about this. Perhaps what they have asked is reasonable.

KENT (*Appalled*): Reasonable? Did we found this colony for others? It is English!

1ST BURGESS: Let me speak! (*Rising; with heartfelt conviction*) Can anyone say that so new a land as this belongs to any one people? To begin with, it truly belongs to the people of John Rolfe's wife, Pocahontas. It was Columbus who brought back news to Europe of a New World. Was he English? No, he was an Italian, sailing under the Spanish flag, with ships manned by men of many races—Spaniards, black men, who knows who else. His charts were the work of Hebrews, Arabs, Greeks— learned men of the whole world. Indeed, it *was* Italians John and Sebastian Cabot who planted our flag here. As for these workers from many lands, one of them even saved the life of Captain John Smith. All have worked and fought bravely.

YEARDLEY (*Nodding*): This man speaks well! Jamestown cannot prosper without labor. These workers are our very lifeblood. (*Pauses, looks around room, then continues seriously*) I will send a petition back, if you are in agreement, to ask the King and the London merchants to allow *all* settlers here to have a vote.

FLETCHER (*Angrily*): Your Lordship, shall we have a vote on this? It will not succeed!

YEARDLEY: No, let us adjourn for today. For I fear that you have not all thought this out. Those people are rightfully angry!

KENT: Gentlemen, there is nothing more to be done here today. Let us adjourn. (*They exit. Curtain.*)

* * * * *

SCENE 2

TIME: *Sometime later.*

SETTING: *Same as Scene 1.*

AT RISE: JAN, STEFAN, THEODORE, HEDI, PETER, NINA, ANNA, FRANZ, MARCO, STELLA, *and* OTHER COLONISTS *stand in groups at left, pantomiming excited discussion. At right are* KENT, FLETCHER, BAKER *and* OTHER BURGESSES *pantomiming discussion.*

JAN (*Wearily*): It has been some time since we laid down our tools. We, too, are suffering. Have we accomplished anything?

STEFAN (*Reassuringly*): Not yet, but if we win, we will have accomplished much. If we lose, we will never truly be free. There is much that is good about Jamestown, but there is much that is bad. We must keep the good and struggle against the evil.

MARCO (*Discouraged*): But I am beginning to feel the pinch. No one buys my wares.

JAN (*With spirit*): But we mustn't give up! We shall never be free if we give up. I would sooner go back and be oppressed in my own country.

HEDI: Well, I wish the matter would get settled. Our lives and the life of the colony have been disrupted.

NINA: When I came from Poland with my husband, I came because he said we would be free here to make a life with no lords and servants, no masters and no serfs. (*With conviction*) We will not settle for less than equality.

JAN (*Smiling*): There will be freedom in America, I am sure of it. (NARRATORS *enter and come forward.*)

1ST NARRATOR: This first chapter in the American struggle for equality and justice for all was only the beginning.

2ND NARRATOR: The struggle would later be expressed in the Declaration of Independence; in our Constitution; in the Emancipation Proclamation, freeing all Americans from slavery; in the Fifteenth Amendment, giving African Americans the right to vote; in the Nineteenth Amendment, allowing women to vote.

1ST NARRATOR: And it goes on, even in our own times. (NAR-
RATORS *move to one side.*)

FLETCHER (*Resigned*): We are going to have to give in to those
protesters. After all, these are people with skills. Our settlement cannot survive without them.

BAKER (*Seriously*): A nation cannot just be composed of one
kind or class of people. Nationality or education does not make
one person better than another—merely different.

KENT (*Looking off*): Here comes Governor Yeardley! (YEARD-
LEY *enters.*)

YEARDLEY (*Gravely*): Gentlemen, not only must this colony
succeed for our sake, but it must succeed because truly we
are founding a nation. Without the work of these men from
many lands, we will not be able to survive. Therefore . . .

KENT (*Eagerly*): Therefore, I will hear a motion that these men
be allowed to vote! (YEARDLEY *smiles, taken aback.*)

BURGESSES: We second it! Aye, aye!

YEARDLEY (*To protesting group; enthusiastically*): Citizens of
Jamestown! (*Led by* JAN, *they move toward* YEARDLEY.)
Gentlemen, you have won your great fight. You shall have the
full privileges and rights of all citizens of Jamestown.

ALL (*Ad libbing*): Long live freedom! Long live Jamestown! (*The
two groups mingle, shaking hands.* NARRATORS *come down
center as curtains close behind them.*)

1ST NARRATOR: Thus, the non-English colonists were successful in the first civil rights demonstration on these shores.

2ND NARRATOR: A great precedent was set by our first citizens from Poland and the other protesters—that all men shall
have equal rights under the law.

THE END

Production Notes

CORNERSTONE OF CIVIL RIGHTS

Characters: 14 male; 3 female; 2 male or female for Narrators; as many male and female extras as desired for Burgesses and Colonists.

Playing Time: 20 minutes.

Costumes: Seventeenth-century Colonial dress. Women wear long skirts and kerchiefs, men wear dark clothes. Governor wears cloak and sword. Soldiers carry pikes and wear military dress. Colonists carry tools and other implements.

Properties: Gavel.

Setting: Meeting room of the Virginia House of Burgesses. A lectern is up right and chairs for Burgesses are set in rows facing it, down left. Door is at left.

Lighting: No special effects.

The Printer on Queen Street

by Grace Alicia Mayr

Young Benjamin Franklin strikes out on his own . . . .

Characters

NARRATOR
BENJAMIN FRANKLIN, *17*
JAMES FRANKLIN, *his brother, 26*
JOSIAH FRANKLIN, *their father*
GILLIAM ⎫
PIERS ⎬ *apprentices*
PATRICK ⎭
JOHN COLLINS
NICHOLAS SCUDDER
DANIEL, *12*

NARRATOR: It is Thursday, September 23, 1723. The cloud-shrouded, watery sun barely peeks over the eastern horizon of Boston Harbor when through the door of a print shop comes 17-year-old Benjamin Franklin. He wears a leather apron and carries a bundle of *New England Courant* newspapers. Two apprentices, Gilliam and Piers, in homespun shirts and knee breeches, wait outside the shop for copies of the *Courant* to deliver to subscribers. This weekly newspaper was established two years ago by London-trained master-printer James

12

Franklin, Benjamin's older brother. Because of James's publication of articles criticizing the clergy and other town officials, and because of his refusal to divulge the identity of his daring contributors, in January of this year James was arrested for a second time and forbidden to publish. Since then the *Courant* has been published over the name of Benjamin Franklin.

Now, as Benjamin shifts the newspapers from his shoulder, he sniffs at the tangy, salty sea breeze.

BENJAMIN: I can fairly taste that fog coming in. Stand aside, Piers. I'm dropping your stack to the cobbles. There you are, for the north side. Gilliam, there's your bundle for the south side. The third stack is Patrick's for the waterfront subscribers. Where *is* that boy?

GILLIAM: I'm sure he'll be along soon, Ben.

PIERS: May we have the morning off, after we finish deliveries, Ben?

GILLIAM (*Eagerly*): Other printers' apprentices have Thursday morning free-time—

BENJAMIN: All right, but stay out of fights and taverns and get to the boarding house for dinner on time or watch out for James's heavy hand.

GILLIAM: I've felt the master's hand too often already.

PIERS: Who hasn't, eh, Ben?

BENJAMIN (*Sighing*): To my sorrow, my brother outranks me in size and strength, and too often he forgets we are brothers.

GILLIAM: He treats you ill, Ben. You, acting as publisher and all, should have proper respect from him.

BENJAMIN: My brother and I have had our differences in the past, but of late I admit, matters grow worse between us.

GILLIAM: At least the master should see that you're fed a good dinner at the boarding house.

PIERS: 'Tis so, Ben. You shouldn't have to eat your dinner here and mind the shop mid-days.

BENJAMIN (*Lightly*): That's an arrangement of my own choice, lads. For a while I ate those big heavy meals with the others until I made a bargain with James—a bargain he well liked.

GILLIAM: And the master's not easy to please!

BENJAMIN: I offered to board myself for half what the boarding house charged him for my dinner. James snapped up my offer.

PIERS: The master's no fool!

BENJAMIN: I taught myself to prepare nourishing food—boiled potatoes or rice, a hasty pudding, and I spend the other half of what James gives me on books.

PIERS: You spend half your dinner money on books!

BENJAMIN: Reading makes a full man. I'm willing to read half my dinner.

PIERS: I'd rather be full of meat and a good big sweet afterward.

BENJAMIN: You can have your roast beef and cider, and slug through the afternoon with a full belly and a dull brain. Here alone, I eat my light repast—a biscuit or a slice of bread, a handful of raisins, and a glass of water. Then I have the rest of the time till you return for study with a clear head and the quicker apprehension because of my temperate eating and drinking.

GILLIAM (*Amused*): You're a rare bird, Ben. There never was and there'll never be another like you.

BENJAMIN: There are those who would rejoice at that thought! (*They laugh. Impatiently*) Now, where *is* Patrick? (*Calling loudly*) Patrick!

PATRICK (*As if from a distance*): Coming, Ben. (*Breathless, but no longer distant*) I'm sorry, Ben. I was—

BENJAMIN (*Knowingly*): I know. You've been down on Long Wharf again, dreaming, watching the ships from distant ports. (*Wistfully*) The wide sea beckons, bewitching us all with its irresistible fascination.

PATRICK: Why, Ben, it sounds as if you've a hankering to follow the sea yourself!

BENJAMIN: Always had, Patrick, but my father wouldn't hear of it. One son—my brother Josiah—lost at sea was enough,

he said, and I must learn a useful trade ashore. But to be free!
I'd love to escape the hemmed-in narrowness of my life here!

PATRICK: Not me. I've a good trade now, so I content myself
with sea-gazing instead of sea-sailing.

BENJAMIN (*Sighing*): Yours, no doubt, is the wise part, Patrick. Contentment makes poor men rich.

PATRICK (*Suddenly*): Oh, I almost forgot. I saw three passengers get off a sloop just in from New York. There was a man,
a lady, young and pretty—his wife, I think—and a boy. The
boy stood there on Long Wharf in his gold-buckled shoes, sur-
veying Boston Town as if he owned the whole of it. The man
looked a gentleman, he did. He called to me, so I ran over,
and guess what he said, right out of the blue, without a will-
you or a won't-you?

BENJAMIN (*Amused*): You'll make a capital newsman, Patrick,
but make it short.

PATRICK: He gave me a message for Mr. Franklin, the printer
on Queen Street!

BENJAMIN (*Thoughtfully*): Whom does James know in New
York?

GILLIAM: Maybe the man has a printing job for us.

PIERS: Or an article for next week's issue or an advertisement.

BENJAMIN: Did he also give you his name, Patrick?

PATRICK: No, but he gave me this Dutch coin, and I'm going
to buy myself a tart from the pastry cook on Pudding Lane.

BENJAMIN: You're never going to get to Pudding Lane or anywhere else if you don't be quick with the message.

PATRICK (*Hurriedly*): The man said, "Tell Mr. Franklin, the
printer on Queen Street, that an old friend will be lodging at
the Green Dragon on Union Street across from the sign of the
Blue Ball, and would welcome his visit."

BENJAMIN: 'Tis someone who knows my father's house at the
sign of the Blue Ball. I must tell James.

GILLIAM: Hist, Ben! (*In fast whisper*) The master stands behind
you now, fire-hot mad as a stuck pig. Come on, Piers. Patrick,
grab your papers.

JAMES (*Angrily*): Tell me what, Benjamin? Say it fast and stop wasting time. You lads—do you think our subscribers are happy to wait for you? Get to work!

GILLIAM (*Urgently*): Hurry along, Piers.

PIERS: I'll see you later on Pudding Lane, Patrick. I've a taste for a bit of pastry myself.

PATRICK: Well, see to it that you have a bit to spend yourself.

JAMES: At last, they're gone. And you, Benjamin, are you too grand to earn your keep? Hustle yourself and get us some new subscribers.

BENJAMIN (*Surprised*): You want me to go about the streets selling subscriptions? Me, the editor and publisher?

JAMES: Someone has to build up our circulation. It's you or I, lad, and who is truly the master-printer in this shop? Inside you go, lazybones, and pick up some copies to distribute as samples.

NARRATOR: Like most Colonial shops, the Franklin print shop has white-washed plaster walls and a wide-beamed pine ceiling. A high desk and a three-legged stool stand in front of the window. The printing press, a large wooden structure, a foot or two taller than a man, stands in the center of the room, dominating the shop. Recently printed sheets hang drying like pieces of laundry. The shelves of the print shop library and the compositor's type box are against the left wall. A door at the rear of the shop leads to an alley. James is sitting on the three-legged stool before his desk. Goose quill in hand, he is working on his books. Benjamin glowers as he noisily assembles additional copies of the *Courant* and stuffs them into the leather pouch slung over his shoulder. The atmosphere is tense with the animosity between the two brothers. Finally James throws down his pen and leaps from the stool.

JAMES: Bah! I'm beset with political enemies who won't let me publish. My financial accounts show heavy loss. And now you give me trouble. Stop thrashing around like a bull-ox. Be off with you!

BENJAMIN: Stop ordering me around like a slave-apprentice!

JAMES: You are legally bound until you're twenty-one by indenture papers you signed yourself.

BENJAMIN: You destroyed those papers, for you knew no apprentice could legally publish a paper.

JAMES: You are conveniently forgetting the second indentures you signed more recently. They're binding.

BENJAMIN: You forced me to sign those. You don't dare let the town officials know there are secret papers! You'd be thrown into jail the minute I let that news out of the bag!

JAMES (*Incredulously*): You dare threaten me—the master—in my own shop!

BENJAMIN: Indisputably, James, this is *your* shop. I can never forget that fact. It's clear that we cannot work together. I must find employment with another printer.

JAMES: Not in Boston, you won't. (*Smugly*) I've talked with all the printers. Not one of them will hire you.

BENJAMIN (*Speaking with difficulty*): This time, James, you have gone too far. Even Papa cannot reconcile me to this blow.

JAMES (*Mockingly*): Go, run and tell Papa.

BENJAMIN (*Hotly*): I will.

JAMES: As long as you're going home, take Papa's copy of today's *Courant* to him.

BENJAMIN: I'll do that. Like you, Papa may have forgotten that my name publishes this paper, not yours!

JAMES (*Angrily*): Benny, I warn you—foot it fast out that door or (*Exhaling loudly*)—he's gone. (*Suddenly calling after* BENJAMIN) What was that message? Ben, come back here!

NARRATOR: But Ben was gone, racing to his father Josiah Franklin's soap and candle shop at the sign of the Blue Ball. Thick fog has begun to roll in as Ben ducks into his father's shop.

JOSIAH (*Pleasantly but firmly*): You have quarreled with James again, Benny. I can tell by the look on your face.

BENJAMIN: Papa, James has gone too far. He dares—

JOSIAH (*Breaking in*): Aye, James dares much. He dares much in the articles he publishes. I know also that James is often

bad-tempered over financial difficulties and seems to take sat-
isfaction in mistreating you. I can arbitrate your differences
to a degree, but you must serve out your apprenticeship, be-
having faithfully to James in all things. It is the law!

BENJAMIN: Is it the law that I should be bound by secret indenture papers?

JOSIAH: James is your brother, Benny, and your master. You
are bound to keep his secrets and protect his interests.

BENJAMIN: Papa, what about *my* interests? I'm blacklisted
with all the printers in town!

JOSIAH: Benny, be patient. Bear with James. How proud I was
when James was in prison and your editorial blazed in fiery
defense of him and his right to publish what he saw fit!

BENJAMIN: Yes, Papa. In this matter I have no quarrel with
James. Wherever I go, all my life, I promise to fight for freedom, not only freedom of the press, but all the rightful free-
doms of man. But now I must fight for myself.

JOSIAH: Benny, only four years are left to your apprenticeship.

BENJAMIN: Four years is too long to wait! I am eager to do
something important—worthy and important. You don't
understand. (*Sighs*) No one does.

NARRATOR: Outside Ben finds the fog has thickened. The sign
over the tavern door across the street, a dragon in hammered
metal, is hardly discernible as a man and a boy step out of
the tavern. The man is Nicholas Scudder, bookseller, and the
boy is Daniel, the twelve-year-old brother of Nicholas Scudder's wife.

NICHOLAS: 'Tis difficult in this fog to know which way to turn,
Daniel. There's someone we can ask. (*Raising his voice*) Hello,
you sir, there! May I beg a favor?

BENJAMIN (*As if distant*): At your service, sir. I'll cross over.

NICHOLAS: Sir, can you direct me to—(*Suddenly*) Benny!
What a stroke of luck!

BENJAMIN (*Confused*): You have the advantage of me, sir.

NICHOLAS: Look closely, Benny. Think back—you were two
years apprenticed to your brother James and hungry for

books, starved for knowledge. I was apprenticed to John Checkley, bookseller. Have you forgotten our little arrangement? You could borrow any book provided you had it back next day before it was missed.

BENJAMIN: Nick! Give me your hand. I can't begin to count the books I borrowed and sat up all night to read. You were my bookish friend in those days.

NICHOLAS: May we always be friends, bookish and otherwise. Benny, this is my wife's brother Daniel. Daniel, this is the friend I told you about.

BENJAMIN: This is a pleasure, Daniel.

DANIEL: Good day to you, Mr. Franklin.

BENJAMIN: Your wife's brother, Nick? You're a married man then. A lot has happened since we last met.

NICHOLAS: Aye, a lot.

BENJAMIN: Where are you headed?

NICHOLAS: I'd like to get to Checkley's book shop, but I'm confused in this fog. That's why I called to you.

BENJAMIN: I'll take you there. Let's walk as we talk.

NICHOLAS: Follow closely behind us, Daniel.

BENJAMIN: Daniel looks a likely lad. He won't lose us. Now, give me your news, Nick.

NICHOLAS: When I finished my apprenticeship, I could find no openings in a Boston book shop, so I sailed to New York. Now, there's a thriving port, bigger than Boston, but no book shop at all, alas!

BENJAMIN: I've heard of a printer in New York, William Bradford.

NICHOLAS: I know him. His son Andrew has a printing establishment in Philadelphia. William Bradford's print shop was next to the goldsmith's shop where I finally found work keeping the accounts.

BENJAMIN: Not very congenial work for you, was it?

NICHOLAS (*Laughing*): On the contrary, most congenial, for the goldsmith had a daughter Anne, and in time he gained a son in me. Anne and I were married in July of this year.

BENJAMIN: You're on a wedding trip!

NICHOLAS: Always the incurable romantic, aren't you, Benny? No, it's not primarily a wedding trip. Anne and I are setting out to make our fortunes. Shortly after we married, Anne's father died. He left everything to Anne and Daniel, but he was heavily in debt. We decided to sell everything, pay off his debts, and open a book shop somewhere else where there is a demand for books, a more literary town.

BENJAMIN (*Concerned*): The competition in Boston will be very keen. I know of ten book shops here now.

NICHOLAS: We're going north to Portsmouth, where cultural interest accompanies commercial activity.

BENJAMIN: Then why stop off in Boston?

NICHOLAS: The sloop we sailed in from New York is owned by a Dutchman who could take us no farther. He is loading cargo now for an immediate return to New York.

BENJAMIN: He'll not sail in this foul weather.

NICHOLAS: The Dutchman claims that within thirty-six hours the fog will have lifted, driven away by a violent storm with thunder and lightning. He vows he'll sail Saturday morning on schedule.

BENJAMIN: Our Boston weather is variable enough, 'tis true— as variable as men's fortunes. Behold me, so close to the wide open sea, the pathway to the whole world, and a prisoner here in Boston, which already has too many printers.

NICHOLAS: In Portsmouth there is no printer.

BENJAMIN: No printer? What an opening that would be for an ingenious fellow—providing, of course, the fellow had some supply of capital.

NICHOLAS: In time I'll have the capital to set up a press, and Daniel here shall be the printer. We'll operate a family business, printing and selling books.

BENJAMIN: It'll be a long time till then, Nick. Daniel looks to be about twelve, the age I was when apprenticed to James.

NICHOLAS: Exactly what I wanted to see you about. You got

my message from that red-headed rascal I spoke to this morning, didn't you?

BENJAMIN: You sent it to the printer on Queen Street.

NICHOLAS: To you—the editor of the *Courant*. I want to ask if you will take Daniel on as an apprentice.

BENJAMIN: As apprentice?

NICHOLAS: Aye, Benny. Surely for old time's sake you'll take Daniel.

BENJAMIN: I cannot, Nick.

NICHOLAS (*Stiffly*): Cannot or will not?

BENJAMIN: Cannot. The plain truth is that I'm still apprenticed to James myself.

NICHOLAS (*Confused*): How's that? In New York I read a February number of the *Courant*. Mr. Bradford has a copy he lent me to read.

BENJAMIN (*Pleased*): So Mr. Bradford knows about the *Courant!*

NICHOLAS: You can't imagine how pleased I was to show him that it is printed over the name of a friend of mine.

BENJAMIN (*Sadly*): That is only subterfuge of James's to evade a prohibition to publish leveled against him.

NICHOLAS: A ticklish business, I see. I'll delve no further, trust me. (*Thinking*) Perhaps James could use another apprentice. I would like to get Daniel settled in a good situation. My wife and I will be moving on to Portsmouth as soon as I have secured more books and merchandise to stock our shop.

BENJAMIN (*Slowly*): Nick, I think James will be wanting an apprentice shortly, within the week perhaps.

DANIEL (*Hesitantly*): Mr. Franklin—

BENJAMIN: Yes, Daniel.

DANIEL: Is your brother James like you? Would he be a good master?

BENJAMIN: James is a good printer, no slovenly self-taught craftsman. You'll find no better master in the colonies.

NICHOLAS: Well spoken, Ben.

BENJAMIN: Nick, I respect and admire my brother. But we are

brothers—too much alike or too little alike perhaps to work in the same shop, but I stand firm beside him and the new breed of young men here in Boston, who believe a strong newspaper should bring controversial issues to public attention by freely publishing the facts so people can form intelligent opinions and act accordingly.

NICHOLAS: I, too, agree with James in this. I look forward to seeing him soon.

BENJAMIN: You'll probably find James with Checkley. On publication day James and his contributors, the Couranteers as they call themselves, meet to discuss the latest issues. The Reverend Cotton Mather calls them the Hell Fire Club because they attack the established church and the royal government. 'Tis dangerous business for James and his friends, and it's becoming so for me, too, of late. Yet, if all printers were determined not to print anything till they were sure it would offend nobody, there would be very little printed. Here we are, Nick, Checkley's book shop.

NICHOLAS: Thank you, Benny. If you ever need help, I'll be glad to do what I can—any time. Come on, Dan, and look alive, boy. You're going to meet my old master Checkley, and maybe get a look at your future master.

DANIEL (*Calling sadly after* BENJAMIN): Goodbye, Mr. Franklin. I wish I could be apprenticed to you.

NARRATOR: Benjamin smiled wryly and turned toward Queen Street, where he found Patrick and Piers engaged in a minor struggle, puffing and grunting as each claimed his share of a meat pie.

PIERS: Hold the pastry still so I can measure the halves.

PATRICK: I want the bigger piece. I paid for most of it.

PIERS: I gave you half of the cider I bought, and you promised me *half* the pie!

BENJAMIN: Patrick! Piers! "Stay out of fights" meant fights with each other, also.

PATRICK: Piers has cut my pie into two pieces with his pocket knife, and he's got the bigger half.

PIERS: The halves are the same. You be the judge, Benny.

BENJAMIN: I'd rather not. I'd rather you'd be reconciled. If one half is bigger I wish you would each generously offer it to the other.

PATRICK: No, no. You must be the judge, Benny.

PIERS: Which piece is larger?

BENJAMIN: Well, then, let's see. This piece that Piers is claiming is bigger by a hair's breadth.

PATRICK: And I should have it, right? Since buying the pie was my idea in the first place.

BENJAMIN: Oh, no. The larger half now belongs to me as my fee for passing judgment. A workman is worth his hire.

PIERS: But—but—

BENJAMIN: I'm sorry, lads, but now you must cut the smaller piece in half and be content to share that.

PATRICK (*Disgusted*): After this, I'll settle my own differences.

BENJAMIN: Ah, such words of wisdom I have never heard from one so young!

PIERS: Good thing it's almost dinner time. This little piece of pie is hardly worth eating.

BENJAMIN: It's just possible that I may not care for this piece of pie for my dinner. In which case, you can share it this afternoon. Right now, I need a favor. Go visit my friend Collins and ask him to come during the noon hour to the print shop. It's urgent I see him.

PIERS: You mean John Collins, the clerk at the Post Office?

BENJAMIN: Yes. Now, be quick about it, and don't blab to my brother.

PIERS: I don't talk, I eat at meal time. Come on, Patrick.

PATRICK: Nary a word I'll speak of it, Ben.

NARRATOR: It's a thoughtful Ben that makes his way into the print shop on Queen Street. Once there, and alone, he is all action. In a short time he has filled a wooden chest with books from the shelves of the shop library. Finally he deliberates over which of the two volumes he holds in his hands shall be the last one added to a separate stack, piled on the windowsill.

He has just decided when John Collins enters hurriedly, casts a quick eye around the shop, then pulls up short when he observes Ben's actions.

JOHN: Patrick and Piers said you wanted to see me . . . Ben, what's wrong? Why are you packing your books in that chest? Don't tell me you've had a final fight with James and you're quitting him!

BENJAMIN: It's not just the trouble with James. I'm quitting Boston. This may be the biggest mistake of my life, but there is nothing else I can do.

JOHN: Where will you go? When? (*Eagerly*) I'll go with you! What do we do first?

BENJAMIN: Listen to me, John. I must go alone. Don't argue. You must not risk your future for me. I am obliged to leave. There is no future for me in Boston. Because you are my friend, let me go alone, John. It's safest.

JOHN: Aye, safest. As usual, you're right. I can always join you later.

BENJAMIN: But I do have something you can do for me that I dare not do myself.

JOHN: Ask me anything, Ben.

BENJAMIN: I need money, and my purse is light. I want you to take these books piled on the windowsill and offer them to Nicholas Scudder at the Green Dragon tonight.

JOHN: You think he'll buy them?

BENJAMIN: If you say the books are the property of his bookish friend, who needs help.

JOHN (*Savoring the intrigue*): It's all very secret. I like that— "his bookish friend."

BENJAMIN: Very secret. With the money Nicholas Scudder pays, go to Long Wharf. A sloop lies tied there. Arrange passage for me to New York.

JOHN: There must be several sloops docked at Long Wharf. What's the captain's name?

BENJAMIN: Nicholas Scudder arrived this morning on the

sloop. I couldn't ask him the captain's name lest he later seem to be involved in my escape.

JOHN: Then how shall I know the sloop?

BENJAMIN: This sloop is out of New York. The captain, a Dutchman, expects to sail Saturday with cargo now being loaded aboard. Make up some suitable story about why I can't arrange passage myself.

JOHN: I'll think of something convincing!

BENJAMIN: Then come to my house afterward. I'll need your help smuggling out my clothes to pack in this chest with my books. We'll have to take everything out on our backs.

JOHN: I'll be there.

BENJAMIN: James and the others will soon be back. You had better hurry with the books. And John, please, tell no one any of this. I've little faith in three-cornered secrets. I have long dreamed of escaping my servitude, but I know the risk I'm running. Who knows better than I the listings printed every week in the *Courant*—names and descriptions of runaway slaves and apprentices with handsome rewards offered for their capture and return.

JOHN: On my honor, Ben, my lips are sealed.

BENJAMIN: Until tonight.

JOHN: Everything's as good as done, Ben.

NARRATOR: The fog dispersed by Friday evening, blustered darkly away by a threatening storm. In the lonely, unlighted streets and under cover of folks' preparations to shutter houses and shops against the onslaught of the coming rains, preluded now by flashing lightning and great claps of thunder, no one took particular notice of two young men carrying a sea chest through the streets toward Long Wharf. With each step Benjamin Franklin was moving inexorably toward the fulfillment of his destiny. Who would have guessed then that this self-taught genius would help build a new nation and be known throughout the world as the American success symbol—a poor boy reared in humble circumstances who became the companion of princes and the friend of the greatest men of his time? Tonight, however, as he boards the Dutchman's sloop that is tugging restlessly at its ropes to be away, Ben knows only that he has one good friend in John Collins.

BENJAMIN: Goodbye, John. Go quickly now before the storm breaks. You mustn't be seen here with me, lest anyone blame you for my escape.

JOHN: Who would blame me for helping a friend escape an intolerable situation?

BENJAMIN: You could be charged as my accomplice.

JOHN: I'll go, but not until the storm drives me away.

BENJAMIN: The span of time between the lightning and the thunder indicates that the storm is now very close. Such bolts of lightning—a mysterious power like fire in the sky! One day someone will capture that fire and harness it for man's use.

JOHN: There's another project for you, Ben. Look, I brought you something—cheese and a few apples. I wish it were more, but like yours, my purse is light.

BENJAMIN: How I enjoy a roasted apple! I have something there in this sack for you. Open it, John. Surprised? Keep them as a memento of our boyhood.

JOHN: Ben, the swim-paddles you made for your hands and feet to give you more speed in the water! I'll never forget the first time I saw you use them.

BENJAMIN: All you did was laugh. But they worked!

JOHN: I'm going to miss you, Ben, you and your audacious, inventive imagination.

BENJAMIN: I'll miss our long talks and debates, John.

JOHN: Where will you go in New York?

BENJAMIN: To a printer there—William Bradford. I'll seek employment with him. Failing that, I'll go to Philadelphia, a city whose name appeals mightily to me. Philadelphia, that's Greek for City of Brotherly Love.

JOHN: You'll write?

BENJAMIN: I'll write, but you must tell no one of my letters. Go, my friend. Think of me often, but speak of me never.

NARRATOR: At dawn on Saturday, the storm having come and

gone, the sloop sailed away before the wind with an easy pleasant gale. Three days later Ben reached New York. William Bradford, the New York printer, had no work to offer Ben and advised him to go to Philadelphia, where his son Andrew had a printing establishment. Benjamin Franklin, who could never resist adventure, especially if it led to freedom, left New York, and after walking across New Jersey reached Philadelphia, the city that would in time claim him for its own. Almost immediately Benjamin was missed in Boston. The next issue of the *Courant* still published under the name of Benjamin Franklin, carried this advertisement: "James Franklin, Printer on Queen Street, wants a likely lad for an apprentice." James could search the whole land over and no likelier lad would he ever find than the one he had just lost. James's loss, however, was the world's gain. In the sixty-seven years that lay ahead for him, Benjamin Franklin made his own fortune before he was forty and then devoted the second half of his life to helping shape the fortunes of his beloved country—supporting the American Colonies faithfully through the War of Independence, assisting in the formulation of the Declaration of Independence, representing the new government as the American Minister Plenipotentiary to the Court of France, and lastly in 1787 at 81 years of age, serving as delegate from Pennsylvania at the Federal Convention to draw up the Constitution for the new Republic of the United States of America. Before he died at 84, the whole world was to acclaim this printer-inventor-scientist-patriot-diplomat-statesman, for with boundless eagerness, Benjamin Franklin had lived out his life, guided by his own glorious precept: The noblest question in the world is, *What good may I do in it?*

THE END

This reading play may also be performed as a stage play by adding simple sets, costumes, and properties, as described in the text.

Adams for
the Defense

by Beatrice S. Smith

John Adams risks his reputation in the name of justice. . . .

Characters

ABIGAIL ADAMS
JOHN ADAMS
HELEN, *nursemaid*
FORESTER, *British sympathizer*
BEN EDES, *Boston newspaperman*
CROWD, *extras*

TIME: *The evening of March 5, 1770.*
SETTING: *The sitting room of the Adams home in Boston. Fire-place is right. Bookcases, sofa, table, and three chairs are placed around room. A window with drapes is in wall up center, near door to outside. A wardrobe with cloaks inside is left. Door, right, leads to the bedroom.*
AT RISE: ABIGAIL ADAMS *is sitting on sofa, sewing, as* HELEN *enters from bedroom.*
ABIGAIL: Are the children asleep, Helen?
HELEN: Yes, Mrs. Adams, though John Quincy took awhile to drop off.
ABIGAIL (*Smiling*): He's a handful, that boy. He—(*Breaks off as bells start clanging offstage*) Are those the fire alarm bells again?

HELEN: Yes, ma'am, they surely are!

ABIGAIL (*Shaking head*): It seems hardly a week goes by without at least one fire. I wonder where this one is.

HELEN (*Going to window*): I can't see any smoke. And the bells don't tell the direction, the way they usually do. (*Nervously*) Should I go see what I can find out, Mrs. Adams?

ABIGAIL: Yes. Yes, do that, Helen. With these March winds and all these wooden houses, a fire could be a disaster. (*As* HELEN *starts out*, ABIGAIL *gets cloak from wardrobe*.) Here, wear this cloak. It's cold.

HELEN (*Putting on cloak*): Thank you, ma'am. (*Exits*)

ABIGAIL (*Calling out door*): Do be careful. (*Watches from door for a second, then closes it, checks fire with poker, sweeps hearth with small broom. Then she jumps as several explosions are heard from offstage. Child crying is heard offstage.*) I'm coming, darling. (*Rushes out right*)

JOHN (*Throwing open outside door, cloak over one shoulder; calling breathlessly*): Abby! Abby! Where are you? (*Goes to bedroom door*) Abby! (ABIGAIL *enters*.) Oh, there you are. Are the children all right? Is Helen with them?

ABIGAIL: No, Helen has gone out to see about the fire. But the children are fine. (*Takes his arm*) John, you look pale. Are you all right?

JOHN (*Removing cloak*): Yes, yes. I'm fine. (*Pats* ABIGAIL's *arm*)

ABIGAIL: What caused that explosion? Where was the fire?

JOHN (*Wiping forehead with handkerchief, still breathing heavily*): It was no fire, Abby.

ABIGAIL: But I heard the fire alarm ringing.

JOHN: I know. (*Throws cloak on sofa*) But there was no fire.

ABIGAIL: What was it? (*Takes cloak and starts toward wardrobe*)

JOHN (*Somberly*): A massacre.

ABIGAIL (*Whirling around*): A massacre! John! You don't mean it! (*Throws cloak on back of chair*)

JOHN (*Quietly*): I do. (*Sits on sofa*) Four men are dead and another wounded, mortally, I fear. (*Hunches over, puts head in hands*)

ABIGAIL: No! What happened?

JOHN (*Shaking head*): It was so senseless.

ABIGAIL (*Impatiently*): What happened, John?

JOHN (*Taking a deep breath*): It was during another one of those conflicts between some of our people and a dozen or so British soldiers from Murray's barracks. (*Sighs, shakes head*)

ABIGAIL: Yes, yes, go on.

JOHN: From what I heard, the soldiers, armed with clubs and cutlasses, happened upon a crowd of young people gathered near the church on Brattle Square—all carrying canes and cudgels, as usual.

ABIGAIL: And no doubt just waiting for a chance to use them, as usual. What then?

JOHN: There was the customary catcalling and shoving, but nothing much happened until a British officer crossed King Street on his way to the barracks. As he passed, a barber's boy whistled through his fingers, called the officer an ugly name, and asked why the officer didn't pay the money he owed the barber for dressing his hair.

ABIGAIL: Did the officer take offense?

JOHN: Yes, of course. And so did the sentinel standing nearby. He was outraged that a mere boy would talk like that to a British officer, and he whacked him with the butt of his musket.

ABIGAIL: The boy yowled, I suppose?

JOHN (*Nodding*): Loud enough to raise the dead. Then the crowd began pelting the soldiers with snowballs. Luckily, the officer had his wits about him and ordered his men into the barracks, promising the crowd that no more soldiers would be let out that night.

ABIGAIL: I'm glad someone has some sense. Did that quiet the situation?

JOHN: It did for a while. Then some idiot hoisted a boy through a window of the Brick Church at the north end of town and told him to ring the bell as if for a fire, which, of course, sent everyone out into the streets, trying to find out what was burning.

ABIGAIL: Was there no calm voice among them, telling them to go home?

JOHN: A few. But in Dock Square just below King Street some other idiot in a red cloak and white wig began addressing the gathering crowd, pointing out the many injustices being done to the country in general, and to the good people of Boston in particular.

ABIGAIL (*Hotly*): Well, there *are* injustices being done! British troops are all over town. British sentries are challenging us on our very doorsteps. And a wicked British Prime Minister is stamping our goods for whatever he decides they're worth! These are surely injustices!

JOHN: I know. But this evening wasn't the time to talk of them. The speech touched off a spark. And suddenly someone in the crowd shouted, "There's the sentinel who struck the barber's boy. Let's go after him." Then someone yelled, "Let's kill the coward!" (*Sighs*) And that was the beginning.

ABIGAIL: They didn't kill the sentinel!

JOHN: They tried. They threw chunks of wood, pieces of ice, anything they could lay their hands on.

ABIGAIL: The sentinel was armed, wasn't he?

JOHN: Yes, of course. He was on duty.

ABIGAIL: But he didn't shoot?

JOHN: No. He shoved the rammer down his musket and primed it, but he didn't shoot. He shouted for help instead.

ABIGAIL: Who wouldn't! Did anyone hear him?

JOHN: Yes. A captain heard him. Captain Preston, I believe his name was. Anyway, he sent seven men across the square, headed, unfortunately, by a very young and flustered lieutenant. The eight of them managed to push the crowd aside; the crowd kept regrouping and jeering and hurling ice. Finally, Captain Preston himself appeared.

ABIGAIL: He didn't order his men to shoot, I hope! British law forbids its soldiers to fire without permission from the governor or someone in civil authority. They're very particular about that.

JOHN: I know. And so was Captain Preston, evidently. However, he did order his men to prime and load—as a scare tactic, I presume.

ABIGAIL (*Shaking her head*): He shouldn't have done that.

JOHN: Well (*Hesitates*)—perhaps not, but remember, there were only nine British, counting Preston. And the crowd numbered about a hundred—all whooping, cursing, whistling, and throwing anything that came to hand.

ABIGAIL: So finally Captain Preston gave the order to shoot?

JOHN: I'm not certain. I wasn't there myself. But the way it was told to me, one of the soldiers was struck by a chunk of ice. He slipped, and his gun discharged accidentally.

ABIGAIL: Oh, dear. (*Takes breath*) Then the other eight soldiers began firing, I suppose.

JOHN (*Somberly*): Yes. Also, they say, a half dozen or so British sympathizers fired into the crowd from the windows of the Custom House. Whether true or not, I don't know. But (*Pauses*)—when the smoke cleared, five men lay sprawled in the snow, one just a lad of seventeen who had been standing in the street looking on.

ABIGAIL (*Upset*): Dear heaven! (JOHN *and* ABIGAIL *start as loud knocking and shouting are heard outside door.*) What's that? (*Jumps to feet*)

JOHN: I don't know. (*Goes quickly to door, opens it.* CROWD *enters, brandishing sticks and clubs, shoving at* FORESTER, *whose clothes are torn.*)

CROWD (*Shouting angrily; ad lib*): Go back where you belong! What do you think you're doing here? Adams won't take to the likes of you! (*Etc.*)

JOHN (*Loudly, above noise*): What's going on here?

FORESTER (*Stumbling toward* JOHN): Mr. Adams, please, sir—I would like to talk with you.

JOHN (*Frowning*): And so you shall, Forester. I would not deny

anyone the right to speak. (*Sternly, to* CROWD) Do any of the
rest of you have anything to say? If so, step forward, one at a
time. (CROWD *mumbles, but no one steps forward.*) If not,
leave my home—at once! (CROWD *backs out, still mumbling.*
JOHN *closes door, turns to* FORESTER.) Forester, what is it
you want?

FORESTER (*Humbly*): Please, Mr. Adams, I must have a word
with you.

JOHN (*Frowning*): All right. (*To* ABIGAIL) This is Mr. Forester, Abigail. Forester, my wife. (ABIGAIL *and* FORESTER
nod. JOHN *continues in a disapproving tone.*) Mr. Forester is
a Tory, a British sympathizer. He has the unfortunate habit,
I am told, of taking a dram too many at the British Coffee
House. Is that correct, Forester?

FORESTER (*Sheepishly*): I'm afraid so, Mr. Adams. (*Firmly*)
But I'm all right now, sir, I assure you.

ABIGAIL (*Politely*): Have a seat, Mr. Forester.

FORESTER (*Sitting*): Thank you, ma'am. (*To* JOHN, *in agitated
manner*) Mr. Adams, you were on King Street this evening.
Do you know what happened?

JOHN (*Hesitating then nodding; grimly*): Why are you here?

FORESTER (*Twisting hands nervously*): I—I came on behalf of
Captain Preston, sir. He's in terrible condition. His face is
bruised, his eyes black and swollen. He was beaten!

JOHN (*Coldly*): Sir, five others were killed!

FORESTER: I know, Mr. Adams. But (*Distressed, grips arms of
chair*)—as God is my witness, Captain Preston is innocent.
He did not give the signal to shoot! His soldiers were only
trying to defend themselves from the mob. Did you see what
they were doing?

JOHN (*Shortly*): I've heard. Why have you come here, Forester?

FORESTER: Captain Preston asked me to help him, sir. I'm a
friend of his. He's in prison. His trial will come up within
ten days.

JOHN: What does this have to do with me?

FORESTER: The Captain has no one to defend him, sir.

JOHN: I still don't understand why you have come here.

FORESTER: There may be dark days ahead. I know of no man better qualified to meet this difficult situation than you, Mr. Adams. Would you consider (*Hesitates as sees growing look of horror on* JOHN's *face*)—will you take this case, sir?

JOHN (*Shocked*): Me? Why me? I'm not a British sympathizer. Quite the opposite! I support liberty—revolution, if necessary! Forester, my beliefs are the very same as those who followed you here, the same as those who harassed Captain Preston. You must know that!

FORESTER (*Steadily*): Yes, I know that, Mr. Adams.

JOHN: Well, then, why come to me? Get a lawyer from the ranks of your own party.

FORESTER: I've already gone to three of them, sir. They refuse even to listen to me.

JOHN (*Incredulously*): All of them?

FORESTER: One, Robert Auchmuty, said he would act for Captain Preston, but only if you would agree to serve as counsel to him.

JOHN (*Angrily*): This is preposterous!

ABIGAIL: You must be mistaken, Mr. Forester. Here in Massachusetts Bay, English law isn't all it should be, but it does give everyone fair judgment. Captain Preston will not be denied counsel. The lawyers for the Crown will step forward eventually, I'm certain.

FORESTER: No, Mrs. Adams, they won't. They're afraid. I don't blame them. There are thousands of people in the streets, many of them around the jail, chanting Captain Preston's name, roaring for his blood. (*Shaking head*) It's frightening to see. Please help us, sir. Captain Preston must have a lawyer the people of Boston respect, someone they know has acted fairly in the past and will act fairly now. (*Pauses, then pleadingly*) I swear to you that Captain Preston acted in self-defence. He is an innocent man, Mr. Adams!

JOHN (*Coldly*): That must be ascertained at his trial.

FORESTER (*Timidly*): I'm afraid there will be no trial, sir. Not a fair one. Not without you.

JOHN (*Scowling*): A man in jail in peril of his life! The bar denying him counsel! How could such things come to pass here in Boston? We have never been a bloodthirsty people. It's disgraceful!

FORESTER: Then will you help us, sir?

JOHN (*Shaking head*): I have to think about it, Forester.

FORESTER (*Rising*): There isn't much time, sir.

JOHN (*Curtly*): I said, I must think about it!

FORESTER (*Sadly*): Yes, well—thank you for listening, Mr. Adams. (*Rises*)

ABIGAIL (*Softly*): John—I think you should help.

JOHN (*Looking at* ABIGAIL *for a moment without speaking, then abruptly to* FORESTER): All right.

FORESTER (*Brightening*): You mean you'll take the case, sir?

JOHN (*Gruffly*): Yes, I'll take it.

FORESTER (*Springing forward, shaking* JOHN'*s hand*): Thank you, oh, thank you, Mr. Adams. (*Searches three different pockets and finally comes up with a coin*) A retaining fee, sir. Only a guinea, but it's all I have. Will it do?

JOHN (*Taking coin, bowing gravely*): Thank you, Forester. Consider the bargain sealed. Tell Captain Preston that I shall see him tomorrow.

FORESTER (*Bowing; humbly*): Thank you again, sir. Thank you. (*To* ABIGAIL) And you, too, ma'am. Goodnight. (*Exits. JOHN sits in chair, staring into space. Finally he turns to ABIGAIL, who has picked up sewing.*)

JOHN: I hope I've done the right thing, Abby.

ABIGAIL: You have, John.

JOHN: There may be trouble, you know.

ABIGAIL (*Concerned*): Do you think so?

JOHN: Oh, yes, indeed! Feeling against Preston is running strong. You saw the crowd that followed Forester here tonight. People won't understand why I've taken the case. What's more, my defending Captain Preston also means I'm defending his soldiers, (*Pauses*) including the one who shot the seventeen-year-old boy.

ABIGAIL (*Emphatically*): Simply because you took the case doesn't mean that you believe what Captain Preston and his soldiers believe, or that they did the right thing. You're merely seeing to it that they get a fair trial!

JOHN: I understand that, Abby. And you understand that. But I'm not sure everyone will. We—(*Breaks off as* HELEN *enters*)

HELEN (*Agitated, to* JOHN): Good evening, Mr. Adams. (*Turns to* ABIGAIL) It wasn't a fire, Mrs. Adams. It was (*Voice rises*) murder, over on King Street. (*Breathlessly*) Those British soldiers, you should have seen them—they shot our people down like they were made of tin! (*Voice breaking*) One of them they killed was a just a boy of seventeen, the same age as my brother. And he wasn't doing anything but—just standing there. (*Covers face with hands and sobs*)

ABIGAIL (*Rising and putting arm around* HELEN, *comforting her*): I know. I heard, Helen. (*Looks at* JOHN *over* HELEN's *shoulder*)

JOHN (*Shrugging*): I—ah—have things to do. Will you be all right without me for a while, Abby?

ABIGAIL (*Still comforting* HELEN): I'll be fine, John. (JOHN *picks up cloak, starts to exit, then half turns, not quite facing* HELEN.)

JOHN: Helen—

HELEN (*Wiping eyes*): Yes, sir?

JOHN (*Clearing throat*): Apparently you haven't heard.

HELEN: Heard what, sir?

JOHN: That I've been asked to defend Captain Preston.

HELEN: Captain Preston? (*Voice rises*) Do you mean the officer who gave the order to shoot?

JOHN: We're not sure what happened. That's what trials are for.

HELEN (*Aghast*): You're not going to take his case!

JOHN: Yes, Helen, I am.

HELEN: You're going to defend a murderer of poor helpless people and—and an innocent seventeen-year-old boy!

ABIGAIL (*Quietly*): No one else will take the case, Helen.

HELEN (*Stiffly*): Why should they? Who but a—a traitor would defend such a man as that Preston? (*Puts her hand to her mouth suddenly*) I'm sorry to offend you, sir, but (*Throws head back defiantly*) it's the way I feel. (*To* ABIGAIL) I can't work here anymore, Mrs. Adams. I just wouldn't feel right.

ABIGAIL: Very well, Helen. Pack your belongings and leave, if you must. I can manage without you. (HELEN, *glaring at* JOHN, *exits right.*)

JOHN: What did I tell you?

ABIGAIL: Helen is a very emotional person, John. I'm certain that her reaction isn't typical of what to expect. I—(*Breaks off as knock is heard at door.* JOHN *looks at* ABIGAIL, *then goes to door, hesitates, opens it, cautiously.*)

JOHN (*Relieved*): Ben, come in. (BEN EDES *enters.*) Glad to see you. (*Turns to* ABIGAIL) You remember Ben Edes, don't you, Abby?

ABIGAIL (*Warmly*): Yes, indeed. I'm happy to see you again, Mr. Edes.

BEN (*Bowing slightly*): And I you, Mrs. Adams.

JOHN (*Jovial*): Well, Ben, how's the best newspaper man in Boston?

BEN: I'm fine, thank you, John. (*Removes cloak*) But you obviously have lost your mind!

JOHN (*Cautiously*): What do you mean?

BEN: I hear you've agreed to defend Preston.

JOHN: News travels fast.

BEN: It's true, then?

JOHN: Yes, it's true.

BEN: Why did they come to you, of all people?

ABIGAIL (*Hotly*): Because everyone knows that John Adams, of all people, is the only one in town with any courage, that's why!

JOHN: Now, now, Abby.

ABIGAIL: It's true!

BEN (*To* ABIGAIL): I believe it, Mrs. Adams. (*Turning to* JOHN) But, John, you're no Tory. Why should you care what happens to those rascals?

JOHN: Because I care about fair play. (*Firmly*) Because I believe all men deserve justice. Because I believe that all men, regardless of belief, are assumed innocent until the law proves them guilty!

BEN: Fine words. But be sensible, John. No one will understand. Worse, they'll hate you for it.

JOHN (*Stiffly*): I hope not. But if so, it can hardly be helped.

BEN: Have you thought what this might mean to your political career?

JOHN: I'm not interested in a political career, Ben. I've already allowed myself to be drawn into more political events than I really want. All I want to be is a good husband and father, a decent citizen, and a fair-minded lawyer.

BEN: The elections are in June. I think you could be elected to the House of Representatives with a little help from your cousin Sam. The Sons of Liberty think highly of you. You'd get their support.

JOHN: Ben, haven't you been listening? I said I have no ambitions along political lines. None!

BEN: And you're determined to go through with the Preston case?

JOHN (*Firmly*): I am. I've already accepted a retaining fee, as a matter of fact. (*Reaches into pocket, holds up small coin*)

BEN (*Incredulously*): A guinea! You, the best lawyer in Boston, accepted one guinea as a retaining fee! (*Shakes head*) Now I know you're mad!

JOHN (*Half-smiling*): Call it a labor of love.

BEN: Love! (*Snorts*) This is the enemy we're talking about! Tyrants!

JOHN: Don't tyrants deserve a fair trial?

BEN (*Vigorously*): No, they don't! Not these tyrants! Have you forgotten how infractions of the Stamp Act are dealt with in their courts—without a jury, and a commission on every fine and condemnation paid to the judge? Have you forgotten that, John?

JOHN: No, Ben, I haven't forgotten. But two wrongs do not make a right.

BEN: You're hopeless. But (*Pauses, not quite meeting* JOHN's *eye*) I do see your point. (*Rubs chin thoughtfully*) I wonder if I can print something in the *Gazette* that will gloss over your actions a little.

JOHN: No, Ben. (*Passionately*) Concealment is not part of my nature. What you print in your paper is this: "John Adams has agreed to act as counsel for Captain Preston, who is being held for murder." You also say that I shall defend the British soldiers lying in the same jail under the same charges (*Vehemently*)—including the soldier who shot the seventeen-year-old boy.

BEN: You're a fool, John Adams. An incredible fool. (*Puts on cloak*) I can see I'm wasting my time talking to you.

JOHN: You're right. You are. (*Goes to door, holds it open*) Good night, Ben! (BEN *exits, shaking head.*)

ABIGAIL: Now everyone will know what you intend to do, won't they?

JOHN: I imagine everyone knows already. (*Picks up cloak*) I must go and confer with my partners, Abby. It shouldn't take long. What I'm going to try to do is get Preston's trial postponed. If it isn't, we shall have no chance at all of a fair trial. Right now, I doubt any jury would even *consider* not convicting him. (*Puts on cloak, kisses* ABIGAIL *lightly on cheek*) Are you sure you'll be all right here alone?

ABIGAIL: I'm sure. (*Anxiously*) Please be careful, John. I suspect by now everyone in Boston is armed.

JOHN (*Gloomily*): I wouldn't doubt it. Perhaps I should see about organizing a citizen's watch before anything else happens. (*Starts to exit, turns to* ABIGAIL) You'd best go and stay with the children. And bolt this door. I'll be back as quickly as I can. (JOHN *exits.*)

ABIGAIL (*Standing at door, waving*): Take care, John. (*Closes door, bolts lock, exits to bedroom. Lights dim to indicate passage of time. Then* ABIGAIL *enters from bedroom door, wearing dressing gown, paces restlessly, checks fire, finally settles in chair and picks up sewing. Suddenly noise of a* CROWD *is heard offstage. As noise comes closer,* ABIGAIL *jumps up, gets poker from hearth, and checks bolt on outside door.*) No hoodlums will get in here—not if I can help it! (*Shouting, scuffling, and knocking are heard outside door.*)

CROWD (*Shouting outside door*): John Adams is a traitor! John Adams is a traitor! John Adams is a traitor! (*Chant increases in volume as it is repeated.* ABIGAIL *stands firm, poker raised. Finally* CROWD *noise diminishes. Relieved,* ABIGAIL *puts poker back on hearth, sits again, picks up sewing. All is quiet. Then suddenly a rock comes crashing through window; there is sound of smashing glass.* ABIGAIL *jumps to her feet, picks up rock, stares at it, trembling with rage.*)

ABIGAIL: Oh—who would do this! (*Goes to window, looks out*) I say, you there! (*Runs to outside door, unlocks it, flings it open, shouting*) Come back here! You—you bloody rowdies! (*Sound of running feet going into distance is heard.* ABIGAIL *slams door, places rock on table, gets broom from hearth and begins sweeping up glass. A few seconds later,* JOHN *enters.* ABIGAIL *puts down broom, runs to greet him.*) Oh, John, you're all right!

JOHN (*Wearily*): I'm fine, Abby. And you? Everything all right?

ABIGAIL: Fine. Everything's fine.

JOHN (*Sighing*): Good. I was worried that those hoodlums who were here earlier might return.

ABIGAIL (*Quickly changing the subject*): You look tired. Would you like a cup of tea, something to eat?

JOHN: No, thank you. I'm too tired to eat. (*Sinks on sofa, squeezes bridge of nose, rubs forehead*)

ABIGAIL (*Sitting next to him*): You've had a bad time, John?

JOHN (*Nodding*): Yes. Worse than I thought. Whistles, catcalls, mud spattered as I passed, a snowball or two, things like that.

ABIGAIL: How terrible for you.

JOHN: It didn't surprise me. I expected hostility. (*Shakes head, looks up, rather bemused*) What I didn't expect was the reaction I got from the Tories.

ABIGAIL: What happened?

JOHN (*Ruefully*): Nine out of ten of them are convinced that I've come over to their side.

ABIGAIL (*Indignantly*): They can't believe such a thing!

JOHN: They do. (*Gets up, begins to pace*) I'm not sure how to convince them otherwise. To protest would be ridiculous. To— (*Breaks off as he sees rock; he picks it up, looks at floor.*) What's this? Glass? (*Goes to inspect window; concerned*) Abby! What has been going on here?

ABIGAIL (*Evasively*): Nothing. Nothing important, John. (*Changing subject again*) Are you sure you wouldn't like a cup of tea? It will take only a minute. (*Starts toward bedroom door*)

JOHN: Abby. (ABIGAIL *stops without turning around.*) What happened? (*Goes to her, puts hands on her shoulders, turns her around to face him; sternly*) What happened?

ABIGAIL (*Shrugging, pretending indifference*): Someone threw a rock through the window, that's all.

JOHN (*Fiercely*): That's all! That's all, you say!

ABIGAIL: Don't get excited, John. It was—just a small rock. And the youngsters who threw it weren't very big, either. I saw them disappear around the corner.

JOHN: But you might have been hurt. Oh, Abby! (*Puts arms around her*) I have no right to sacrifice my family this way, and I won't!

ABIGAIL (*Frowning*): What do you mean?

JOHN: I mean I intend to tell Preston to find someone else to defend him.

ABIGAIL (*Horrified*): You what?

JOHN: You heard me. I'm not going to take Preston's case.

ABIGAIL: Why? Because of me?

JOHN: Abby, those rowdies could have hurt you!

ABIGAIL: Pooh! I'm the equal of a hundred rowdies!

JOHN (*Smiling*): I believe that, still—

ABIGAIL (*Interrupting*): Still what? John Adams, if you don't take Preston's case, you'll see just how—how equal I am!

JOHN (*Chuckling*): Who would have thought the quiet little parson's daughter I married six years ago would turn out like this?

ABIGAIL (*Pertly*): You thought so—or you never would have married me.

JOHN (*Tenderly*): Perhaps you're right. (*Silence for a moment, as they look at one another*) Seriously, Abby, I'll grant that perhaps you can handle a mob, but are you also up to being the wife of the most unpopular man in Boston?

ABIGAIL (*Stoutly*): I certainly am!

JOHN: It's not going to be easy, you know, facing repudiation from even our closest friends. (ABIGAIL *looks at him for a second or two, then goes to bookcase, picks up a book.*)

ABIGAIL: I want to show you something.

JOHN: A book? (*Smiles*) Do you know it was your interest in books that first made me notice you?

ABIGAIL (*Chuckling*): I don't know if that's a compliment or not. (*Holds up book*) Do you remember this particular book, John?

JOHN (*Nodding*): I do. It's a volume by an Italian philosopher named Beccaria.

ABIGAIL (*Opening book, turning pages*): There's a passage in it that you once read aloud to me. Would you like to hear it?

JOHN (*Smiling broadly*): I think I know which one you mean.

ABIGAIL (*Reading*): "If by supporting the rights of mankind . . . " (JOHN *joins in from memory.*)

ABIGAIL *and* JOHN (*Together*): "I shall contribute to save from the agonies of death one unfortunate victim of tyranny or of ignorance, his blessing and tears will be sufficient consolation to me for the contempt of all mankind." (*In the distance, church bell rings, as* JOHN *and* ABIGAIL *finish reading. Curtain*)

THE END

Production Notes

ADAMS FOR THE DEFENSE

Characters: 3 male; 2 female; male and female extras.

Playing Time: 30 minutes.

Costumes: Colonial dress. John wears cloak when he enters. Forester's clothes are torn; he has coin in pocket.

Properties: Sewing, rock, book.

Setting: Sitting room of the Adams home in Boston with appropriate Colonial furnishings. A fireplace with poker and small broom on hearth is in right wall, and there are bookcases, sofa, table, and chairs. Wardrobe closet is at left. Door to outside, with bolt, is up center. Window with drapes is in wall beside it. Door right leads to bedroom.

Lighting: Lights dim as indicated.

Sound: Clanging bell, explosion, breaking glass, footsteps running away, church bell.

One Life to Lose

by *Anne Coulter Martens*

Nathan Hale: American hero

Characters

MS. DALTON, *history teacher*
JANIE
OWEN
WILL } *students*
SAM
LAUREN
HOT DOG VENDOR
FLAG SELLER
NATHAN HALE
SIS, *his sister*
BONNY, *his girlfriend*
ZEB, *a friend*
BRITISH GUARD
STAGEHAND

TIME: *The present.*
BEFORE RISE: MS. DALTON *enters from front auditorium door, map in hand.* JANIE *follows.* WILL, LAUREN, *and* SAM *trail behind.* OWEN *saunters in last.*
MS. DALTON: This way, everybody. (*She leads others up steps to stage.*)
WILL (*Wearily*): What are we going to see *now?*
OWEN (*Unenthusiastically*): Want to bet it's another statue?
LAUREN: It's bound to be.

44

OWEN (*Dryly*): There are so many here, it's a wonder there's room for the people.

WILL: Ms. Dalton, when do we get to do something fun, like take the boat trip around the Statue of Liberty?

LAUREN: And go to the top of the World Trade Center?

MS. DALTON (*Firmly*): Later.

OWEN: I'm tired of visiting this dead person's house and that dead person's statue.

JANIE: Pay no attention to him, Ms. Dalton. (*Sarcastically*) Owen thinks history began when he was born.

OWEN: Now, just a minute. I'm willing to admit all these historical characters did something important a long time ago. But what does that matter to us *now?*

MS. DALTON (*Earnestly*): Owen, you have to understand that this country is great today because of the people who helped found it.

OWEN (*Under his breath*): Start of lecture.

MS. DALTON: All right, all right. The statue should be somewhere near here. (*Consulting map*) O.K., we're only a couple of blocks away. Come on, everyone. (*All exit right as curtain opens.*)

* * * *

SETTING: *City Hall Park in New York City. Large statue, almost completely covered with canvas, is up right. Bench is center, and a table and another bench are up left.*

AT RISE: MS. DALTON, JANIE, OWEN, WILL, LAUREN, *and* SAM *enter right and stop when they see statue.*

MS. DALTON (*Disappointed*): Oh, no! They're working on it!

WILL: You still haven't told us whose statue this is, Ms. Dalton.

OWEN: Another general, most likely.

LAUREN: Is it George Washington?

MS. DALTON: Why do you ask that, Lauren?

LAUREN: Because Washington fought a battle on Long Island, didn't he? And in New York.

MS. DALTON: This person (*Gestures to statue*) was not a general.

LAUREN: Was he a great writer?

MS. DALTON: He wrote a few letters, but they were torn up and never delivered.

JANIE: He must have done *something,* if New York put up a statue of him.

MS. DALTON: There's another statue of this man in Hartford, Connecticut, where he was born in 1755.

JANIE (*To* OWEN): I doubt they'll ever put up a statue of *you* anyplace.

OWEN (*Bored*): So?

MS. DALTON (*As* SAM *goes near canvas*): Don't touch the canvas, please, Sam. (SAM *rejoins others.*)

SAM: Since we can't see the statue, I guess we won't be staying here long.

MS. DALTON (*Disappointed*): No, it appears we won't be.

JANIE (*Still guessing*): Ms. Dalton, was this person a Revolutionary War hero?

MS. DALTON: Yes, he was, Janie.

JANIE: And he did something very great?

MS. DALTON: No, actually, he failed in what he set out to do.

OWEN (*Interested for the first time*): Don't tell me they put up a statue to a failure! (HOT DOG VENDOR *enters left, pushing cart.*)

VENDOR: Get your hot dogs here. New York hot dogs. Anybody here for a hot dog?

OTHERS (*Ad lib*): No thanks. We already had lunch. (*Etc.*)

MS. DALTON (*Smiling*): Sorry. No sale here, I'm afraid.

VENDOR (*Glumly*): Business has been terrible since they draped the statue.

MS. DALTON: I'm sorry to hear that.

VENDOR: Me, too. (*Goes right, calling*) Hot dogs! Come get your hot dogs. (*Exits right*)

JANIE (*Looking off after* VENDOR): It doesn't seem right to sell stuff here. Unpatriotic, somehow.

OWEN: To make a buck where you can find it? There's nothing wrong with that. (*Points to statue*) Anyway, our hero's been dead for more than two hundred years. He doesn't care. (FLAG SELLER *enters right, carrying flags and box for contributions.*)

FLAG SELLER: Anyone want to buy a flag?

OWEN (*Puzzled*): Why are you selling flags? Is this some kind of holiday I don't know about?

FLAG SELLER: My high school class is selling flags to help pay for the cost of cleaning this statue.

WILL (*Wryly*): I can just see myself carrying a flag around New York.

FLAG SELLER (*Disappointed*): So no one's interested?

JANIE: Not now. Thanks anyway.

FLAG SELLER: That's what everyone says. (*Sighs and exits left*)

OWEN: How much longer do we stand here looking at nothing?

JANIE: Until we figure out who this mysterious man was. I keep wondering why he's famous, if he was a failure. Could you give us some more clues, Ms. Dalton?

MS. DALTON: Well, let's see. . . . He died near here. Some think a little farther north, toward the East River.

JANIE: But what did he *do?*

MS. DALTON: When he was about twenty years old, he joined the Continental Army, under Washington, and attained the rank of captain. But he was captured by the British. . . . (*Stage lights go out. Students and* MS. DALTON *move right. In the darkness,* NATHAN HALE *enters, carrying traveling bag containing papers, and sits on bench at center.* STAGEHAND *puts candle, inkwell, and quill on bench and exits. Spotlight shines on bench, where* NATHAN *sits writing, using traveling bag as a writing table.* BRITISH GUARD *enters spotlight.*)

GUARD (*Harshly*): Prisoner, get up! (NATHAN *rises, his bag falling to the floor; he stoops to pick it up.*) Stay on your feet when I talk to you!

NATHAN HALE: I'm standing.

GUARD: Don't forget it.

NATHAN: What time is it?

GUARD: Too late for you.

NATHAN: Will you answer my question?

GUARD: Dawn's in fifteen minutes.

NATHAN: I thought as much.

GUARD: You have a visitor. Though why anyone would want to see *you* is beyond me. (ZEB *enters. Sarcastically, to* ZEB) Here's the fine schoolmaster you came to see.

NATHAN (*Surprised*): Zeb!

ZEB: It's me, all right. (*Uncomfortably*) Strange place for us to meet. (GUARD *moves out of spotlight.*)

NATHAN: You recognized me in the tavern last night?

ZEB (*Looking down*): That I did.

NATHAN: I saw you, but I thought I'd escaped your notice.

ZEB (*Softly*): You didn't.

NATHAN: In a few more hours I would have been back behind my own lines. (*Sighs*) So it was you who reported me to the British.

ZEB: Yes. (*In frustration*) What would you expect me to do?

NATHAN: Only what you did, Zeb.

ZEB: I heard General Howe himself talked to you last night.

NATHAN: Yes.

ZEB (*Hesitating*): And—that papers and maps of the British camps were found in your shoes. (NATHAN *nods.*) Nate, why did you *do* it?

NATHAN: Somebody had to, Zeb.

ZEB: I came to call you a traitor, as the British did. (*Softening*) But, Nate, we were boys together. Remember?

NATHAN: That seems such a long time ago.

ZEB (*Flatly*): You should never have joined Washington's army. You wouldn't be in this trouble now.

NATHAN: To me, it was necessary.

ZEB: You were doing passably well as a schoolmaster at home. Do you love war so much?

NATHAN: I hate war, but I love freedom.

ZEB (*Sharply*): Precious little you have of it now.

NATHAN (*Nodding; slowly*): I know.

ZEB (*Gesturing toward letters*): What were you writing?

NATHAN: Letters. My mother, my little sister. And Bonny.

ZEB: Sit down again and get on with them, then. Time's short.

NATHAN: Yes. (*Sits down*)

ZEB: I'll ask the guard to let you have these few minutes alone.

NATHAN: Thank you. Will the officer have my letters delivered?

ZEB: Your guess is as good as mine, Nate. (*After a pause*) I suggest you finish those letters. You haven't much time. (*Leaves spotlight*)

NATHAN (*Softly, to himself*): This isn't what I used to dream about for the future. (*Picks up paper, a letter partly written*) Mother . . . what can I say to you now? (*Puts paper down and picks up another letter*) Sis, you thought I'd be rich and famous some day, didn't you, and that you could point to me with pride? You're still too young to understand. (*Picks up third letter*) Bonny . . . will you understand? I can't write it all down on paper, why I had to do what I've done. I keep thinking of that first day after I came home from school. I wanted to rush over to see you, but I paused a moment over my books. (*Spotlight goes out, then comes up right on* MS. DALTON *and students. As she speaks,* NATHAN *moves to sit at table up left.* STAGEHAND *puts books on table.*)

MS. DALTON: He was about eighteen when he was graduated from Yale with honors. A studious boy, but an athlete, too. Eager for fun, but also eager to make a name for himself. (*Spotlight goes out, then comes up on* NATHAN. *Knock is heard off.*)

BONNY (*Calling offstage*): Nate! (*She enters left.* NATHAN *rises, crosses to* BONNY *and takes her hands.*)

NATHAN (*Happily*): Bonny! I was going over to see you in a few minutes.

BONNY (*Excitedly*): When I heard you were home, I just couldn't wait. (*Studies him*) You're taller.

NATHAN: And you're even prettier.

BONNY (*Demurely*): Thank you, kind sir. But why do you always call me Bonny, when that's not my name?

NATHAN: I've told you and told you. You want more compliments, miss?

BONNY (*Sitting on bench*): I love them.

NATHAN: Bonny is a Scottish word, meaning fair and lovely. There, does that please you?

BONNY: Of course. (*Glances at books*) Why the books, when you're through with college?

NATHAN: I'll never be through with books.

BONNY: Your family must be glad to have you back again.

NATHAN: So they say. Mother and Sis are at a neighbor's house, but they'll be back shortly. Have you missed me, Bonny?

BONNY: Yes, and I've saved all your letters.

NATHAN: And I yours.

BONNY: Honest and true?

NATHAN: Always that. (*Hesitates*) I know we're both quite young yet . . .

BONNY: Too young, my father would say.

NATHAN: And I still have to make my plans for the future.

BONNY: Have you decided what you're going to do? Become rich, like the Tory merchants?

NATHAN: Not that. I hope what I decide to do will *matter*.

BONNY: To yourself?

NATHAN: Yes, and to others. (*Ruefully*) Do I still sound like a schoolboy dreamer?

BONNY: If you do, I like you all the better for it. . . . They say there's a position as schoolmaster open.

NATHAN: So I've heard.

BONNY: Are you interested?

NATHAN: I ask myself, what else am I qualified for? And yet I know the boys I teach will yawn, and look out the window, and think about fishing in the stream, even as I once did.

BONNY: I'm sure you will make a great impression on your students!

NATHAN: Maybe one or two will remember me and say, "He used to be my schoolmaster."

BONNY: Isn't that worthwhile?

NATHAN: For now, perhaps. But you know the pay is low.

BONNY: You may move on to a bigger school, or even to a college.

NATHAN: I've thought of that.

BONNY: You may even write books.

NATHAN (*Laughing*): I have to live a little more of my life before I write for anyone else to read.

BONNY: That's true.

NATHAN: When I'm a fat, middle-aged man, you may laugh at me for still lazying over my books. (*Indicates books on table*)

BONNY (*Looking at titles*): Shakespeare, Plato, the Bible . . . I won't laugh, Nate. (SIS *enters left, followed by* MRS. HALE, *who carries market basket.*)

SIS (*Happily*): Bonny's here! (*Goes to* BONNY *and hugs her*)

MRS. HALE: I'm glad you came over, Bonny.

BONNY (*To* MRS. HALE): This son of yours would have lost himself in his books, and forgotten all about me.

NATHAN (*Laughing*): You know that's not so.

MRS. HALE: Nate never forgets important things.

SIS (*Picking up a book, glancing through it*): I don't understand why you want to read all these books. (*Puts it down and glances through another one*) Especially when no one is making you!

NATHAN (*Laughs*): Oh, Sis. Someday maybe you will even read a book for pleasure!

MRS. HALE: Come, Sis. We have things to do.

SIS: I'll sit here with Bonny for a while, Mother. (*Sits on bench beside* BONNY)

MRS. HALE: Oh, no, you won't. I want you to watch the way I knead the dough for the bread to rise.

SIS (*Impatiently*): What do I care about how to make bread?

MRS. HALE: You'll have to know how when you grow up.

SIS: I'll have a servant in the kitchen, because I'll be rich. Will you be rich too, Nate?

NATHAN (*Smiling*): Naturally.

SIS: Will you get married?

MRS. HALE (*Firmly*): Come, Sis. Now! (*Takes* SIS *by the arm and leads her off left*)

NATHAN (*Seriously, to* BONNY): I *do* hope to get married.

BONNY (*Teasingly*): Do you have anyone special in mind?

NATHAN: You know I do. (*Knock off left*) Come in! (ZEB *swaggers in.*)

ZEB: So, our schoolboy's home!

NATHAN: Schoolboy no longer, Zeb. I'll be going to work soon.

ZEB: Will you make enough money to buy Bonny a fine new hat with feathers?

NATHAN: You still measure success with money, don't you?

ZEB (*Laughing*): Is there any other measure?

BONNY: Not for you, I'm afraid.

ZEB: I think *I'm* on the right road to making plenty.

NATHAN: How?

ZEB (*Proudly*): Apprenticed to a rich merchant. Someday I expect to own the shop.

BONNY (*Concerned*): Like a Tory?

ZEB (*More seriously*): The rowdies who talk against the King will come to no good end. As for anyone who sympathizes with them—

NATHAN: Yes?

ZEB (*Meaningfully*): He'd be wise to keep his mouth shut. This colony is loyal to the Crown.

NATHAN (*Bristling*): Is that what you came over to say?

ZEB (*Laughing*): Upon my word, no! I came to congratulate you, Nate, and to wish you well in the future. (*Holds out his hand*)

NATHAN (*Shaking* ZEB's *hand*): Thanks, Zeb.

ZEB: No arguments today about what you call unjust taxes, and laws you don't agree with. Just good luck.

NATHAN (*Sincerely*): I appreciate your words, Zeb.

ZEB: Word's around that you may try for the schoolmaster's position.

NATHAN: I may.

ZEB: And where will that get you? Poor pay, a shabby suit, and fortunate to keep a roof over your head.

NATHAN (*Shrugging*): It's a beginning.

ZEB: To what? Hold out for something that will make money. Don't take the fool's road, Nate.

NATHAN: I don't look at it that way.

ZEB: Well, you have my opinion. I'm quite sure it's not your own.

NATHAN: No.

ZEB: I'll see you now and then. Goodbye. Bonny, you *could* do better. (*Laughs and leaves the spotlight*)

BONNY: Nate, I think you *have* made your decision.

NATHAN: Yes, I think I have. For a while, at least, I'll be a schoolmaster.

BONNY: It's a good beginning.

NATHAN: More money should come later when I grow older.

BONNY: I'm quite sure of it. (*Stands*)

NATHAN: Bonny . . . will you wait?

BONNY: Yes, Nate, of course I'll wait. (*He takes her hands as spotlight goes out and comes up right on* MS. DALTON. *As she speaks,* NATHAN *exits, and* MRS. HALE *enters and sits at table. Books are removed.*)

MS. DALTON: He did move on to a better school. For two years he was a schoolmaster, and a good one, even though his suit was rather shabby, and there was little spending money in his pocket. But war clouds gathered over the colonies and he grew restless. . . . (*Spotlight comes up on* MRS. HALE, *sitting with a basket of darning.* BONNY *stands near her.*)

BONNY: Shall I set the table for your supper, Mrs. Hale?

MRS. HALE: No, thank you, dear. Sis will do it when she comes back.

BONNY (*Pacing nervously*): I wonder what's keeping Nate?

MRS. HALE: A meeting, perhaps.

BONNY: He meets with some of the men very often these days. (*Upset*) Do you know why?

MRS. HALE: I think I do.

BONNY: But he's only twenty. Surely he shouldn't become involved!

MRS. HALE (*Gently*): Bonny, I'm afraid we're all involved.

BONNY: I worry so about Nate.

MRS. HALE (*Wearily*): Do you think I don't?

BONNY: Sometimes when I talk to him, he hardly seems to hear me.

MRS. HALE: He's listening to other sounds, dear.

BONNY: Good ones?

MRS. HALE: For a mother, good sounds are the talk and laughter of her family, gathered around the table, safe and warm, in a time of peace.

BONNY: You frighten me a little.

MRS. HALE: Maybe because I myself am frightened. (SIS *comes into the spotlight from left.*)

SIS (*Excitedly*): Guess what? One of the boys told me that Nate made a speech in the town square!

BONNY (*Worried, glancing at* MRS. HALE): What was it about?

SIS: I don't know. (*Proudly*) But a lot of the men cheered.

MRS. HALE (*Putting head in hands*): Oh, dear. It's coming. Very soon.

SIS (*Concerned*): Mother, what's the matter?

MRS. HALE (*To* BONNY): You know what I mean.

BONNY (*Unhappily*): I'm selfish enough to hope you're wrong. (NATHAN *enters spotlight.*)

SIS: Nate! We heard about your speech.

NATHAN (*Surprised*): The word has spread already?

BONNY (*Worried*): Nate, what did you say?

NATHAN (*Boldly*): The same things many others are saying these days.

MRS. HALE: Tell us about it.

NATHAN (*Enthusiastically*): Well, we had a meeting out in the open. Most of the men felt as I do, but there were a few Tories there to jeer.

BONNY: At you?

NATHAN: Not at me personally, but at what I believe in.

MRS. HALE (*Upset*): Nate, you're so young! Couldn't you have waited till you're older?

NATHAN (*Vehemently*): Mother, the time is now. The colonies have knuckled under to the King too long.

SIS (*Confused*): When you talk about colonies, I get all mixed up. Connecticut's one, isn't it?

NATHAN: Yes, and Massachusetts, and New York. And Pennsylvania, New Jersey, and Virginia. There are thirteen colonies divided, hoping to get together.

MRS. HALE: That's what you talked about?

NATHAN: In part. (*Laughs*) My words came so fast that I can't recall them all.

BONNY: Maybe something about unjust taxes or the Stamp Act?

NATHAN (*Ardently*): In themselves, those things aren't of first importance. It's the principle behind them, that we should have the right to do our own taxing and make our own laws.

SIS: It sounds as if you're making the speech now.

NATHAN (*Considering*): I do remember the last part of what I said. (*Hesitates, then speaks as if addressing audience*) These colonies of ours should be united for our own welfare! No longer should we submit to the whims of a King. There are fighting men in action under General Washington. Why are they fighting? Not because of a law, not because of a tax, but for the right to be free! (ZEB *comes into spotlight.*)

ZEB (*Angrily*): Have you taken leave of your senses? Rabble rouser!

NATHAN (*Evenly*): You're wrong, Zeb.

ZEB: How long do you think you'll last as a schoolmaster?

NATHAN: That scarcely matters now. Does the word freedom mean nothing to you, Zeb?

ZEB (*Shaking head*): Talk, crazy talk.

NATHAN (*Fiercely*): No, Zeb. It's true talk.

ZEB (*To the others*): I've warned him to keep his mouth shut.

MRS. HALE: Nate has always done his own thinking.

NATHAN: I have nothing in common with you, Zeb.

ZEB: You mean because I'm a Tory? Yes, I am one. And when I'm rich and prosperous, where will you be? (*Turns his back on* NATHAN *and goes out of the spotlight left*)

BONNY: Nate, what does he mean?

NATHAN: I'm leaving to join General Washington's army in Boston.

MRS. HALE (*Upset*): I knew it!

BONNY (*Taking* NATHAN's *hand*): When, Nate?

NATHAN: Now.

SIS (*Clinging to him*): Oh, Nate, you'll come back to us, won't you?

NATHAN: When our freedom is assured. Now, I have to go. My traveling bag is already packed, under my bed.

MRS. HALE: I'll get it. (*As* NATHAN *starts to speak, she holds up her hand for silence.*) It may be a long time before I'm able to do anything for you again. (*Exits*)

BONNY (*Upset*): Nate, why must you go?

SIS: We need you here. And wars are bad.

NATHAN: Sometimes there's no other way, Sis. (BONNY *starts to cry.* NATHAN *tilts up her chin.*) Smile, my Bonny. Other men have gone off to war.

BONNY (*Trying to smile*): I know.

NATHAN: Think of the days to come when I'll be a middle-aged college professor, getting a little bald.

BONNY: That's so far ahead to think.

NATHAN (*Trying to be cheerful*): We'll have our own house then, and children running in and out slamming doors, and you'll call to them to be quiet when Father is preparing his lectures.

BONNY (*Her voice breaking*): I'll try to think of that. (MRS. HALE *comes into the spotlight with small traveling bag, which she gives to* NATHAN.)

NATHAN: Thank you, Mother.

SIS (*In tears*): Promise you'll come back soon, Nate.

NATHAN: I'll come back, Sis, though it may be quite a little while.

SIS: What if I'm all grown up?

NATHAN: You will still be my little sister. (*Kisses her on cheek, then takes* MRS. HALE's *hand*) Mother—

MRS. HALE: I hear that things aren't going too well with Washington's army.

NATHAN: All the more reason why I must go. (*Kisses her on cheek*)

MRS. HALE: Godspeed, my son. (*Embraces him*)

NATHAN (*Taking* BONNY's *hand*): You won't forget me, Bonny?

BONNY (*Unsteadily*): Not ever. (*He kisses her on cheek and leaves spotlight.* MRS. HALE *sits with her hands covering her face.* SIS *sits with her arms around* MRS. HALE, *and* BONNY *stands by them, her hand on* MRS. HALE's *shoulder, looking after* NATHAN. *Spotlight goes out, then comes up on* MS. DALTON. *As she speaks, the women hold this pose, and* NATHAN *enters to sit on bench at center, with traveling bag. Lighted candle and letters are beside him.*)

MS. DALTON: He was a dependable soldier, and soon was made a captain. When Washington was defeated at the Battle of Long Island, it was necessary that someone infiltrate the British camps to find out their plans. Nate volunteered. Wearing his schoolmaster's suit, he captured the plans, but before he could return to his own lines, an informer recognized him, and he was arrested by some British soldiers. . . . (*Spotlight falls on* NATHAN, *looking toward left.* ZEB *comes into the spotlight.*)

ZEB: Nate. Did you finish your letters? (NATHAN *doesn't reply.*) The guard is coming back. Do you hear me? (NATHAN *does not reply, and* ZEB *shakes his head.* GUARD *enters spotlight and* ZEB *exits.*)

GUARD: Rise, dog of a spy! Stand up! (NATHAN *slowly rises, still looking left. Another small spotlight falls on* MRS. HALE, BONNY, *and* SIS.)

NATHAN (*Softly, to women*): Goodbye.

GUARD: Step forth, Nathan Hale!

NATHAN (*Speaking to women*): I'm sorry I must bring you grief, that I cannot keep the promises I made. If you remember me—if anyone remembers me in the years to come—I only regret that I have but one life to lose for my country. (*Looks at women a moment longer, then turns and follows* GUARD *out of spotlight. Spotlight and light on women go out, and they exit. Candle on bench center is the only light; after a moment, it is extinguished, leaving stage in total darkness. All properties are removed from the stage. When stage lights go on,* MS. DALTON *and students stand on either side of draped statue.* HOT DOG VENDOR *and* FLAG SELLER *have joined the group.*)

OWEN (*Moved*): Nathan Hale!

JANIE: He died for his country as truly as if he had fallen in battle.

OWEN (*Passionately*): Ms. Dalton, this man did *not* fail! (*He takes bill from pocket and gives it to* FLAG SELLER, *who hands him a flag. He leans flag against statue. Then all stand looking up at draped statue. Offstage, recording of "America" may play softly as curtain falls.*)

THE END

Production Notes

ONE LIFE TO LOSE

Characters: 5 female; 6 male; 3 male or female for vendor, flag seller, stagehand.

Playing Time: 20 minutes.

Costumes: Present-day characters, casual modern dress. Nathan, knee breeches, long-sleeved shirt, narrow string tie. His hair is tied back with ribbon. Zeb's dress is similar, but more elegant. Mrs. Hale, Bonny, and Sis, long dresses. Guard, British officer's uniform, cocked hat.

Properties: Map, hot dog cart, small flags, electric candle, books, traveling bag, paper, inkwell, quill pen, darning basket.

Setting: City Hall Plaza, New York. Large statue up right is covered with workmen's canvas. Bench is center; table and bench are up left. Exits are right and left.

Lighting: Spotlights and electric candle.

Sound: Recording of "America," if desired.

Ordeal at Valley Forge

by *Bill Van Horn*

Weary soldier finds courage and love in midst of war. . . .

Characters

OLD NATHAN, *narrator*
YOUNG NATHAN, *soldier*
SILAS LUDWIG
JOSHUA BUCKWALTER
PATRICK, *drummer boy*
GEORGE WASHINGTON
BARBARA BAILEY
LIBBIE BUCKWALTER, *Joshua's wife*
PATRICK'S MOTHER
ABBIE FERGUSON
MRS. FERGUSON, *her mother*
ANNE }
MARY } *nurses*

SCENE 1

TIME: *Winter 1777–78.*
SETTING: *At left, campground at Valley Forge, with trees, logs, and campfires. Down left is a desk or small table.*
AT RISE: *Spotlight shines on* OLD NATHAN, *writing at desk.*

60

OLD NATHAN: I, Nathan Thomas, write these words at the insistence of my beloved children and grandchildren. It is the year 1826, fifty years after the signing of the Declaration of Independence. This has been a year of celebration and sadness, for on July 4th, both Thomas Jefferson and John Adams died. How strange, but somehow, how fitting. . . . (*Soft drumbeats are heard.*) My narrative begins in the year 1777. I was 21, cold, tired, wet and hungry like all soldiers of the Continental Army. We had been on the march for a week. It took that long to cover the thirteen miles from Whitemarsh to Valley Forge. We had suffered much from lack of clothing and shoes . . . and left bloody footprints in the snow. (*Lights come up left on* YOUNG NATHAN, JOSHUA, *and* PATRICK, *who enter, rubbing their hands, stamping feet, etc.* JOSHUA *has a blanket over his ragged clothes.* PATRICK *carries a drum.*)

JOSHUA (*Shivering*): So this is Valley Forge! Where is the welcoming committee? (*To* PATRICK, *who is shivering*) Ah, cheer up, Patrick, my boy. (*Slaps him on the back*) I'll call for our dinner. (*Takes stick from* PATRICK *and taps it on his drum, then calls out*) Ho, there, varlet! Are you deaf? I demand dinner!

PATRICK (*Shivering*): I'm so cold.

JOSHUA (*Kindly*): Then it is your turn for the blanket, Patrick. (*Puts blanket on* PATRICK) Now, come, dance with me. (*Whirls* PATRICK *around.* SILAS *enters.*)

SILAS: What's all this? (JOSHUA *and* PATRICK *stop.*)

JOSHUA: A bit of levity, sir. To keep our feet from freezing.

SILAS: I'm Captain Silas Ludwig, your new commander. And you?

JOSHUA: Private Joshua Buckwalter, Reading, Pennsylvania.

NATHAN: Private Nathan Thomas, sir, Reading, Pennsylvania.

PATRICK: Patrick Allen Murphy, sir, York, Pennsylvania.

SILAS: York, eh? That's where our Congress is, now that the British occupy Philadelphia. Patrick Allen Murphy, how old are you?

PATRICK: Old enough, sir, and I'd much rather fight than play the drum.

JOSHUA (*Ruffling* PATRICK's *hair*): The only tune he can beat time to is "Yankee Doodle." Pardon me if I don't whistle, but my lips are frozen, just like all the rest of me.

SILAS: And there's no need for it! There are barrels and barrels of clothes and shoes lying about in the road behind us. Lying and rotting there because there aren't enough horses nor carts to haul them.

NATHAN: And what about food?

SILAS (*Bitterly*): Ask the farmers around here that have sold their goods to the British. Ask our inept commissary and quartermaster corps.

NATHAN: Is there no food in the countryside? Can't we send out foraging parties?

SILAS: We can, and we will. But there's precious little food or fodder to be found. The British have stripped most of the farmers dry. It promises to be a hard winter. (*Shakes head*) Very hard.

JOSHUA: A toast to the coming winter! (*Holds up hand*) Ah, for the good old days. (*Dramatically*)
What happy golden days were those
When I was in my prime.
The lasses took delight in me,
I was so neat and fine.
I roved about from fair to fair;
Likewise from town to town.
Until I married me a wife,
And the world turned upside down.
(*Pulls his tattered hat down over his face and bows. Others laugh.*)

NATHAN (*After a moment's pause*): Why Valley Forge for a winter camp, then? (*All freeze as spotlight comes up on* GEORGE WASHINGTON, *who enters left and addresses audience.*)

WASHINGTON: Why, indeed? The Pennsylvania Assembly

threatened to cut off troops and supplies unless I positioned my army twenty-five miles away from the British to protect Pennsylvania's inland farms. And they urge me to wage battle against the British. Do they think my men are insensitive to frost and snow?

OFFSTAGE VOICES (*Shouting*): No bread, no soldier! No meat, no soldier!

WASHINGTON: I have barely 8,000 men fit for duty. Three thousand are unfit—sick, barefoot, or without uniforms.

OFFSTAGE VOICES: No bread, no soldier. No meat, no soldier!

WASHINGTON: I must inform Congress that a lack of food has caused a dangerous mutiny, which was suppressed with difficulty. Something must be done to take the troops' attention away from their misery. (*Spotlight goes out. WASHINGTON exits. Lights come up again on JOSHUA, NATHAN, SILAS, and PATRICK, who become animated.*)

SILAS (*Reading from paper*): General Washington has offered a prize of twelve dollars to the group that finishes its cabin first. Each cabin must be built according to strict army specifications.

JOSHUA: Ah, the army way! The right way, the wrong way, and the army way!

PATRICK (*Excitedly*): Twelve dollars! Let's go!

JOSHUA: Hold your horses, Patrick. We've got to plan this out. First we have to find some white pine. White pine works easier than most wood. And we're going to need cedar.

PATRICK: Why cedar?

JOSHUA: Cedar gives off a smell that helps keep away the fleas. We'll use cedar for shingles and for the bunks.

PATRICK (*Rubbing his hands together*): Where are the axes?

JOSHUA: You're too small, Patrick. Cutting down trees is man's work.

PATRICK (*Defiantly*): Just give me an axe and I'll show you what a man I am!

JOSHUA: No. There are plenty of other important jobs to be done.

PATRICK: Like what? (BARBARA *enters, carrying tree branches.*)

BARBARA: Well, we'll need strong arms to drag in the logs and fill in the chinks with mud. And not just anybody can build a fireplace.

SILAS (*Touching hat*): Howdy, Mistress Bailey. How's the hospital cabin coming along?

BARBARA: It's almost finished. My husband and his men arrived yesterday. But we could use some more help. (*To* PATRICK) And I think I can find some hot soup for you.

PATRICK (*Eagerly*): Can I go with her, Captain?

SILAS (*Kindly*): You're on your way, son.

BARBARA (*Smiling*): Thank you, Silas. And I think there's enough soup for you and your men.

JOSHUA (*Gratefully*): Hot soup? Ah, nectar of the gods. (*He bows.*) I am yours forever. (BARBARA *laughs and exits left with* PATRICK.)

SILAS (*Looking after her*): She's Sergeant Bailey's wife. Been with him for over a year. She and the rest of the camp women cook, nurse, wash, and make things more tolerable. Now, let's get to work on that cabin. (*He,* JOSHUA, *and* NATHAN *exit left.*)

OLD NATHAN: The whole camp went to work. Everybody did something. By Christmas almost all of the men were sheltered, and only then did Washington leave his tent and take shelter in the Forge master's house. (JOSHUA, NATHAN, *and* PATRICK *enter.* NATHAN *wears the blanket.* JOSHUA *is whittling. They all sit by the campfire.*)

PATRICK (*Musing*): It's Christmas. I was with Washington last Christmas when we crossed the Delaware and beat the Hessians. That man, Tom Paine, wrote some important words on my drumhead. I always carry them with me. (*To* NATHAN) Will you read them to me, Nathan? (*Takes paper from pocket, handing it to* NATHAN)

NATHAN: Of course, Patrick. (*Reads from paper*) "These are the times that try men's souls. The summer soldier and the sunshine patriot will, in this crisis, shrink from the service of their country; but he that stands it *now,* deserves the love and thanks of man and woman. Tyranny, like hell, is not easily conquered; yet we have this consolation with us, that the harder the conflict, the more glorious the triumph." (*A short silence. Drum beats are heard.*)

PATRICK: What are you whittling, Joshua?

JOSHUA: Trying to make some toys. Maybe next Christmas I can give them to my children, Rachael and Jason. (*Whittles vigorously. SILAS enters left. He holds two letters.*)

SILAS: I've got a present for you, Patrick.

PATRICK: What is it, Captain?

SILAS: A letter from your mother. (*Holds out letter. The men freeze. Spotlight comes up down right on PATRICK'S MOTHER.*)

PATRICK'S MOTHER: Dear Patrick, Hope this finds you well. We all miss you so much and can't wait until you come home. I'm making a quilt for your bed, and your Paw is adding on another room to the cabin. He's even putting in another window. You won't know the old place when you come home. Your sisters send their love. Your old dog, Sam, sleeps in your bed, and I know he can't wait either. God bless you, son. Love, Mother. (*Spotlight goes out. MOTHER exits. PATRICK takes letter from SILAS and clutches it to his chest.*)

SILAS: Got one for you, too, Joshua. (*Hands letter to JOSHUA, who looks up expectantly*) It's from Libbie. (*Spotlight comes up down right. LIBBIE enters, smiling.*)

LIBBIE: Dear Joshua, We all send you our deepest love. Rachael is walking now and babbles constantly. Jason has taught her the word "Daddy," but I'm not sure she knows what it means. Jason is quite the little man and helps all he can. He says to hurry home so you two can go fishing. The farm is doing well, and we had good crops. Please be careful, and always remember how much we love you and eagerly await your safe return. God's blessing on you, my dear husband. Love, Libbie.

(LIBBIE *exits. Spotlight goes out.* JOSHUA *sighs, and exits left.*)

NATHAN: Joshua? (*Starts out after him, but is restrained by* SILAS)

SILAS: Let him be, Nathan. He needs to be alone. (SILAS *and* NATHAN *freeze.*)

OLD NATHAN: There was no letter for me. Loneliness gripped my heart, and I was envious of Patrick and Joshua. But my self-pity was short-lived. (*Action continues.*)

SILAS: Nathan! Joshua! (JOSHUA *reenters.*) Dispatch from General Greene. He's in command of all foraging parties. We're to search the countryside for food and fodder. If we can't transport it, we're to burn it. If we can't feed our army with it, then we'll destroy it so the British can't have it. I'm from this area and know the country well. Who'll volunteer?

NATHAN: I'll go.

JOSHUA: Count me in!

PATRICK: Me, too!

SILAS: Patrick, you stay. It's too dangerous. The British are out there too, stealing and burning all they can.

PATRICK (*Protesting*): But . . .

SILAS (*Sternly*): That's an order! (*To* NATHAN *and* JOSHUA) Come on, you two. (*They pick up rifles and exit left.* PATRICK *stays by campfire, looking unhappy, as curtain closes.*)

* * * * *

SCENE 2

TIME: *A short while later.*

SETTING: *Stage is now divided: Campground is at left, and at right, interior of a colonial farmhouse with fireplace, table and chairs, rocking chair and bench. There is a rifle hanging over fireplace. Lights come up either left or right, depending on action, then dim at conclusion of action.*

AT RISE: ABBIE FERGUSON, *wearing heavy jacket and pants,*

her hair completely covered by a cap, enters right, supporting
MRS. FERGUSON, *and helps her into rocking chair. After a*
moment, loud knocking is heard. ABBIE *goes to fireplace,*
takes down rifle.

ABBIE (*Shouting off*): Who's there? (*Knocking continues.*) I
said, who's there?

NATHAN (*Offstage*): The Continental Army!

ABBIE: Come in! (NATHAN *enters.*) Hold it! Right there! (NA-
THAN *freezes.*) Who are you?

NATHAN: Nathan Thomas!

ABBIE: And what outfit are you with?

NATHAN: The Pennsylvania Line. Put down that rifle!

ABBIE: When I'm good and ready. This could be a trick. (SILAS
enters, addresses ABBIE.)

SILAS: It's all right. He's one of ours.

NATHAN (*Addressing* SILAS; *gesturing toward* ABBIE): You
know him?

ABBIE: Him? I'm not a him. I'm Abbie Ferguson. Silas and I
are neighbors.

NATHAN (*Surprised*): Abbie? But those clothes . . .

ABBIE (*Sarcastically*): Dear me, I beg your pardon. If I had
known you were coming, I'd have worn my Sunday best. What
better clothes to wear, seeing that I have to do all the work
around here.

SILAS: Where's your father, Abbie?

ABBIE (*Bitterly*): Dead! Killed by the British. A few weeks ago
a foraging party came by stealing all they could get their
filthy hands on. Father went out to protest, and one of them
knocked him over with his horse and then trampled him.
Trampled him! And then rode off laughing!

SILAS: I'm sorry. (JOSHUA *enters.*)

ABBIE: Sorry's not enough! I want to join the army and have re-
venge!

NATHAN: The army's no place for a girl.

ABBIE (*Angrily*): I'm a woman, not a girl. And I'll bet I can shoot as straight as most men. And if it weren't for Mother, I'd—

SILAS: What's wrong with your mother?

ABBIE: See for yourself, Silas. (SILAS *goes to* MRS. FERGU-SON, *who stares straight ahead.*) She doesn't recognize you. She hasn't spoken a word or done anything except sit there and rock, since Father's death.

SILAS: Is there anything we can do?

ABBIE: Yes. State your business, and you (*To* NATHAN), watch your tongue. (JOSHUA *laughs.* NATHAN *glares at him.*)

SILAS: We're looking for food and fodder.

ABBIE: Isn't everybody? (*Takes off cap and fluffs hair.* NA-THAN *gapes at her in admiration.*) I'll share all I can spare. Father and I hid lots of food and grain in the caves out by the barn. I'd be much obliged if you'd leave some food for Mother and me.

SILAS: Of course. And no one else will ever know.

ABBIE: You always were a good neighbor, Silas. And I'd appreci-ate it if you'd not take the cow.

SILAS (*Pretending ignorance*): Cow? What cow?

ABBIE (*Smiling*): You're a good man, Silas. (*Shakes his hand*)

SILAS: And you're a courageous woman, Abbie.

JOSHUA: And a beautiful one. (ABBIE *ignores the comment.* JOSHUA *nudges* NATHAN.)

NATHAN (*Clearing throat*): Mistress Ferguson?

ABBIE (*Looking up*): Yes?

NATHAN: May I wish you a—a happy Christmas?

ABBIE: You may indeed, Private Thomas. (*Smiles at him*) And I wish you the same. Come along, now. (*They exit left.* MOTHER *stays in chair.*)

OLD NATHAN: The new year of 1778 saw little change in the miserable conditions at Valley Forge. (*Lights up on camp-ground.* JOSHUA, NATHAN, *and* SILAS *join* PATRICK *at campfire.*) It was not the British that we battled here, but despair, hunger, and sickness. (BARBARA *enters left, carrying a small traveling bag.*)

BARBARA: I've come to say farewell. I'm going to Yellow Springs with my husband.

PATRICK: Yellow Springs?

BARBARA: A village some ten miles away. The army has a hospital there. A hospital for those who suffer from typhus. (*Her voice breaks.*) My husband has typhus. (SILAS *puts his arm around her.* PATRICK *looks at the ground, as does* NATHAN.)

JOSHUA: Is there anything we can do?

BARBARA: Yes. Take good care of Patrick (*Hugs him*) and your-selves. Goodbye and God bless you. (*Exits left. They watch her exit.*)

SILAS: There goes a wonderful woman. Sergeant Bailey's lucky to have such a wife.

NATHAN: Are you married, Captain? (JOSHUA *whittles.*)

SILAS: I was. But Martha took sick and died in the summer of '76. That's when I joined the army. (*Wistfully*) Barbara reminds me some of Martha.

JOSHUA (*Whittling more vigorously*): She reminded me of my Libbie. (*Stops whittling, sighs*) Libbie . . . I wonder if I shall ever see her again? (*After a short silence he laughs and gets up. Bitterly*) Ah, yes, the army! Sign up, men! Sign up for five dollars a month and good rations. A pound or so per day of pork, beef, or fish, plus a pound of bread or flour, and a pint of milk or a quart of beer or cider. Plus a weekly allowance of vegetables! And what do we have to eat at this winter resort? Firecakes—a little flour mixed with water! Firecakes! Fire-cakes for breakfast, dinner, and supper!

SILAS (*Worried*): Are you all right, Joshua?

JOSHUA: All right and happy. A soldier who gripes is a happy soldier, right? (*Tries to laugh, but coughs*)

SILAS: I'm looking for volunteers for another foraging party.

PATRICK (*Eagerly*): I'll go, Captain!

SILAS: No! And don't ask me again, Patrick! (PATRICK *looks crestfallen.*)

NATHAN: I'll go.

JOSHUA (*Teasing him*): I'll bet you will. (*Laughs again, then coughs*)

NATHAN: Why do you say that?

JOSHUA: Because Silas told me earlier that he was going in the direction of the Ferguson farm.

NATHAN: So? (SILAS *and* JOSHUA *laugh*.) Are you coming with us, Joshua?

JOSHUA: No.

SILAS (*Surprised*): No?

JOSHUA: No. I'll stay here and keep Patrick company. And whittle away at these toys. That is, if you don't mind, Captain.

SILAS: It's all right. Come on, Nathan, let's find some more men. (*They exit*.)

PATRICK: We'd better get some more firewood, Joshua. (*He and* JOSHUA *exit. Curtain*)

* * * * *

SCENE 3

TIME: *A short while later.*

AT RISE: ABBIE, *wearing a dress, with her hair long, bustles about the cabin. She drapes a quilt around her mother.*

ABBIE: There. That should keep you warmer, Mother. (*Loud knocking is heard.*) Who is it?

NATHAN: The Continental Army!

ABBIE: Oh, for heaven's sake! (*Calls out*) You may come in, but leave the rest of the army out there! (NATHAN *enters, hat in hand.*)

NATHAN: Mistress Ferguson.

ABBIE: How can I help you, Private?

NATHAN (*Uncomfortably*): I wanted to say . . . I wanted to say. . . .

ABBIE (*Smiling*): Yes?

NATHAN (*Blurting it out*): Well, it's nice not to have a rifle barring my entrance. (*He laughs weakly.*)

ABBIE: And it's nice not to have any remarks about my appearance. (*She laughs. He joins her.*)

NATHAN: Why, you look—you look—

ABBIE: Yes?

NATHAN: You look beautiful, Mistress Ferguson.

ABBIE: Thank you. And for that you may call me Abbie.

NATHAN: Abbie. A pretty name.

ABBIE: Thank you. You flatter me.

NATHAN: I speak only what I feel. (*They look at one another.*) Ah, how is your mother?

ABBIE (*Sighing; looking at her mother*): The same. Silas stops by now and then to help. He said you might come on another foraging party.

NATHAN: I was glad to come. Silas is out in the barn. We need what food and fodder you can spare.

ABBIE: Is that the only reason you have come?

NATHAN (*Quickly*): Oh, no. That is, I mean—

ABBIE (*Saving him from embarrassment*): Please, have a seat. I will bring you some cider.

NATHAN: Much obliged. (*He sits at table. She pours cider into a mug and hands it to him. He drops it.*) Oh, I'm so sorry!

ABBIE: It's all right. (*They drop to floor to retrieve mug. Their fingers touch; he takes her hand. They gaze at one another. At that moment,* SILAS *bursts in with a huge package.* ABBIE *and* NATHAN *rise, she holding the mug.*)

SILAS: We'd best be off, Nathan. Many thanks for the supplies, Abbie.

ABBIE: I'm happy to be of help. Come again. (*Looks at* NATHAN) You are always welcome. (*He backs out, looking at her.* SILAS *pulls him out right. She blows him a kiss and skips over to* MRS. FERGUSON. *Lights out right.* ABBIE *and* MRS. FERGUSON *exit.*)

OLD NATHAN: I was as light as a feather! I wanted to sing, to shout with joy! I was in love! I attempted a cartwheel and ended up head first in a snowdrift. But I felt no chill—that would come when I arrived at the camp. (NATHAN *rushes in left.*)

NATHAN (*Happily*): Joshua! Joshua! (PATRICK *enters.*)

PATRICK (*Upset*): Joshua's gone, Nathan.

NATHAN (*Surprised*): Gone? Gone where?

PATRICK: They've taken him to Bethlehem, almost fifty miles away.

NATHAN (*Shocked*): Bethlehem!

PATRICK (*Quietly*): To the hospital there. The doctor says it's typhus.

NATHAN (*Upset*): Typhus! Oh, no, not Joshua.

PATRICK: He said not to worry because he'd be back soon. Do you think he'll come back, Nathan? Do you?

NATHAN (*Putting his arm around* PATRICK): He has to! If anyone can survive, it's Joshua. (*They exit left.*)

OLD NATHAN: Survival for all of us became a never-ending battle. And without Joshua's antics, we were drawn more and more into our own agonies and doubts. A cold January blew into a colder, icier, more brutal February, and conditions worsened. Typhus continued to spread throughout the camp. Most of those afflicted died, as did many who nursed them. There were rumors about camp that Joshua was recovering and would soon return. We needed his humor—the men argued and fought constantly.

    Because our unit was placed on special guard duty, I had no chance to visit Abbie. As the temperature dropped, so did my morale. I write the following shamefully. (NATHAN *and* SILAS *enter left.*)

SILAS: Two thousand of our men have deserted to the British in Philadelphia, and it is getting worse.

NATHAN: I suffer. I serve. I try to do my duty. It is not easy.

SILAS (*Grimly*): Nathan, here is a note from Joshua. (*Pulls note from his pocket, hands it to* NATHAN)

NATHAN: From Joshua? (*Reads*) "Do what I cannot. Go where I cannot. Finish what must be done." (*Looks up*) What does this mean? (SILAS *pulls bundle out from under his jacket.*)

SILAS: This. (*Hands bundle to* NATHAN, *who unwraps it, pulls out small wooden toys*)

NATHAN: The toys! The toys Joshua was making for his children.

SILAS (*In somber tone*): The toys he will not be able to finish. (*He clasps* NATHAN's *shoulder.*)

NATHAN (*Miserably*): Not Joshua! Not Joshua! No, no! (*He runs off.*)

SILAS (*Running off after him*): Nathan! Nathan!

OLD NATHAN: I ran until I could run no more! I cried until I had no tears. I shouted, "Unfair! Unfair!" until I had no voice. I could take no more. No more! I wandered senselessly and furtively in the frigid countryside for two days, without food or water. And then, delirious and exhausted, I came to a decision. (*Lights up right.* ABBIE *enters, goes to* MRS. FERGUSON, *in chair, gives her drink of water. There is loud knocking on door.* NATHAN *bursts in.*)

NATHAN: Abbie! Abbie! (*He collapses. She kneels over him.*)

ABBIE (*Concerned*): Nathan! What is it?

NATHAN: I can't take any more! I'm running away. Come with me!

ABBIE: Nathan, what are you saying?

NATHAN: I've deserted! (*She shakes him.*)

ABBIE: No, you haven't, Nathan! You can't! I won't let you! (*He slumps over.*) Nathan? Nathan! (*Holds mug of cider to his lips, but he's unconscious.* ABBIE *calls off.*) Barbara! Barbara, I need your help! (BARBARA *runs in.*) It's Nathan. He's unconscious. (BARBARA *takes off her apron, dips it in bucket of water and mops* NATHAN's *brow. After a few moments, he stirs, sees* BARBARA.)

NATHAN: Barbara? What are you doing here?

BARBARA: We're setting up a hospital in Abbie's barn.

NATHAN: Why aren't you with Sergeant Bailey? (ANNE *and* MARY *enter with blankets.*)

BARBARA: My husband is dead, Nathan. He died from typhus.

NATHAN: I'm sorry, Barbara. Joshua died of typhus, too.

BARBARA (*Sadly*): Too many die from typhus. (*Indicates* ANNE *and* MARY) That's why we're hoping to help with a hospital here.

NATHAN: And you, Abbie, will you be a nurse, too?

ABBIE: Yes, Nathan.

NATHAN: But you may all die!

MARY: We will do what we can.

ANNE: With what we have.

NATHAN: Don't do it, Abbie! Come away with me! (*He gets to his feet and grabs* ABBIE. *She pushes him down.* SILAS *enters, carrying rifle.*)

SILAS: Ah, Nathan. Where have you been? We've been looking for you. It's easy to become lost in this countryside.

NATHAN: I was not lost and I do not want to be found!

SILAS: But you'll be coming back.

NATHAN (*Forcefully*): No!

SILAS: There will be charges against you, you know.

NATHAN: I'm not going back!

SILAS: And I say you will!

NATHAN: No! (*Wrests* SILAS's *gun from him, points it at him*) Nothing—no one—is going to stop me! (*Sound of hoofbeats is heard, then a scream and shots, after which hoofbeats fade away.*)

SILAS: Patrick! (*Runs out*)

NATHAN, ABBIE, *and* BARBARA (*Ad lib; upset*): Oh, no! It can't be Patrick! What's happened? (*Etc.* SILAS *reenters, carrying* PATRICK, *who is limp. Others surround him.*)

SILAS: I never should have let him come, but he begged me! He begged me! (*Lays* PATRICK *down*) He wanted to go on a foraging party like the big boys, he said. And now look.

BARBARA (*Wailing*): Oh, what happened?

SILAS: A British foraging party. My men scared them off, but not until one of them trampled Patrick with his horse. (*Closes eyes and shakes head*) Why Patrick? Why not me? Why not me? (PATRICK *murmurs.*)

BARBARA: He's calling for his mother. (*She rubs his forehead,* ABBIE *holds his hand.*)

SILAS: It's all right, Patrick. Here's a new letter from your mother. (*Takes a piece of paper from his pocket, reads*) "Dear Son. We're all fine back here at home. Your captain has written us and told us what a brave and loyal soldier you are. A real soldier, not a summer one. We're all so proud of you. Hurry home soon and I'll bake your favorite apple pie. First thing you know, you'll be back and out in the fields playing with old Sam. God bless you, son. Love, Mother." (PATRICK *murmurs again.*)

BARBARA: He's smiling. But he said he's cold.

ANNE (*Offering blanket*): Here. Put this on him.

MRS. FERGUSON (*Rising out of rocking chair*): No. Let me. (*She walks over to* PATRICK, *covers him with blanket, then takes his hand. After a moment, she speaks.*) He's gone. (*Drumbeats are heard.*)

SILAS: We'll take him back to camp and bury him.

MRS. FERGUSON: No. No common grave for this boy. We'll bury him here. (*Looks down at him*) And we'll bury him in decent clothes.

ABBIE: Silas?

SILAS: Yes, Abbie?

ABBIE: There was no letter, was there? There was nothing written on that paper?

SILAS: No, Abbie. There wasn't. (*All hold pose around* PAT-RICK'*s body. Actors exit.*)

OLD NATHAN: We buried his small body under the largest tree on the farm and marked his grave with the largest boulder we could find. (*Echoes of drumbeats are heard.*) Silas and Abbie's mother read the services. I was too ashamed to ask Abbie's forgiveness. The hurt in her eyes told me all I needed to know. I went back to camp and resumed my duties as a soldier. Silas never mentioned my desertion to anyone. For a long time I could not meet the eyes of those loyal emaciated soldiers shivering in front of their pitiable fires, and huddling in their drafty cabins. They did not know, but I did, and so did Abbie. Silas made me work extra hard, as well I should have, and my pain lessened as I reached out and helped the others. And then, one day in May . . . (SILAS *and* NATHAN *enter left.*)

SILAS: Nathan, you've been working hard and long, and you show qualities of leadership. I'm recommending you for promotion.

NATHAN: But I—

SILAS: Say no more. You've proved you're no summer soldier. And I've something that will make you feel even happier than a promotion. (*Hands him note, then exits*)

NATHAN (*Reading*): "If at all possible, I would like to see you again. Yours, Abbie." (*He runs off.*)

OLD NATHAN (*Happily*): "Yours, Abbie"! I ran to Silas, but that wonderful old saint had already written the orders. I was free to go! I ran the entire three miles to Abbie's farm. (*Lights up right.* NATHAN *runs in.*)

NATHAN (*Looking around*): Abbie? Abbie! Where are you? (*Runs out*)

OLD NATHAN: It was deserted. The barn and the outbuildings had been burned down, the caves looted, and the cow had been killed. And Abbie? Gone. But there was no time to investigate. We moved out of Valley Forge and into battle. Three years later, in 1781, I was at Yorktown when Cornwallis surrendered. We had won! On my way home I carried the completed toys to give to Joshua's children. And that caused me sorrow. I felt sorrow, too, when I stopped at the Ferguson farm and found it empty still. But I entered the cabin for one last look. Providence willed that I should call out.

NATHAN (*Entering cabin, carrying a pack*): Abbie? Abbie! (MRS. FERGUSON *enters, smiles when she sees* NATHAN.)

MRS. FERGUSON (*Hugging* NATHAN): Nathan! Thank God you're all right. (*Calling as she runs out*) Abbie! He's here! Nathan's here! (*Exits.* ABBIE *runs in, throws herself into* NATHAN's *arms.*)

ABBIE: Oh, Nathan! Thank God you've returned!

NATHAN (*As he strokes* ABBIE's *hair*): Where were you? What happened? No word for three years! I thought you were dead!

ABBIE: The British made one last raiding party. They forced us to reveal where we had hidden our food, and were furious to see how much there was. They took everything and burned down the barn.

NATHAN (*Suddenly*): The hospital?

ABBIE (*Shaking head*): Fortunately, we were no longer using the barn as a hospital. The British took us prisoner and made us work in the army camps.

NATHAN (*Upset*): Oh, Abbie, no!

ABBIE: Mother and I were treated tolerably well, but there was no way I could contact you.

NATHAN: How long have you been back?

ABBIE: Just since this morning. (*Hugging him*) Oh, Nathan, it's a miracle! We're together again. I'm so happy.

NATHAN (*Gravely*): I'm not.

ABBIE: Oh, why? Is there anything I can do?

NATHAN: You're the only one who can.

ABBIE: And what is that?

NATHAN (*Smiling*): Marry me, Abbie.

ABBIE (*Exuberantly*): Oh, yes, Nathan! Yes! (*Spirited Revolutionary music is heard as curtain falls.*)

THE END

Production Notes

ORDEAL AT VALLEY FORGE

Characters: 6 male; 7 female.

Playing Time: 30 minutes.

Costumes: Period clothing. Soldiers wear tattered clothes, stockings. etc. Silas, an officer's coat. In last scene, Nathan wears officer's coat. Abbie first wears heavy jacket, pants, with hair up under cap, then changes to long skirt, blouse, and apron.

Properties: Drum and sticks; blankets; tree branches; pieces of wood and whittling knife; rifles; letters; small traveling bag; quilt; mug; bundle of wooden toys; bucket of water;

Setting: Scene 1, campground at Valley Forge is left, with trees, logs, and campfires. Down left is a desk or small table. Scenes 2 and 3, stage is now divided: Campground is at left, and at right, interior of a colonial farmhouse with fireplace, table and chairs, rocking chair and bench. There is a rifle hanging over fireplace. Lights come up either left or right, depending on action, then dim at conclusion of action.

Lighting: Lights up and down on action as it takes place either stage left or right; spotlights, as indicated.

Sound: Drumbeats; hoofbeats; gunshots; Revolutionary music.

Molly Pitcher Meets the General

by Marjory Hall

Revolutionary heroine earns her nickname . . .

Characters

WILLIAM ⎫
JAMES ⎬ *ragged soldiers*
RICHARD ⎭
MOLLY PITCHER
GEORGE WASHINGTON
CHARLES
FRANK
MAJOR SMITH, *Washington's aide*

SCENE 1

TIME: *Early evening in June, 1778.*

SETTING: *Interior of a hut. Fireplace is right, with bench nearby. Soup pot hangs over fireplace. It is dark, the only light coming from fireplace and lantern.*

AT RISE: WILLIAM *and* JAMES *sit quietly on bench.* WILLIAM's *shoes are on floor in front of him.* RICHARD *leans back against wall, his eyes closed. Mug and spoon are beside him.* MOLLY PITCHER, *her sleeves rolled up and an apron tied over her long skirt, stirs soup pot. She turns, looks at* RICHARD *with worried expression, and walks over to him.*

MOLLY: Here, lad, try some more soup. You'll feel better if you get something hot into you. Come on, just to please Molly? (RICHARD *shakes his head and says nothing.* MOLLY *picks up mug and spoon and starts to feed him, by spoonfuls, which he swallows reluctantly.)*

WILLIAM: I could fancy some more soup myself, if you'd help *me* that way.

MOLLY (*Sharply*): There's not so much in the kettle that you can have third and fourth helpings.

JAMES: You want us to leave, I suppose?

MOLLY: No, no, I didn't mean that. You're welcome to sit there until the space is needed.

WILLIAM: Or until they come for us and tell us to start chasing that British general. I don't see why we should chase him at all.

MOLLY: To keep him from getting away, of course. Besides, they say that General Clinton has food and guns and a whole lot of other things that would come in mighty handy for our own boys. He's trying to skedaddle, so they tell me, after living like a king in Philadelphia all winter. I heard, too, that it has something to do with the fleet the French have sent to help us. The British general doesn't like that a bit.

WILLIAM (*Sneering*): I've no use for generals, no matter which side they're on. I don't think they know any more about soldiering than I do. Take Washington. How'd *he* get to be a general?

JAMES: He's been a soldier for years. He fought the French and the Indians, and he made a good job of it, too.

WILLIAM: Well, I hear he's a high and mighty Virginian.

JAMES: High and mighty? Why, they say at Valley Forge he walked around talking to the soldiers, away from his aides. My cousin told me Washington sat down at his campfire one night just to talk to the men. (*Proudly*) Now, there's a real leader. Why, he could be at this camp this very minute and walk right in *here.*

WILLIAM (*Scoffing*): Oh, sure! Maybe he could shine up our shoes for us, or stir the soup for this lady.

JAMES: There's not much use talking to you, I can see that. (*He looks around cabin, turns to* MOLLY.) When I looked in this morning, this place was full of rubbish. How'd you get it cleaned up so quickly?

MOLLY: Cleaning up comes naturally when you've been at it a lifetime.

WILLIAM: Not so long a lifetime, in your case. How old are you, twenty?

MOLLY (*Smiling*): Close enough.

WILLIAM: I wouldn't mind having a girl like you around to clean up and make good soup for me. Would you be interested?

MOLLY (*Laughing*): I don't think my husband would like that.

JAMES: So that's why you're here. I heard a lot of wives came up here in wagons last night. Where'd you come from?

MOLLY: New Jersey. And it's a good thing for you we did come, too. This place looked as if you could use a few brooms—and some food.

RICHARD (*Weakly*): We just got here ourselves, ma'am. There's been no chance for us to do any cleaning yet.

MOLLY (*To* RICHARD): I'm glad to hear you talk, soldier. You look better, too. I knew the soup would help. Would you like some more?

WILLIAM (*Roughly*): You just told me that there wasn't enough for another helping.

JAMES (*Firmly but quietly*): Can't you see he needs it to get his strength back?

MOLLY (*Turning back to* RICHARD): Let me have your mug, soldier. (*She picks up* RICHARD'*s mug and begins to ladle more soup into it, as* GEORGE WASHINGTON *enters quietly right and goes to sit on empty bench, left, in dim light, his back mostly to audience. He wears a cloak with collar upturned, and others do not recognize him.* MOLLY *gives him a brief glance, then turns back to kettle and continues to ladle soup into* RICH-

ARD's *mug. She hands mug to* WILLIAM.) Here, take this to him. (*She points to* RICHARD.)

WILLIAM: Do you want me to feed him, too?

MOLLY: Oh, he can manage for himself now, I reckon. (*Turns to* RICHARD) Can't you, soldier? (*As* WILLIAM *walks over to* RICHARD *and gives him mug,* MOLLY *picks up another mug and fills it, picks up spoon, then hands them to* WASHING- TON. *He nods thanks, and begins to eat.*)

WILLIAM: Say, missus, how far away is this place you come from?

MOLLY: Thirty, forty miles, I guess. It seems longer, riding in a farm wagon on a road that feels as if it's made out of tree trunks.

WILLIAM (*Bitterly*): You should try *walking* that far. (*He sits down, rubs his hands over his stockinged feet, then starts to put his shoes on, groaning as he does so.*)

MOLLY: Where'd you come from? All the way from Valley Forge?

WILLIAM: No. I thank my stars for that, anyway. I just joined up two weeks ago, and that's three or four weeks too long to be in this dratted army.

MOLLY (*To* JAMES): You, too?

JAMES: Me, too. What about your husband, if you really have one? Did he ride over in that wagon with you?

MOLLY: Indeed not! He's been in the army since last Novem- ber—seven and a half months he's been gone from me. Yester- day was the first time I'd seen him since he left Carlisle. That's where we live.

RICHARD (*Slowly*): Was your husband at Valley Forge?

MOLLY: He was. It must have been as terrible as they say, because he won't speak of it. "Over and done with," he says, "over and done with." And that's all I get out of him, so I know it must have been bad.

RICHARD (*Shuddering*): Bad! You could never know, ma'am, how it was.

MOLLY: You were there, too?

RICHARD: Yes, I was there. And I understand about your husband, ma'am, because I can't speak of it either. My younger brother died there, just from being cold and hungry, and that's the truth. What do I tell my mother, when I get back to Massachusetts—if I ever do get back there? He died, and I didn't, and she'll think I could have shared my food with him and taken care of him somehow. Lots of others died, too, or froze their toes off. I was lucky—I just got sick.

MOLLY: But you're all right now.

RICHARD (*Sighing*): Yes, I guess I'm all right now, but I don't get along so well on this marching. (*Shakes his head*) Maybe tomorrow, or whenever we move on again, it won't be so bad. (*He stands, hands* MOLLY *mug, sways a little.* JAMES *tries to help him, but he pushes him aside.*) I'm right enough. It was your soup that did it, ma'am—gave me my strength back. Your husband is a lucky man. (*He walks out slowly.*)

JAMES (*Looking after him*): That one won't make many more miles, if you ask me.

WASHINGTON (*Speaking for the first time, so that others turn quickly at sound of his voice*): He might. Men do more than they can, sometimes.

JAMES: Yes, they do. I suppose we'll all be like that after a while, although it was that snow and cold at Valley Forge that did him in. Were you there too, soldier?

WASHINGTON: Yes, the whole time. I was fortunate. I had shoes and food. There were many that lacked both. (*To* MOLLY) What's your husband's name, ma'am?

MOLLY: Hays. John Hays. He's just been made a lieutenant!

WASHINGTON: And I'm sure he is worthy.

WILLIAM (*Scoffing*): It doesn't follow. A man buys his commission, and then sits by the fire and lets others do his work for him.

JAMES (*Angrily*): That isn't true. They told me the highest-ranking officers gave the men their food and even the shoes off their feet and the clothes off their backs. Most of the time they never ate any better than the men did. You sure have a grudge about officers. What did any one of 'em ever do to you?

WILLIAM: You just don't look at the facts head-on. (*To* WASHINGTON) Does he?

WASHINGTON: There are men who are bad officers, and men who are good ones. No one was really ready for this war, you know. The best we could do was take the men who had some knowledge of fighting and put them in charge.

WILLIAM: The officers ride their horses and let us walk.

JAMES (*Firmly*): The officers ride those same horses ahead of men right into the fighting, too, you know. (*Impatiently*) There's no use arguing with you, William. Come on, we might as well go find the others and get some sleep. We have a lot more walking to do tomorrow, I expect. (*To* MOLLY) Thanks for the soup, ma'am. It sure was good.

MOLLY (*Kindly*): Good night to you. (JAMES *and* WILLIAM *walk out, and she stirs the pot again. Over her shoulder, to* WASHINGTON) A bit more soup, soldier?

WASHINGTON: Won't it be needed for others?

MOLLY: If one man comes in, I could give him only half a mug, and that would only aggravate him, I reckon. I didn't let on to the others we were down to the bottom of the kettle, because that weak one needed all he could get into him. That was plain to see. Here, give me your mug. (*She takes his mug and ladles the last of the soup into it.*) I brought everything my father could spare from his farm and hid it under the false bottom in the wagon, just in case there were any thieving Redcoats on the road. I had enough to fill that kettle for today and tomorrow anyway. When do you think you'll move on, soldier?

WASHINGTON: As soon as we can. Two days, maybe. It depends on what news the scouts bring back. The men have done well, but we must take care of them, give them as much rest as possible before—(*He pauses.*)

MOLLY (*Quietly*): Before the battle, which will be a big one. Is that what you didn't finish saying? (*She sighs.*) A big battle that means lots of killing and wounding. My husband told me something fearful is just ahead; he's sure of it.

WASHINGTON: We always hope not.

MOLLY: You sound like a doctor, worrying about the men. Are you?

WASHINGTON: No. You don't have to be a doctor to know that men have limits to their endurance.

MOLLY: My husband knows a lot about doctoring. He's a barber, you see. A barber-surgeon. He pulls teeth and treats many ills. He's well thought of back in Carlisle.

WASHINGTON: He does important work. And such men are badly needed in the army. Has your husband been barbering and doctoring in the army, Mistress Hays?

MOLLY (*Sighing*): Alas, no. He is a gunner. (*Shakes her head sadly*) My John never even liked to shoot squirrels or rabbit for food, and now he's shooting men.

WASHINGTON (*Sympathetically*): Even the gentlest of men are fighting for the cause of freedom and independence these days. That's the way of a true patriot. What must be done, he will do. You are lucky to have such a husband.

MOLLY: Oh, I *know*.

WASHINGTON: And he is lucky in his wife. (*Rises*) Your soup was most welcome, Mistress Hays. I believe it was the best I have tasted since long before Valley Forge—almost since I can remember. (*Sighs*) Somehow the weeks and months are all run together in a nightmare of hope and hunger and despair. (*He turns to go.*)

MOLLY (*Sharply*): Since you are the only man here and you say you enjoyed my soup, would you help me with the kettle before you go?

WASHINGTON: Oh, I beg your pardon. I didn't think. (*He walks back to hearth.*)

MOLLY (*Holding one side of kettle*): It must be lifted down and put there (*Points to bench or floor*) so I can scour it later. (WASHINGTON *lifts kettle down from crane and sets it on bench or floor.*)

WASHINGTON: There. Now, is there anything else I can do for
you before I go?

MOLLY: Thank you, no. And I'm sorry I snapped at you. (*She
puts her hands to her back, wearily.*) This has been a long day,
tiring as well as worrisome. I hope you understand.

WASHINGTON: Of course, I understand, Mistress Hays, and
I'm sorry I didn't think to do it myself. What is your given
name, may I ask?

MOLLY: Molly. I am Mary Ludwig Hays, but always called
Molly. And what is your name, soldier?

WASHINGTON (*Walking toward door, then turning back*):
George. (*He exits, then puts his head in doorway, smiling
broadly.*) Since you told me both of your names, I should in
all fairness do the same. My name is George Washington.
(*He exits. MOLLY claps her hands to her mouth, looks after
WASHINGTON in amazement, as he exits and the curtain
falls.*)

* * * * *

SCENE 2

TIME: *Two or three weeks later.*

SETTING: *A clearing in a wooded area. There are bushes all
around and a log on the ground at right.*

JAMES: What a day! So hot, so confounded hot. But not as bad
as yesterday. Never was such a day as that.

WILLIAM: If you say that again, I'll shoot you, I swear it.

JAMES: With what? You have no ammunition left, any more
than I have. I'll bet there isn't a bullet left in the whole army.
(*There is a long silence.*)

WILLIAM: Well, we won, didn't we? Though I guess we almost
didn't. I heard tell that General Charles Lee went the wrong
way, or something that made General Washington terribly
angry. But we won just the same—chased those Redcoats out
and took their whole wagon train away from them.

JAMES: Chased them! (*Laughing*) They didn't run, they just melted away in those heavy red coats, if you ask me.

WILLIAM: So did a lot of our own men, and our clothes were much better for 94 degrees in the shade. But no matter how you're dressed, this is no weather to be rushing around with guns and dragging cannons up hills. I hope what they call our independence is going to be worth all this.

JAMES (*Wryly*): It won't be to all those who died of the heat. I'd rather be killed by a bullet any day than die that way. I was never so happy to see anything in my whole life as the pitcher of water that woman carried to the soldiers.

WILLIAM: They called her Molly—Molly Pitcher. That's a funny name.

JAMES: It was fitting, though the men didn't even look at her. Everyone was so exhausted and thirsty.

WILLIAM: It was almost dark when she got to us, anyway. But the water was just as welcome as the soup that woman gave us back in Pennsylvania. Remember that?

JAMES: I'll never forget it. She saved our lives. (JAMES *gets up and walks about, looking at bushes and off.*) The spring must be close by. Come on, let's get some more of that water.

WILLIAM (*Getting up*): I think we'd better move from here, anyway. We didn't find the guns the officers sent us for, and if they see us, they're sure to give us something else to do. (*Pauses, looks off right, listening*) I hear hoofbeats. (*Walks right, peers out, then turns back*) There are horses and officers coming this way. Come on, let's go. (*They rush out left. CHARLES, better dressed than soldiers, but dirty and hot, walks in right. He looks around, then beckons toward right. FRANK enters.*)

CHARLES: This will do. Tell the General's aide to bring the woman here, then go for the General. I hope he's still on his feet. He slept under a tree wrapped up in his own cloak last night. What a man!

FRANK: What's all this about, anyway?

CHARLES: Some woman took her husband's place at his gun yesterday.

FRANK: Oh, I heard about it. What happened to her husband?

CHARLES: Shot, I guess. Or perhaps the heat got him, like so many of the rest. Anyway, seems somehow she knew how to swab the gun, and stuck at it for a couple of hours. General Washington heard about it, and decided to give her some recognition, too, I guess.

FRANK: But, why here?

CHARLES: It's close to headquarters, that's all. Now you'd better make haste and fetch the woman. (FRANK *exits right.* CHARLES *starts to sit on log, then jumps to attention, as* WASHINGTON *enters right.*)

WASHINGTON: This is hardly what you'd call a parade ground, but it will serve. Where's the woman?

CHARLES: On her way, sir.

WASHINGTON: What's her name?

CHARLES: Mrs. Pitcher, sir.

WASHINGTON: Do we know her husband's condition?

CHARLES: Can't find a Pitcher on the rolls, sir, to inquire, but—

WASHINGTON: But of course that doesn't mean much. Our records leave a little something to be desired.

CHARLES: I'm sorry, sir, but—

WASHINGTON (*Kindly*): I'm not blaming *you,* man. Not unless *you* made the decision to have us fight this war before we were ready for it. Someone did, but I presume it wasn't you.

CHARLES (*Uneasily*): No, sir. (*Looks off*) Here comes someone, sir. It's Major Smith, and I suppose that's Mrs. Pitcher with him. (MOLLY *and* MAJOR SMITH *enter.* MAJOR *and* WASHINGTON *exchange salutes, then* MAJOR *steps to one side.* MOLLY *is wearing a soldier's jacket and hat, both much too big for her. She looks frightened and tired. When she sees* WASHINGTON, *she makes a quick, awkward curtsy.*)

WASHINGTON: Mistress Pitcher. (*Looks at her closely*) Pitcher? But surely you're . . .

MOLLY: Molly Hays, sir. Yes, sir.

WASHINGTON (*Smiling*): You didn't always call me sir, and I wish you would not do so now. But why are you called by the name of Pitcher?

MOLLY: Oh, well, it's just that I carried water to the men, sir, and somehow they began to call to me that way to get me to bring the pitcher of water.

WASHINGTON: How is your husband, the lieutenant?

MOLLY: He will be all right, General.

WASHINGTON: And does he know what you did yesterday?

MOLLY: Yes, sir, and he's provoked with me (*Smiles*), though of course not really, sir.

WASHINGTON: Good. Then I'll let you go back to him, where you belong. (*Takes paper from his pocket*) But first I want to give you this honorary commission as a sergeant in our army, as a token of our great appreciation of your courage in battle. A grateful country will never forget what you did yesterday, and this bit of paper is an inadequate way of expressing our thoughts on the matter. I believe it will not reward you as much as the expressions on the faces of the men to whom you gave water, when they needed it so badly.

MOLLY (*Overcome, speaking softly*): Thank you, sir. (*He hands document to her.*) I will cherish this forever.

WASHINGTON: I hope you aren't disappointed that we had no great ceremony for you. We have little time for such things, not today or tomorrow, not for some time to come, I'm afraid. You do understand?

MOLLY: Yes, General Washington.

WASHINGTON: I liked it better when you were making me move your kettle for you. (*Officers smile.*) We were friends then.

MOLLY (*Shocked*): Oh, sir, if I had ever known—if I had dreamed—

WASHINGTON (*Holding up hand; smiling*): Molly Hays, if you ever wish to have another kettle moved, I insist that you call on me. I will be forever at your service. (*He holds out his hand, which she takes.*)

MOLLY (*Curtsying*): Thank you very much, General Washington. (*She goes to exit right, then turns to face* WASHINGTON *again, grins impishly, salutes; he returns it, with dignity. They look at each other seriously for a moment, holding salutes, as curtain falls.*)

THE END

Production Notes

MOLLY PITCHER MEETS THE GENERAL

Characters: 7 male; 1 female.

Playing Time: 20 minutes.

Costumes: Soldiers wear shabby uniforms of Continental army. Charles, Frank, and Major Smith, officers' uniforms. In Scene 1, Washington wears cloak over uniform; it has turned-up collar to hide lower part of his face. Molly, long dress with full skirt, large apron. In Scene 2, soldiers' and officers' uniforms are dirty and disheveled. Molly wears soldier's uniform and hat that are too large for her.

Properties: Document.

Setting: Scene 1, dimly lighted hut: fireplace up center, with soup pot hanging from crane; rough wood table against wall left, on which are mugs, plates, spoons, and lighted lantern; two wooden benches in right corner, and third bench in shadow left, facing fireplace. Scene 2: Clearing surrounded by bushes, with log on ground.

Lighting: Dim light, Scene 1.

An Imaginary Trial of George Washington

by Diana Wolman

Revolutionary heroes take the stand . . .

Characters

JUDGE, *appointed by the King of England*
BAILIFF
LORD NORTH, *lawyer for the Crown*
JOHN ADAMS, *lawyer for the defense*
GEORGE WASHINGTON, *the defendant*
TOM PAINE
JOHN HANCOCK
RICHARD HENRY LEE
THOMAS JEFFERSON
PATRICK HENRY
BENEDICT ARNOLD
PAUL REVERE
MARY HAYS (*Molly Pitcher*) } *witnesses*
ETHAN ALLEN
RACHEL SALOMON
MARQUIS DE LAFAYETTE
DEBORAH GANNET
BENJAMIN FRANKLIN
CITIZENS

TIME: *1780*.

91

SETTING: *A courtroom in Colonial America. Judge's bench, a large table, is at right. There is a chair behind table, and a British flag stands beside chair. The witness stand is at center. Several rows of chairs at left, facing center, represent the gallery. In front of the first row of chairs are two tables, for defense and prosecution, with paper and documents on them.*

AT RISE: JUDGE *sits at bench. Witnesses and* CITIZENS *sit in gallery.* ADAMS *and* WASHINGTON *sit in first row, at one table.* LORD NORTH *stands center, holding document.* BAILIFF *stands near* JUDGE. BAILIFF *holds long wooden staff.*

BAILIFF (*Striking floor with staff*): Hear ye, hear ye! The trial of George Washington for treason against the British Crown is now in session.

JUDGE (*Striking gavel on table*): Lord North, as lawyer for the Crown, will you please read the bill of particulars?

NORTH (*Reading from legal document*): First: After pledging loyalty to his country and his king, as subject and officer, George Washington has taken up arms against his government in an effort to overthrow it. Second: He has conspired with other subjects of His Majesty to overthrow the rightfully established government of England by force and violence. Third: He has surrounded himself with people of low character—anarchists, robbers, smugglers—who have incited the people to riot and made treasonous statements in public. (NORTH *places document on* JUDGE's *table.*)

JUDGE: George Washington, step forward. (WASHINGTON *steps forward to face* JUDGE.) How do you plead, guilty or not guilty?

WASHINGTON: Before God and man, as history is my witness, I am *not* guilty!

JUDGE: Take the stand. (WASHINGTON *walks to witness stand, sits.* NORTH *approaches witness stand.*)

NORTH: Your full name, please.

WASHINGTON: George Washington.

NORTH: Where and when were you born?

WASHINGTON: February 22, 1732, at Bridges Creek, Virginia.

NORTH: Occupation?

WASHINGTON: Farmer.

NORTH (*Surprised*): A farmer, did you say?

WASHINGTON (*Proudly*): Yes. To me there is nothing more rewarding than to plant my fields and watch living things grow. I would like above all to be able to return to my beloved Mt. Vernon.

NORTH (*With sarcasm*): And can you explain just how you, a lover of the land, became Commander-in-Chief of this handful of rebellious subjects?

WASHINGTON: This honor came to me by default, so to speak. *All* of us are farmers, or workers, or merchants. We are not soldiers by training or desire. I, at least, had some experience as an officer under General Braddock in the recent French and Indian War. In the spring of 1775, five years ago, the second Continental Congress appointed me Commander-in-Chief of the Continental Army, and this responsibility I undertook with great humility and a sense of duty.

NORTH (*Interrupting angrily*): May I interpose here, Your Lordship, that this man is most responsible for all our troubles today. I can show that it was Washington and probably Washington alone who kept the Revolution alive. He was the only man among these rebels who combined military experience with a sense of organization and an ability to deal with men. Oh, I am willing to admit his personal superiority of character and love for justice. But, in the year and a half from November 1776 to the spring of 1778, the Revolution would have collapsed had we killed or captured only this one man.

PAINE (*In gallery; rising*): Aye, those were the times that tried men's souls. I remember well that bitter winter at Valley Forge. The summer soldier and the sunshine patriot will always shrink from service to his country.

JUDGE: You, there, what is your name?

PAINE: Tom Paine. And I wish to say that—

JUDGE (*Angrily*): Your turn will come. Indeed, it will! (PAINE *sits.* NORTH *takes seat in first row of gallery at left.*) Mr. Adams, as lawyer for George Washington, do you have anything to say at this time?

ADAMS (*Rising*): I would like to ask the defendant some questions, if I may. (*Approaches witness stand*) General Washington, what duties have you performed in the past?

WASHINGTON: I have been a surveyor, a soldier, an officer. . . .

ADAMS: And how did you carry on these activities?

WASHINGTON: Very faithfully, Mr. Adams. I have always been loyal to my work and to my superiors.

ADAMS: What was your attitude toward the conflict with the English government at first?

WASHINGTON (*Slowly*): At first I never dreamed of separation from our mother country. Even after I became Commander-in-Chief, we officers would nightly toast King George's health. (*Soberly*) But now I am convinced that separation is the only possible solution.

ADAMS: Thank you. That will be all. (*Nods to* WASHINGTON, *who leaves stand and returns to seat.* NORTH *rises, walks over to stand before* JUDGE.)

NORTH: Your Honor, I intend to prove to you that Washington has surrounded himself with men of low and treasonous character and I have witnesses to prove it. I now call to the stand John Hancock. (HANCOCK *comes to witness stand.* NORTH *picks up copy of Declaration of Independence and approaches* HANCOCK.) You are a smuggler by trade. Is that not correct?

HANCOCK: No, sir, a merchant, a rather wealthy merchant, I am glad to say, but one who respectfully disregards the hated duties imposed on our imports.

JUDGE (*Sarcastically*): I see. I shall write down—John Hancock, smuggler. (*Picks up pen*)

HANCOCK (*Angrily*): You may write what you please, but I, too, have written, knowing full well what the consequences might be. I was the first to sign the Declaration of Independence, and I signed it in large bold letters to make sure that George the Third could read it without his spectacles. (*Laughter from gallery*)

JUDGE (*Striking table with gavel*): Order in the court!

NORTH: That will be all, Mr. Hancock. (HANCOCK *leaves witness stand, returns to his seat.*) Indeed, I wish to speak about that hateful document, which I now hold in my hand. Will Richard Henry Lee please take the stand? (LEE *rises and walks to witness stand.*) Mr. Lee, can you identify the document that I am now holding?

LEE: Certainly. That is the Declaration of Independence.

NORTH: And what was your connection with this piece of treachery?

ADAMS (*Jumping up*): I object, Your Honor, to the prosecutor's use of such prejudiced language to describe this noble expression of the free spirit of man.

JUDGE (*Dryly*): Objection overruled. (ADAMS *sits.*)

LEE: I am proud to state here that I am the one who made the original motion concerning independence, at the Continental Congress. May I read it to you? (*Takes paper from pocket and reads*) "RESOLVED: that these united colonies are, and ought to be, free and independent states; that they are absolved from all allegiance to the British Crown, and that all political connection between them and the state of Great Britain, is, and ought to be, totally dissolved."

NORTH (*Angrily*): You will live to regret this rash notion of yours.

LEE (*Proudly*): On the contrary, I am glad that I said on that momentous occasion (*Continues reading*), "Let this happy day give birth to a new nation." In my opinion, July 4th will, in the future, be regarded as the birthday of these United States.

NORTH (*With disgust*): That is quite enough.

ADAMS (*Stepping forward to witness chair as* NORTH *sits down*): Now I would like to ask the witness: What is your opinion of General Washington?

LEE (*Admiringly*): Washington is more than a general. He is the embodiment of all that is noblest and best in the American people. Not only has he willingly served without any pay, but from his own pocket he has bought clothing for his men and sent aid to the destitute families of his companions in battle. I prophesy that Washington will go down in history as first in war, first in peace, and first in the hearts of his countrymen.

ADAMS: Thank you, Mr. Lee. (*Spontaneous applause from gallery as* LEE *returns to seat.* ADAMS *follows.* NORTH *rises.*)

NORTH: I call Thomas Jefferson to the stand. (JEFFERSON *walks up to stand, sits down.*) I ask you, sir, whether you recognize this paper.

JEFFERSON: Yes, I do.

NORTH: Will you read the opening words?

JEFFERSON (*Reading*): "In Congress, July 4, 1776, Unanimous Declaration of the United States of America . . ."

NORTH: Would you please state briefly in your own words, Mr. Jefferson, the purpose of that declaration.

JEFFERSON: We wished to make known to the world why we moved to declare our independence from the government of Great Britain. We listed the reasons for our act, including the tyrannical action of the present British king. We presented also—

NORTH (*Interrupting; impatiently*): Would you say, Mr. Jefferson, that the words of the Declaration of Independence are, in truth, *your* very own words? Is it not true that *you,* in fact, are the author of this treacherous paper? (*Brandishes paper*)

JEFFERSON: Sir, I had the honor to be chosen by my colleagues at the Continental Congress to help in the writing of this document.

NORTH: Do you accept the doctrines announced in the paper?

ADAMS (*From seat*): Objection!

JUDGE: (*Reluctantly*): Lord North, this line of questioning should not be continued, since Mr. Jefferson is not now on trial.

NORTH (*To* JUDGE): Very well. I wish, sir, to submit this Declaration to be marked Exhibit A.

JUDGE: Is there evidence that the defendant, George Washington, signed this document?

NORTH: No, sir, he did not sign it, but we shall introduce conclusive evidence that the defendant in fact supported the views of the Declaration.

JUDGE: Admitted. (NORTH *hands document to* JUDGE.)

NORTH (*To* JEFFERSON): I have no further questions for the witness. (JEFFERSON *leaves stand and returns to his seat.)*

JUDGE: Who is your next witness, Lord North?

NORTH: Patrick Henry, of Virginia.

JUDGE: Patrick Henry, step forth! (HENRY *stands up at his seat.)* Take the stand. (*He goes to witness stand.)*

NORTH: You are a Virginian?

HENRY: The distinction between New Yorkers, New Englanders, Virginians, and Pennsylvanians, is no more. I am not a Virginian, sir. I am an American.

JUDGE: Yes, I hear you've been inventing that word lately. And you have been making treasonous statements, haven't you?

HENRY: What I said is merely that Caesar had his Brutus, Charles the First his Cromwell, and George the Third . . .

JUDGE (*Striking gavel on table*): Treason!

HENRY (*Continuing calmly*): George the Third may profit by their example. If *this* be treason, make the most of it.

JUDGE: Do you realize what you are saying, you bold young man? You shall hang for this!

HENRY: Is life so dear or peace so sweet as to be purchased at the price of chains and slavery? Forbid it, Almighty God! I know not what course others may take, but as for me, give me liberty or give me death!

JEFFERSON (*Speaking from his seat*): He speaks the way Homer wrote.

JUDGE: You will hang, all right, you may be sure of that. (*To* JEFFERSON) And you, too, Mr. Jefferson.

FRANKLIN (*From his seat*): We must all hang together, or assuredly we shall all hang separately. (*Applause from gallery*)

JUDGE (*Enraged*): Order in the court or I shall clear the room!

NORTH: Your Lordship, I can prove that the rebels who follow Washington are not only traitors to their king and government, lawbreakers and men of low character, but they are

godless creatures, unnatural in their behavior and blasphe-
mous to God himself. In proof, I now call forth the next witness, Thomas Paine. (PAINE *goes to the witness stand, faces*
JUDGE. JUDGE *holds up book.*)

JUDGE: I have here a copy of an abominable piece of writing
by one Thomas Paine, in which the author denies all religion
and all established churches of God. Are you the author of
this, Mr. Paine?

PAINE: I am. And if I am on trial for having written it, then I
say that I am guilty of believing that this is an age of reason—
that human beings should use their common sense and not
merely follow what other generations before them believed
or said.

NORTH: What do you believe in exactly, Citizen Paine?

PAINE: As I have written: The world is my country. All mankind are my brethren. To do good is my religion. I believe in
one God and no more.

NORTH: You have only recently come to this land, haven't you?

PAINE: Four years ago, in 1776.

NORTH: And what was your work in England?

PAINE: At various times I have been a stay-maker, a cobbler,
a civil servant, and a laborer in a weaver's shop.

NORTH: How did you get to America?

PAINE: I was fortunate enough to secure a letter from Benjamin
Franklin when he was in England.

NORTH: And you have been preaching armed rebellion ever
since, have you not?

PAINE: It is my belief that the period of debate is closed. Arms,
as the last resort, must decide the contest.

NORTH: You admit that, then, do you?

PAINE: Admit, indeed! I boast of it. Why, it is only common
sense. Why should a huge continent be tied to a little island
thousands of miles away? Why should the colonists submit to
laws which hurt their trade and industry? Why—

JUDGE: And just what do you think will happen when rabble
like you take over and make your *own* government?

PAINE: Independence would result in a democratic form of government and establish in America an asylum for mankind, a haven of refuge for the oppressed peoples of the world. We have every opportunity and encouragement before us to form the noblest, purest constitution on the face of the earth. We have it in our power to begin the world all over again.

NORTH: If you are finished, Mr. Paine, you may leave the stand! (PAINE *leaves witness stand and returns to his seat.*)

JUDGE: Who is your next witness, Lord North?

NORTH: The next witness will be someone who actually heard George Washington incite soldiers to fight their king, someone who saw him make plans to rebel against the rightful government of these colonies, one who can identify him as the chief ringleader of the rebellion—a man who only last week had breakfast with him. I now call to the stand—Benedict Arnold. (BAILIFF *crosses left.*).

BAILIFF (*Calling offstage*): Benedict Arnold! (ARNOLD *enters, as witnesses and* CITIZENS *stare at him in surprise.*)

CITIZENS (*Ad lib; shouting*): Traitor! Informer! (*Etc.* JUDGE *pounds gavel angrily.*)

JUDGE: Order in the court! (ARNOLD *takes witness stand.* CITIZENS *grow quiet.*)

NORTH: What is your name?

ARNOLD: Benedict Arnold.

NORTH: Have you ever seen the defendant before?

ARNOLD: Many times.

NORTH: What do you know about him?

ARNOLD: I have heard him make plans for the defeat of the British Army. I heard him order that Paine's book, *Common Sense,* be read aloud to all his troops to make them more willing to fight.

NORTH: Is there anything else?

ARNOLD: At a time when officers and men had not been paid for a long period, and their wives and families were close to starving, a number of Continental officers were ready to revolt. They were stopped from doing so by a letter from George

Washington, asking them to act for the good of their cause and not according to their personal desires.

NORTH: Thank you. You have done a real service to His Majesty today.

ARNOLD: I am glad to have this chance to serve my King and to make amends for my former disloyalty.

ADAMS (*From seat; sarcastically*): *And* to get paid 6,000 British pounds.

JUDGE: You are out of order, Mr. Adams. Proceed, Lord North.

NORTH: Mr. Arnold, what was your position with Washington?

ARNOLD: I was a commanding officer. I took part in the famous battle of Saratoga and was largely responsible for Burgoyne's surrender.

NORTH: How do you feel about those activities now?

ARNOLD: I am willing to speak freely of the days when I erred. Truly I was a dupe. I now realize that I was wrong when I worked for the overthrow of His Majesty, King George III. I was blinded and full of false ideas. I wish to atone for those days and will eagerly identify any of the rebels you may wish me to point out.

NORTH: Thank you, Mr. Arnold. That is all for now. (BENEDICT ARNOLD *steps down from stand and takes a seat in gallery.* CITIZENS *glare at him.*) Your Honor, the prosecution rests. (NORTH *crosses to sit in first row of gallery, behind prosecution table.* ADAMS *rises, crosses center.*)

JUDGE: As attorney for the defense, you may now proceed, Mr. Adams. (ADAMS *approaches* JUDGE.)

ADAMS: On trial today stands a man whose name will go down in history as the father of his country, whose picture will be revered throughout the civilized world as the image of liberty and freedom. He is guilty only of following the belief that truth should be told and that freedom be proclaimed throughout the land. I will show you that the colonies suffered long and grievously before they took the extreme measure of armed rebellion, and that they took this step only after all other measures failed because of the obstinacy of the British government. I will show that the followers of Washington are men and women from all walks of life, from town and country, from north, south and even the frontier. They are Presbyterians, Jews, Frenchmen, Germans, Poles, Negroes, frontiersmen and housewives.

JUDGE (*Testily*): Yes, yes, Mr. Adams—get on with your case.

ADAMS: Your Honor, allow me to present character witnesses who will explain in their own words why they support George Washington and his struggle, of their own accord, without hope of award or glory. First I call to the stand that outstanding citizen of Boston, Paul Revere.

REVERE (*Walking up to the stand*): I am glad to appear here on Washington's behalf and also to correct a false impression that the court may be getting.

JUDGE: What impression is that, Mr. Revere?

REVERE: Perhaps you have assumed up to now that all of us in the Revolution are merchants—or smugglers, as you choose to call them—or even rich farmers. As a matter of fact, the majority of us are workers, and it is we—mechanics, carpenters, rope makers, printers and joiners—who organized the Sons of Liberty.

JUDGE: I have heard of you. What is your trade—that is, when you are not riding a horse?

REVERE: Silversmith, sir . . . and as for the incident you are referring to, I was acting for the North End Club of the Sons of Liberty, and I am proud to say that it was our organization that prevented your men from capturing John Hancock at Lexington.

NORTH (*Jumping up*): Your Lordship, this insurrection has been brewing for a long time. Before you sits a member, nay, a leader of this mob, this mixed rabble of Scotch, Irish and other foreign vagabonds.

ADAMS: I object, Your Honor. Paul Revere and his type are the very strength of our community. It is the firm patriotism of these workers that will save our country. (NORTH *sits down*.)

REVERE: Indeed it will. (*Boldly*) We are determined to fight up

to our knees in blood rather than be ruled by tyrants, foreign or domestic. As our song goes (*Chants*)—
Come, rally, Sons of Liberty,
Come all with hearts united,
Our motto is "We Dare Be Free,"
Not easily affrighted!

ADAMS: Thank you, Mr. Revere. (REVERE *leaves stand, and returns to his seat.*) Allow me to present one such person who is not easily affrighted—Mrs. Mary Hays! (MOLLY PITCHER *goes to witness stand.*) Please tell the court your full name.

MOLLY: Mary Ludwig Hays, sir.

ADAMS: By what name are you better known?

MOLLY: Molly Pitcher.

ADAMS: And I am sure our grandchildren will remember you as Molly Pitcher. Tell me, how did you acquire this unusual nickname?

MOLLY: It was at the Battle of Monmouth, in New Jersey. As you may remember, the day of the battle was very hot. Our noble patriots, fighting for independence, naturally suffered from the heat. I moved among them, offering water from my pitcher.

ADAMS: And a brave thing that was, too. But I also know that you did even more. Tell the court about the rest of your action in that battle.

MOLLY: My husband was firing a cannon. Suddenly, he fell to the ground. Immediately, I ran to his cannon and continued to fire it. (*Proudly*) For this action George Washington gave me the rank of sergeant.

ADAMS (*Admiringly*): It was well deserved, and the cause must be a noble one to inspire a woman like you to take such drastic action. Thank you. That is all. (MOLLY PITCHER *bows and leaves stand, returning to her seat.*)

JUDGE: Who is your next witness?

ADAMS: Your Lordship, I wish to call to the stand Mr. Ethan Allen of Vermont. (ETHAN ALLEN *goes to witness stand.*)

JUDGE: Proceed with this witness.

ADAMS (*To* ALLEN): Tell the court your full name and place of birth.

ALLEN: My name is Ethan Allen, and I was born at Litchfield, Connecticut, on January 10, 1738.

ADAMS: Do you know the defendant, George Washington?

ALLEN: Yes, Mr. Adams, quite well.

ADAMS: Please tell us what you did during the years of 1771 through 1775 that brought you into contact with George Washington.

ALLEN: I was the leader of the Green Mountain Boys of New Connecticut, now called Vermont. It was our boys who captured Fort Ticonderoga on May 10, 1775.

ADAMS: What happened later?

ALLEN: On September 25, 1775, I was captured by the British near Montreal, and I remained their prisoner until I was exchanged on May 6, 1778.

ADAMS: Do you think your sacrifice worthwhile?

ALLEN (*Fervently*): I would do it all over again, if I had to, for the cause of the Revolution and for George Washington.

ADAMS: Your opinion of Washington is evidently high.

ALLEN (*Firmly*): The highest. He is a man of great courage and conviction to leave his comfortable home at Mr. Vernon to risk danger in war.

ADAMS: Thank you, Mr. Allen. (ETHAN ALLEN *returns to his seat.*)

JUDGE: Have you more witnesses?

ADAMS (*To* JUDGE): Yes, Your Lordship. My next witness is not a man of war but a woman who came here of her own free will, to explain how she and others like her feel about George Washington. I call to the stand Mrs. Rachel Salomon. (RACHEL SALOMON *approaches witness stand.*)

RACHEL: Thank you, Mr. Adams. (*She sits.*)

ADAMS: Will you explain why you came here today?

RACHEL: My husband, Haym, is now in jail, but I know that he wants me to tell the world why he and other Jews, like

Benjamin Nones, for instance, have gladly supported the Revolutionary cause.

ADAMS: Tell us something about your husband.

RACHEL: My husband was born in Poland. Ten years ago, we were forced to flee that country because of the large part he was taking in the struggle for Polish independence. In 1772 we came to New York, where Haym became a financier, gradually becoming wealthy. Then he became interested in the cause of independence. In 1776 he was arrested by the British and was supposed to be put to death, but he was released by the Hessians, whose language he could speak. Then, two years ago, he was put in jail again.

ADAMS: And does he believe in American independence?

RACHEL: Deeply. My husband is not a fighting man, but he has helped the cause by giving of his own money and by helping to raise more. I'll never forget that Yom Kippur night. Yom Kippur, Mr. Adams, is the holiest of holidays for us. Nothing in the world, I had always thought, would ever make my husband interrupt these services. But a messenger came right into the synagogue, informing us that Washington needed money desperately for his army. Right then and there, my husband took up a collection, and Washington had his needed funds to carry on longer.

ADAMS: Why has Mr. Salomon been willing to risk his life, his wealth, all he has worked so hard to attain?

RACHEL: Perhaps the court will understand better when I read a part of a letter that George Washington sent to the Jewish community of Newport, Rhode Island. (*She takes letter from pocket.*) In his own words he has stated that (*Reads*) "the government of the United States will give to bigotry no sanction, to persecution no assistance." He has pledged to make America, once it is independent, a haven for all people of different faiths. At last Jews will have one country in which they can live and bring up their children without fear of persecution and banishment.

ADAMS: I am sure that your sentiments are shared by thousands of our fellow Americans. You may step down, Mrs. Salomon. (*She returns to her seat.*)

JUDGE (*To* ADAMS): Who is your next witness?

ADAMS: Your Lordship, our patriots have come from all over Europe. People who love mankind and hate oppression have come to our shores to help the cause of liberty. My next witness is the Marquis de Lafayette. (LAFAYETTE *goes to witness stand.*) Will you give your full name, please?

LAFAYETTE: Marie Joseph Paul Yves Roch Gilbert du Motier, Marquis de Lafayette.

ADAMS: Why did you leave your home and family to come to America?

LAFAYETTE: I came to America in 1778, at great effort to myself and in defiance of my own king, because I wanted to help the cause of human freedom. At the first news of this quarrel, my heart was in it.

ADAMS: How did you manage to get here?

LAFAYETTE: I fitted out a ship which carried eleven other officers and me to these shores.

ADAMS: Who were some of the people who came with you, or some other Europeans you met here?

LAFAYETTE: With me came the Baron de Kalb, who since died of his wounds at the battle of Camden. Also from Europe came Baron von Steuben of Prussia. From Poland came Thaddeus Kosciusko, an excellent artillery officer, and Count Casimir Pulaski, who unfortunately died at the battle of Savannah.

ADAMS: What happened to your ship?

LAFAYETTE: We were captured by the King of France, but managed to escape and resume our journey. After we landed at Georgetown, I traveled to Philadelphia and offered my services as a volunteer.

ADAMS: Tell us about your career in Washington's army.

LAFAYETTE: I immediately became a major-general and one of Washington's most trusted men, even though I was only nineteen. It was then that I came to respect and honor him.

He is a genius as a military man, but even more important, he is the soul of fairness and humility.

ADAMS: I am glad that a man of your distinction was able to come to this courtroom today to speak in behalf of the defendant, George Washington. (LAFAYETTE *rises and leaves stand.*)

LAFAYETTE (*As he returns to his seat*): I consider it an honor to speak for George Washington.

ADAMS: I now call Miss Deborah Gannet to the stand. (DEBORAH GANNET, *a young black woman, comes to witness stand.*) Will you give the court your full name, please?

DEBORAH: Deborah Gannet.

ADAMS: What is your occupation, Miss Gannet?

DEBORAH: Fighting for my country's freedom is my favorite one, sir, although I used to be a slave.

ADAMS: How do you know George Washington?

DEBORAH (*Proudly*): He is my commanding officer.

ADAMS: How can that be possible for you, a woman?

DEBORAH: After the Governor of Virginia offered Negroes their freedom and fifty dollars to serve in the King's army, the American army gave Negroes the same chance. I decided to disguise myself and enlist as a soldier under George Washington.

ADAMS: How long did you serve in the army?

DEBORAH: For seventeen months I was a member of the Massachusetts regiment without anyone suspecting my real identity.

ADAMS: Do all the regiments have both white and black troops?

DEBORAH: Most of them. Only Georgia and South Carolina bar slaves from signing up. As a Bostonian, I'm sure you know that among the first to fall in the Boston Massacre was a former slave by the name of Crispus Attucks. And I am proud that it was one of my people, Peter Salem, who killed that boastful British Major John Pitcairn. And—

JUDGE (*Sharply*): That is enough!

ADAMS: Just one more question. Why were you willing to lead a hard soldier's life for so long?

DEBORAH: I can't help thinking of the words of your wife, Abigail Adams, when she wrote: "I wish most sincerely there was not a slave in the province; it always appeared a most iniquitous scheme to me to fight ourselves for what we are daily robbing and plundering from those who have as good a right to freedom as we have."

ADAMS: Thank you, Miss Gannet. That's all. (*She returns to her seat.*)

JUDGE: Who is your next witness, Mr. Adams?

ADAMS: I call Mr. Benjamin Franklin. (FRANKLIN, *wearing bifocal glasses and leaning on cane, comes up to stand.*) How old are you, Mr. Franklin?

FRANKLIN: Seventy-four years old.

ADAMS: And interesting years they have been, too—as well as useful ones.

FRANKLIN (*Modestly*): Well, you know what I say: Early to bed and early to rise makes a man healthy, wealthy and wise.

ADAMS: Tell the court something of your background, please.

FRANKLIN: I was apprenticed to my older brother in Boston, but I ran away at the age of seventeen. Since then I have been a writer, the publisher of a newspaper, and an inventor of sorts.

ADAMS: You are very modest, but this assemblage knows that you are the author of *Poor Richard's Almanac*, that you started our first public library, that you are the inventor of the famous Franklin stove, bifocal glasses—the kind Lord North is wearing (*Laughter from gallery*)—and a number of other household helps. But right now we are interested most in your official duties.

FRANKLIN: I represented the colonies in England in 1765.

ADAMS: What was your advice to the British Parliament concerning the Stamp Act?

FRANKLIN: I told them then that it could never work. It was

my warning that if the British Army were sent to enforce it, a revolution might result.

ADAMS: Did you try in any other way to prevent this conflict?

FRANKLIN: Several times. The most recent was several years ago. I was negotiating with Lord Howe, on Staten Island. I suggested then that the matter could be peacefully settled on the basis of independence. But all he was instructed to offer was the King's clemency if we would stop fighting, with no guarantee of future liberty within the Empire. For years, Mr. Adams, I have striven to prevent just such a conflict as we are having now between brother and brother.

ADAMS: Despite your efforts, the conflict was not averted. What is your opinion of the situation today?

FRANKLIN: Once I wrote, "There never was a good war or a bad peace." Now I realize that rebellion against tyrants is not only justified, it's crucial. (CITIZENS *and other witnesses cheer.*)

ADAMS: Thank you, Mr. Franklin. Two continents value your opinion. (FRANKLIN *returns to his seat.*)

JUDGE: Have you completed your case, Mr. Adams?

ADAMS: I have one final witness—the defendant, George Washington. Will you come forward, General Washington? (GEORGE WASHINGTON *goes to witness stand.*)

WASHINGTON: I appreciate this opportunity to thank the many friends of liberty who have spoken here today. (ADAMS *takes Declaration from table.*)

ADAMS: General Washington, you did not sign this Declaration of Independence. Why not? Did you think it was not justified?

WASHINGTON: No, sir. I could not sign the Declaration of Independence because I was on the battlefield with my soldiers when it was written. But I believe with all my heart in the ideas expressed in the Declaration. May I see it, please? (ADAMS *hands Declaration to* WASHINGTON.) This document specifically states (*Reads*): "Governments long established should not be changed for light and transient causes; . . . experience hath shown, that mankind are more disposed to suffer, while evils are sufferable, than to right themselves by abolishing the forms to which they are accustomed. But when a long train of abuses ... evinces a design to reduce them under absolute despotism, it is their right, it is their duty, to throw off such government, and to provide new guards for their future security."

JUDGE (*Interrupting*): General Washington, consider for a moment to what chaos such a doctrine may lead. If a dissatisfied people can, of their own will, overthrow their established government, what rule of law and order could possibly prevail?

NORTH (*Ominously*): If the court please, we can easily foresee the terrible consequences of this traitorous doctrine. Should this doctrine spread to other lands, the kingdom of Spain might lose the allegiance of Mexicans and of the Argentine. Brazilians might declare: Brazil for Brazilians! What would the world come to?

JUDGE: Indeed, this is the very heart of their treason.

ADAMS: You both forget that there is a right higher than the right of kings over their subjects. A government exists not for the sake of the rulers but only for the good of the people, and only by the consent of the governed. Governments exist to help the people secure the rights which are theirs as human beings.

JUDGE: What rights?

WASHINGTON: In answer to your question, allow me to quote what I think is the *heart* of this Declaration of Independence (*Reads*): "We hold these truths to be self-evident, that all men are created equal, that they are endowed by their creator with certain unalienable rights, that among these are life, liberty, and the pursuit of happiness. That to secure these rights, governments are instituted among men, deriving their just powers from the consent of the governed, that whenever any form of government becomes destructive of these ends, it is the right of the people to alter or to abolish it ... " (WASHINGTON *returns to seat.*)

ADAMS (*To* JUDGE): The defense rests.

JUDGE: Then let the defendant, George Washington, come forward. (GEORGE WASHINGTON *rises, goes to* JUDGE's *table and stands facing* JUDGE.) George Washington, as defendant in this trial, do you have anything further to say before we pass judgment?

WASHINGTON: Only history can pass judgment on our noble cause. But I believe firmly that history shall prove our cause was just, our path honorable, and that what we have started and fought for here and now will in the future lead this nation to greatness and leadership among the free peoples of the world. (*Music of "America the Beautiful" is played as curtains slowly close.*)

THE END

Production Notes

AN IMAGINARY TRIAL OF GEORGE WASHINGTON

Characters: 15 male; 3 female; as many male and female as desired for Citizens.

Playing Time: 30 minutes.

Costumes: Colonial dress. The Judge wears a long black robe and a white powdered wig. Other characters wear appropriate costumes: fashionable British suits, uniforms of British and Colonial armies, American costumes, etc. Lord North and Benjamin Franklin wear bifocal glasses. Franklin also uses cane.

Properties: Long wooden staff, gavel, documents, parchment copy of Declaration of Independence, book, quill pen, Bible, letter. Witnesses and Citizens may carry various posters and flags, such as a sign reading, NO TAXATION WITHOUT REPRESENTATION, a Vermont flag, etc.

Setting: A courtroom. There is a large table at right, for Judge, with chair behind it. Beside chair is the British flag. There are several rows of chairs in the gallery section, at left side of stage. Two tables are placed in front of the first row of chairs, for defense and prosecution. At center is witness stand, raised platform with chair on it.

Lighting: No special effects.

Sound: "America the Beautiful," played from a recording, and sung if desired, as indicated in text.

The Constitution Is Born

by Carol J. Brown

Forming a more perfect union . . .

Characters

NARRATOR
GEORGE WASHINGTON, *President of the Constitutional Convention, delegate from Virginia*
WILLIAM JACKSON, *secretary of Convention*
WILLIAM PATERSON ⎫
WILLIAM LIVINGSTON ⎭ *delegates from New Jersey*
ALEXANDER HAMILTON, *delegate from New York*
EDMUND RANDOLPH ⎫
JAMES MADISON ⎬ *delegates from Virginia*
GEORGE MASON ⎭
RUFUS KING ⎫
ELDRIDGE GERRY ⎭ *delegates from Massachusetts*
GEORGE READ, *delegate from Delaware*
BENJAMIN FRANKLIN ⎫
JAMES WILSON ⎭ *delegates from Pennsylvania*

NARRATOR: One of the most momentous periods in American history began on May 14, 1787, when fifty-five delegates, representing all of the thirteen colonies but Rhode Island, met in Independence Hall in Philadelphia as a Constitutional Convention. It was eleven years after the signing of the Declaration of Independence in 1776 and four years after the end of

111

the American Revolutionary War in 1783. During that hot summer, this remarkable body of statesmen deliberated, debated, and finally compromised to produce the Constitution of the United States of America, which became the fundamental law of our land. (*Pause*) The mission of the Convention was, in Alexander Hamilton's words, "to render the Constitution of the Federal government adequate to the exigencies of the union." The delegates also sought to protect the mutual interests of the states. George Washington, former Commander-in-Chief of the Continental Army and a delegate to the Constitutional Convention from Virginia, was chosen President of the Convention . . .

WASHINGTON: Gentlemen, we are met for a grave purpose, that of framing a constitution for our United States. The Articles of Confederation and Perpetual Union, ratified by the states during the war, have proved inadequate to meet our nation's needs. It is your choice that I be chosen President of this convention, and I am honored to be able once again to serve you. No man has felt the bad effects of our present confederation more than I. We may justly ascribe the prolongation of the war to the want of powers in Congress. Almost the whole of the difficulties and distress of my army had their origins there. (*Pause*) Let us have the secretary call the roll of the states.

JACKSON: New Hampshire (*As each name is called, a delegate responds, "Here."*) . . . Connecticut . . . New York . . . New Jersey . . . Pennsylvania . . . Massachusetts . . . Delaware . . . Maryland . . . Virginia . . . North Carolina . . . South Carolina . . . Georgia . . . Rhode Island. (*There is no reply. Pauses*) I call Rhode Island.

WASHINGTON (*Surprised*): Is Rhode Island not here?

PATERSON: Mr. President.

WASHINGTON: Mr. Paterson of New Jersey.

PATERSON: Rhode Island is not here. Rhode Island prefers not to join the union at this time.

WASHINGTON (*Firmly*): But that must not be! We must all

work together. We all have the same needs, the same ideas about laws, freedom, religion, and self-government. We must come together and make some agreement.

HAMILTON: Mr. President.

WASHINGTON: Mr. Hamilton of New York.

HAMILTON (*With spirit*): Mr. President, it is imperative that we have a strong central government.

RANDOLPH: But, Mr. President . . .

WASHINGTON: Mr. Randolph of Virginia.

RANDOLPH (*Firmly*): There are many here opposed to Mr. Hamilton's proposal of strong federalism. The rights of the individual states must be preserved.

HAMILTON (*Soothingly*): Mr. President, we are here for one purpose—to form a more perfect union. I am sure we shall work harmoniously to achieve this.

WASHINGTON: Then, gentlemen, let us proceed.

NARRATOR: Throughout the summer of 1787, the delegates to the Constitutional Convention met and worked and debated the articles of the New Constitution. Many divergent views had to be reconciled.

GERRY: Mr. President.

WASHINGTON: Mr. Gerry of Massachusetts.

GERRY: It is the fear of the smaller states that they will be overpowered by the larger states.

READ: Mr. President.

WASHINGTON: Mr. Read of Delaware.

READ (*Indignantly*): We want equal representation! And Mr. Paterson of New Jersey and Mr. King of Massachusetts agree. We must protect the smaller states.

PATERSON *and* KING (*Together*): Yes! Yes!

RANDOLPH: Mr. President.

WASHINGTON: Mr. Randolph of Virginia.

RANDOLPH: As delegate from Virginia, one of the larger states, I should like to present the Virginia Plan. It provides that Congress shall be comprised of two houses—an upper and a lower house to vote on all proposals affecting the nation.

GERRY (*Heatedly*): I object!

RANDOLPH (*Continuing*): Representation in these houses would be based, of course, on the population of the state.

READ (*Angrily*): Never! My state of Delaware should send as many delegates as Virginia!

PATERSON (*Heatedly*): And my state of New Jersey as many as New York!

LIVINGSTON, KING *and* GERRY (*Shouting*): Yes, yes!

HAMILTON, MASON, *and* MADISON (*Heatedly*): No, No!

WASHINGTON (*Trying to restore order*): Gentlemen, gentlemen. (*Pause*) Mr. Read, do you wish to address this Convention?

READ (*Forcefully*): I do, indeed! Under Mr. Randolph's plan, the small states would cease to exist. The large states would control the Congress.

RANDOLPH: But the representation should be based on population.

PATERSON: New Jersey objects!

LIVINGSTON: Mr. President.

WASHINGTON: Mr. Livingston of New Jersey.

LIVINGSTON: My fellow delegate, Mr. Paterson, has a proposal to make.

WASHINGTON: Let us hear your proposal, Mr. Paterson.

PATERSON: Mr. President, I propose instead of the Virginia Plan submitted by Mr. Randolph that we have a Congress of one house, with equal representation from each state.

MASON: No, we want the Virginia Plan.

READ: No, the New Jersey Plan!

WASHINGTON (*Trying to calm them*): Gentlemen, please let us remember that the fate of a nation is at stake. We meet to raise a standard of government. Let us raise a standard to which the wise and honest can repair.

NARRATOR: Days passed in sessions filled with bitter arguments: What would the form of representation be? The debates lasted for hours, with neither side agreeing to compromise. At last, Benjamin Franklin, a delegate from

Pennsylvania and eighty-one years old, rose to his feet. He was quite frail and had not taken much part in the debates, but he was always in attendance at these heated and prolonged meetings.

FRANKLIN: Mr. President.

WASHINGTON: Dr. Benjamin Franklin of Pennsylvania.

FRANKLIN (*Slowly and calmly*): I confess that there are several parts of this Constitution which I do not at present approve, but ... the older I grow, the more apt I am to doubt my own judgment, and to pay more respect to the judgment of others. I agree to this Constitution with all its faults, if they are such, because I think a general government necessary for us. I doubt too whether any other Convention we can obtain may be able to make a better Constitution. For when you assemble a number of men to have the advantage of their joint wisdom, you inevitably assemble with those men all their prejudices, their passions, their errors of opinion, their local interests, and their selfish views. (*Pauses*) Since we cannot agree on the Virginia Plan or the New Jersey Plan or any other of the plans proposed in the course of this Convention, let me propose a compromise. Let our Congress be composed of two houses: a Senate, or an upper house, with two representatives from each state; and a House of Representatives, or a lower house, with the number of members determined according to population.

LIVINGSTON: I do not approve of equal representation.

PATERSON (*Interrupting*): I do not see the need for two houses.

MADISON: Mr. President.

WASHINGTON: Mr. Madison of Virginia.

MADISON: Since we cannot agree to Mr. Randolph's Virginia Plan nor accept Mr. Paterson's New Jersey Plan, it seems to me that Dr. Franklin has given us the only alternative. I move that we accept the compromise proposed by Dr. Franklin.

WILSON: Mr. President, I second the motion.

WASHINGTON: All those in favor say, "aye."

ALL (*Except* GERRY, MASON *and* RANDOLPH): Aye.

WASHINGTON: Opposed, say, "no."

GERRY, MASON *and* RANDOLPH (*Loudly*): No.

WASHINGTON: The ayes have it.

KING: Mr. President.

WASHINGTON: Mr. King of Massachusetts.

KING: Is it to be inferred that those states possessing slaves shall include them as part of the population?

RANDOLPH (*Quickly*): Why, certainly!

GERRY (*Objecting*): Mr. Randolph, it seems to me that only free persons shall be counted.

WILSON: Mr. President.

WASHINGTON: Mr. Wilson of Pennsylvania.

WILSON: Mr. President, it is my feeling that all human beings should be included. The national government is not an assemblage of states but of individuals for certain political purposes.

ALL (*Ad lib*): I disagree. Only free persons. The whole population must be counted. (*Etc.*)

FRANKLIN: Gentlemen, let us compromise on this question also. Let us count only three-fifths of the slave population. In other words, for every five hundred slaves, only three hundred shall be counted in fixing population.

READ (*Hurriedly*): Mr. President, I move that this convention accept Dr. Franklin's compromise.

KING: Second the motion.

WASHINGTON: You have heard the motion. All in favor say, "aye."

ALL: Aye.

WASHINGTON: All opposed, "no." (*There is silence.*) The ayes have carried on the second compromise. I declare this session closed.

NARRATOR: The debate on various parts of the Constitution continued. After several months, George Washington called the final session of the Convention to order on September 17, 1787.

WASHINGTON: Gentlemen, a government has been formed, and a Constitution has been written. In time it shall be voted upon by all states. May it endure for ages. Let the words of the Preamble serve as a standard for human beings to strive for. . . .

JACKSON: "We, the people of the United States, in order to form a more perfect union, establish justice, insure domestic tranquility, provide for the common defense, promote the general welfare, and secure the blessings of liberty to ourselves and our posterity, do ordain and establish this Constitution for the United States of America."

WASHINGTON: Are the delegates ready to sign it?

RANDOLPH: Mr. President.

WASHINGTON: Mr. Randolph of Virginia.

RANDOLPH: I cannot accept the compromises. I will not sign.

MASON: Mr. President.

WASHINGTON: Mr. Mason of Virginia.

MASON: I cannot agree to sign this document.

GERRY: Nor I, Mr. President.

WASHINGTON: I am grieved, Mr. Gerry, that we do not all have the same ideas.

NARRATOR: Again it was Dr. Franklin, beloved sage of two continents, who finally turned the tide toward agreement and the signing of the Constitution on that history-making day. . . .

FRANKLIN: Mr. President.

WASHINGTON: Dr. Franklin.

FRANKLIN: From such an assembly can a perfect production be expected? It therefore astonishes me, sir, to find this system approaching so near to perfection as it does; and I think it will astonish our enemies, who are waiting with confidence to hear that our councils are confounded like those of the builders of Babel . . . . The opinions I have had of its errors, I sacrifice to the public good. . . . Much of the strength and efficiency of any government in procuring and securing happiness to the people depends . . . on the general opinion of the goodness of the government, as well as on the wisdom and integrity of its governor. I hope therefore that for our own sakes as a part of the people, and for the sake of posterity, we shall act heartily and unanimously in recommending this Constitution.

NARRATOR: Dr. Franklin had indeed calmed the tempers of the delegates. He then moved that the remaining thirty-nine of the original fifty-five delegates sign the Constitution and record the signing of this momentous document "by unanimous consent."

FRANKLIN: Mr. President, since each state has at least one delegate who will sign, I move we record that this document is in accordance with all states represented and is the unanimous consent of all states present. Your name shall go first, Mr. President.

JACKSON: "Done in convention by the unanimous consent of the States present the Seventeenth day of September in the year of our Lord one thousand seven hundred and eighty-seven. . . . In witness whereof, we have hereunto subscribed our names."

WASHINGTON: George Washington, President and deputy from Virginia.

KING: Rufus King of Massachusetts.

HAMILTON: Alexander Hamilton of New York.

LIVINGSTON: William Livingston, New Jersey.

PATERSON: William Paterson of New Jersey.

FRANKLIN: Benjamin Franklin of Pennsylvania.

WILSON: James Wilson, Pennsylvania.

READ: George Read, Delaware.

MADISON: James Madison, Jr., Virginia.

NARRATOR: One by one, all but three of the thirty-nine delegates from the twelve states represented made their way to the front of the convention hall to sign the document—delegates from New Hampshire, Connecticut, Massachusetts, New York, New Jersey, Pennsylvania, Delaware, Maryland, Virginia, North Carolina, South Carolina, and Georgia. Again the frail Dr. Franklin rose and spoke a bit wearily but triumphantly.

FRANKLIN: Mr. President, after these long, hard months of debate, we have at last framed a Constitution for our nation.

WASHINGTON: We could not have accomplished this without you and the compromises you introduced. And when I am asked why the legislative branch of the government needs two houses, I shall point to our habit of pouring hot tea from a cup into a saucer to cool it. With two houses, one can check the other, as the hot tea is cooled by being turned from the cup to the saucer.

FRANKLIN: It is not, as I have said, a perfect document, but in years to come it can be and, I have no doubt, will be refined with amendments to make it better serve the needs of the people. At least we have a beginning.

NARRATOR: As the last of the delegates were putting their signatures to the Constitution, Dr. Franklin, observing from the side, spoke to a few of the delegates standing near him.

FRANKLIN: You see the picture of the sun painted at the back of General Washington's chair? Artists have always found it difficult to distinguish in their painting a rising from a setting sun. I confess that I have often in the course of the session looked at that sun behind the President without being able to tell whether it was rising or setting; but now at length I have the happiness to know that it is a rising and not a setting sun.

THE END

Freedom Train

by Craig Sodaro

Family takes a stand against slavery . . .

Characters

LAURA CAMPBELL, *14*
JESSIE CAMPBELL, *her sister, 12*
MARY CAMPBELL, *their mother*
LEVI CAMPBELL, *their father*
ANNIE, *a "conductor"*
OLD NED, *slave*
TEDDY, *his grandson, 8*
BIRDIE, *his granddaughter, 10*
JACK NELSON, *slave catcher*
SHERIFF HARDCASTLE

TIME: *A stormy night in 1851.*
SETTING: *The Campbell Grocery and Dry Goods Store in an Ohio river town. Long counter center has scales, sacks of sugar, boxes of thread, and bolts of material on it. Shelves behind counter are stocked with canned goods, blankets, and household supplies. In front of counter are sacks of flour and a barrel. Hams hang from hooks above counter. Table and two chairs are down right. Window with shade or curtain is left. Lantern hangs on wall, right. Wing entrances are right and left, right leading to rest of house, left leading outside.*
AT RISE: *LAURA CAMPBELL sweeps floor. JESSIE CAMPBELL looks out window.*

LAURA: Jessie, stop looking out the window. You'll make folks suspicious.

JESSIE: Nobody's out tonight in this weather. Besides, I'm scared. What if we get caught?

LAURA (*Firmly*): We won't. (*As* JESSIE *takes blankets from shelf,* MARY CAMPBELL *comes out from under counter.*)

MARY: I think this will work just fine! We can put these flour sacks over the trap door.

LAURA: Pa will be surprised when he sees the counter over here.

JESSIE (*Fearfully*): He'll know exactly what we did.

MARY: But it will be over and done with. Besides, I know deep down he would help . . . if he could.

LAURA: Are you sure?

MARY: Your Pa always does what's right, Laura. I am glad, though, that he's had to help your uncle with the calving. He won't be back for at least two days, and by then they'll be gone.

JESSIE: Here are some blankets, Ma.

MARY: Good. And we have plenty of bacon and bread in the cellar to fill their haversacks. I'm sure they'll be hungry and tired when they arrive.

LAURA: When will they get here? (LAURA *moves to window.*)

MARY: I have no idea.

LAURA (*Nervously*): Ma, someone's coming!

MARY: Now, remember, girls, these people are to be treated as our guests. We must be courteous and hospitable. (LEVI CAMPBELL *enters, wearing hat and rain slicker.*) Levi! We didn't expect you for another two days!

LEVI (*Removing hat and slicker*): It's not fit for man or beast out there!

LAURA (*Tentatively*): Welcome home, Pa!

LEVI (*Fondly*): It's good to be home. Mother Nature worked much faster than we anticipated and all the calves were born.

MARY: Sit and rest yourself, Levi. I'll fetch you a cup of coffee.

(MARY, *nervously glancing at* LAURA *and* JESSIE, *exits right.* LEVI *sits at table.*)

JESSIE: How is Uncle Peter?

LEVI: As grouchy as ever. I wish he would join us here in the city. He worries too much about the weather. (*Looks around*) It looks as if you three have been moving things around here. (*He indicates counter.*)

LAURA: Yes, we have.

LEVI: It must have been hard to move the counter over the trap door.

JESSIE: Oh, it wasn't that hard. (MARY *enters with mug.*)

LEVI (*Suspiciously*): Mary, change for a reason is fine. Change without reason raises suspicions.

MARY: We have our reasons, Levi.

LEVI (*Tensely*): I see. We've been over all this, haven't we?

MARY: I know, but—

LEVI: You know, of course, it is a crime to hide fugitive slaves. . . .

MARY: Yes, but—

LEVI (*Rising; sternly*): If we are caught breaking the law, regardless what you think of the law, we will lose our livelihood. Then what will we do? Become fugitives ourselves?

JESSIE (*Firmly*): But, Pa, slavery is wrong.

LEVI (*Defensively*): There is no slavery in Ohio.

LAURA: You know what Jessie means, Pa. It's wrong anywhere.

LEVI: We aren't responsible for what the people in other states do.

MARY (*Picking up lantern and lighting it*): You heard Reverend Pettibone say our country is like a body, Levi. If an arm is hurt or sick, the rest of the body won't take care of itself. If part of it is sick, the entire body will become sick and die. (MARY *exits left.*)

LEVI (*Calling after her*): Where are you going, Mary? What are you doing? (MARY *returns, without lantern.*)

MARY: It's a signal. The light hanging by the door will let the conductor know that this is the station. (*She pulls window shade down.*)

LEVI (*Alarmed*): Conductor? Station? What are you talking about?

LAURA: You know—a station on the Underground Railroad, Pa.

JESSIE (*Excitedly*): We are one of the stations now!

LEVI (*Sitting at table; upset*): This will ruin us!

MARY: Reverend Pettibone asked if we could help out because slave catchers have been watching his place too closely.

LEVI (*Banging fist on table*): I won't have it!

LAURA: But, Pa!

LEVI: I have worked hard for what we have! I cannot risk everything to help fugitives from justice.

MARY (*Hotly*): Justice? Since when is it just for men to buy and sell other human beings? Is it just to sell children? Is it just to beat innocent people, or to refuse to teach children to read?

LEVI: When those people arrive, you tell them to go elsewhere, you hear? (*Knock is heard off left.*)

MARY (*After a slight pause; firmly*): You'll have to tell them yourself. (MARY *exits left. In a moment she reenters, leading* ANNIE, TEDDY, OLD NED, *and* BIRDIE. *They all carry small satchels, except* TEDDY, *who has his things wrapped in an old print shirt. They place their bundles on the floor.*) Were you followed?

TEDDY: Nobody trailed us, ma'am, except a puppy.

ANNIE (*Proudly*): I'm a mighty careful conductor, ma'am, though the slave catchers are getting pretty crafty . . . especially now that they're getting paid so much to bring folks like these back to their masters.

BIRDIE (*Fearfully*): I don't want to go back!

OLD NED (*Comfortingly*): Now, Birdie, we aren't going back. I made myself a promise a long time ago to die a free man. And I'm keeping that promise.

TEDDY (*Proudly*): Me, too! It's freedom or die!

ANNIE (*With spirit*): Nobody's going to die on me, Teddy. In all my trips as a conductor I've never lost a passenger. We're in Ohio now, so the worst part of the journey's over. Folks here want to help you. (*To* LEVI) We're mighty grateful to you, sir!

LEVI (*Nervously, after a tense pause*): Ah . . . sit down. My daughters Laura and Jessie will fetch some stew for you. (*He looks at them.*)

LAURA (*Happily*): Yes, Pa!

JESSIE: Four stews, coming right up! (JESSIE *and* LAURA *exit right.*)

ANNIE (*Sitting at table*): From the sound of things, the slave catchers have been watching Reverend Pettibone's house.

MARY: He found a slave catcher lurking outside the parsonage, and recognized him as an ex-convict who had been in prison for robbery and assault.

OLD NED (*Sitting at table*): And how else can a convict make a living but chasing down runaways?

BIRDIE: My friend Tooley told me if we get caught by a slave catcher we'll be whipped like cream and beaten like eggs.

TEDDY: I won't let anything happen to you, Birdie.

LEVI (*Tentatively*): Don't worry. We'll make sure you're safe.

MARY: You'll spend the night in the cellar. The trap door is under the counter, and it's covered with a false floor. Even if someone should come looking, they won't be able to tell there's a trap door under it.

LEVI: It isn't the warmest place . . .

MARY (*Picking up blankets*): But it is dry, and we've got a blanket for each of you. Diggs Malone will be around tomorrow at dawn with his wagon. It's got a false bottom, so you can be taken to the next station without fear of discovery.

ANNIE: Oh, that Diggs is a good man. It's not a comfortable ride, but it's safe. (LAURA *and* JESSIE *enter right with four mugs and spoons, which they serve to others.*) This smells delicious!

LAURA: It's Mother's famous recipe.

OLD NED: A bit of heaven, ma'am! (*Starts to eat*)

TEDDY (*Eating*): I'm so hungry . . .

BIRDIE (*Tasting stew*): I've never had anything like this before.

JESSIE: It's just plain stew.

OLD NED: We're used to rice, child—rice and bread. And I remember times when I was young like Birdie when I didn't get anything at all. That was the way I was kept in line.

LAURA (*Shocked*): Your Ma didn't feed you?

OLD NED (*Shaking his head*): My Ma? Oh, child . . .

ANNIE: At a very early age slaves are taken from their mothers. And most of them never know their fathers.

BIRDIE (*Brightly*): I remember seeing my mama once!

TEDDY (*Excitedly*): Me, too!

BIRDIE: She was the most beautiful woman in the whole world.

TEDDY: She brought us each a peppermint stick.

OLD NED: My daughter, Ruthie, walked ten miles each way to see her children . . . and she had to do that between sundown and sunup, because no master gives us time for visiting. 'Course, that was when she lived close. But then she was sold to a master miles and miles away. We haven't seen her in over two years.

BIRDIE: But Annie will find her and bring her to freedom, too.

ANNIE: I'll sure try, Birdie.

MARY: How many trips have you made on the Railroad, Miss Annie?

ANNIE (*Proudly*): This is my tenth, ma'am.

LAURA: Where are you all going?

OLD NED: Canada, miss.

ANNIE: There are colonies across the border where free men, women, and children are building new lives.

TEDDY (*Excitedly*): We're going to go to school!

BIRDIE: Annie says we'll learn to read!

LEVI (*To* ANNIE): It must take a great deal of courage to keep leading slaves to freedom when you know if you're caught you will end up a slave again.

ANNIE (*Firmly*): Again? Sir, I was never a slave! I was born a free woman, and I intend to stay a free woman.

MARY: So you risk—everything.

ANNIE: And if I didn't what would I be risking, then? Look at these two. (*She indicates* TEDDY *and* BIRDIE, *who are gobbling the stew.*) They're the future. They're our hope. (*Loud knock is heard off left. Everyone freezes for a moment.* LAURA, *who is near window, peeks out.*)

OLD NED (*Nervously*): Folks sure shop late here in Ohio.

LEVI: It's not a customer.

LAURA: It's a man. He's holding his arm, as if it's hurt.

MARY: Get away from the window, Laura. (*To* ANNIE) This way. Quickly! (ANNIE *gathers up all satchels except* TEDDY's. MARY *leads* ANNIE, OLD NED, TEDDY, *and* BIRDIE *behind the counter.*)

BIRDIE (*Fearfully*): We won't have to go back, will we? (MARY *ducks behind counter.*)

OLD NED: No, child!

ANNIE: They don't call me Lucky Annie for nothing! (*Slaves duck behind counter, out of sight.*)

MARY (*Rising*): The door is open. Climb down, quickly! (*Knock is heard again.*)

LEVI (*Moving left*): We're closed!

JACK NELSON (*Off left*): Open up! I need help!

JESSIE (*Worried*): Oh, Mother!

MARY: Laura, help me with this floor. (LAURA *ducks behind counter.*) Jessie, Levi . . . bring those flour sacks here. Cover the floor. (JESSIE *and* LEVI *drag sacks behind counter.*)

NELSON (*Off left; urgently*): Please help me! Open up! (MARY, JESSIE, LAURA, *and* LEVI *come out from behind counter.*)

MARY: Now, act natural. Laura, sweep. Jessie, clear the stew away. (LAURA *begins to sweep.* JESSIE *collects mugs.*)

NELSON (*Off left*): I've been hurt!

MARY: Open the door, Levi. (LEVI *exits left, reenters immediately with* NELSON, *dressed in a long coat and floppy hat. He holds his arm.*)

NELSON: I can't tell you how glad I was to find your light burning outside the door. Almost like a signal to travelers.

MARY: We . . . we just had some visitors.

LEVI: How did you get hurt? (NELSON *removes his coat. The sleeve of his shirt is bloody and torn.*)

NELSON: Caught myself on a nail sticking out from a fence-post. Tough to see details in this weather.

MARY (*Examining his arm*): There's quite a bit of blood. Sit down. (NELSON *sits, his coat across his lap.*)

LEVI: Let me hang your coat to dry.

NELSON (*Quickly*): Don't touch my coat! (*Others exchange puzzled looks.*)

LAURA: Shall I get some stew, Pa?

LEVI: Yes, I'm sure our guest is hungry. (LAURA *exits right.*)

MARY: Jessie, would you fetch me a pan of hot water? There's some on the stove.

JESSIE: Yes, Ma. (JESSIE *exits right.* MARY *goes behind counter and gets bandage.*)

LEVI: It's an odd time of night to be out working your way through fences.

NELSON: Not so odd in my line of work, sir.

LEVI: And what line of work is that?

NELSON: I find things. Things that have gotten lost.

MARY: Are you a lawman?

NELSON: Not exactly.

LEVI: What type of things do you find?

NELSON: Whatever people ask me to find. It's surprising how much men pay to get back what's theirs. (JESSIE *enters right with pan of water and cloth.* LAURA *follows with mug of stew, sets it down in front of* NELSON.)

LAURA: There you go, sir.

NELSON: Smells very good. Do you often cook stew at this time of night, ma'am? Seems to me you'd have eaten hours ago. (*He eats hungrily.*)

MARY: Didn't I mention we just had guests?

NELSON: So you did.

MARY (*As she wrings cloth out in water*): This will hurt a bit.

NELSON: Don't mind that at all. (*She dabs cloth on* NELSON's *wound. He grimaces.*)

MARY: It's not much of a wound, really. Just a little scrape. (MARY *continues to clean the wound, then wraps* NELSON's *arm.*)

LEVI: That's good. A little wound won't detain you.

NELSON: You must not be in the habit of detaining people.

MARY: What do you mean?

NELSON: Your guests . . . I would have thought they'd stay the night.

LAURA (*Quickly*): Oh, they live close by.

NELSON (*Indicating* TEDDY's *pack*): Is that why they brought a pack all tied up?

MARY (*Worriedly*): Why, that doesn't belong to our guests.

JESSIE: It's mine. I keep my things in it.

NELSON: Let me see it, child.

LEVI: I don't see that it's your concern, sir.

NELSON (*Rising*): But it is. This country's got laws, see? And if a man is missing a piece of property, he can go after that property himself, or he can hire someone to go fetch his property back for him.

MARY: Property is one thing, sir. Human beings are another.

NELSON: Sometimes they're one and the same.

LEVI (*Firmly*): Sir, you've been bandaged and fed. Now, be on your way.

NELSON: But I have business here.

LEVI: We're closed for business.

NELSON (*Rising, holding his coat tightly*): You think I'm a fool, don't you? But I'm not! I'm good at what I do!

MARY: And very thorough. You cut your own arm, didn't you?

NELSON: I wasn't sure this was the new station on the so-called Underground Railroad, so I had to find some way to get in. But now I know . . . (*Prowling about room*)

LAURA: You don't know any such thing!

NELSON: That pack belongs to a slave as sure as I'm standing here. That's the very shirt I was warned to watch for. A Sunday shirt made of cotton. Just that pattern.

LEVI (*Shouting*): Get out!

NELSON: Not without my employer's property.

MARY: I'm sure your employer owns enough other property.

NELSON: He wants what's his! (*Stomps foot*)

LEVI: I'll tell you one last time. Get out!

NELSON (*In challenging tone*): Or what? You'll call the Sheriff? Should I remind you that the Fugitive Slave Law, passed just this year, guarantees that I have the right to capture and return my employer's property, even if Ohio is a free state? The Sheriff must obey the law! Now—where did you hide them? (*Stomps the floor*)

MARY (*Nervously*): Sir, we do not have any fugitives from justice under this roof!

NELSON: I think under the floor . . . (*Stomps again*)

LEVI (*Angrily*): There's nothing below but dirt.

NELSON: The sound is hollow. There's a cellar down there!

LAURA (*Nervously*): Just a crawl space.

JESSIE: Barely big enough for a cat!

NELSON: We'll see about that! (*He draws pistol from inside his coat, which he drops.*)

LEVI (*Shocked, nervously*): We don't permit guns in this house!

NELSON (*Smiling*): If you're telling the truth, nobody will get hurt! (*He fires gun into floor. JESSIE and LAURA scream and run to MARY. LEVI grabs NELSON, and they scuffle.*)

MARY (*Frightened*): No! Stop that!

LAURA: Don't you hurt my father!

JESSIE: Stop it! Stop it! (NELSON *strikes* LEVI *with gun.* LEVI *crumples to the floor.* MARY, JESSIE, *and* LAURA *rush to* LEVI'*s side, terrified.*) Pa!

MARY: Levi!

NELSON (*To* MARY, *angrily*): Bring them up here now! (MARY *goes behind counter. She moves flour sacks, false floor, and then opens trap door. One by one,* ANNIE, OLD NED, TEDDY, *and* BIRDIE *appear from behind counter. Meantime,* LAURA *and* JESSIE *help* LEVI *up.*)

MARY: Did any of you get hurt by the bullet?

ANNIE: No, ma'am. He hit the other corner of the room.

OLD NED (*Noticing* LEVI): What's happened?

NELSON: He'll be all right. That's what comes of aiding and abetting runaways!

BIRDIE (*Terrified*): I don't want to go back! I don't want to go back!

TEDDY: Sh-h-h, Birdie. It'll be all right.

OLD NED (*Somberly*): Don't tell her lies, Teddy. It won't be all right.

ANNIE: Ned, please!

OLD NED (*Angrily*): It won't be! Birdie's right! I don't want to go back, either! (*Knock is heard off left.*)

NELSON: But you will! If my guess is right, that's the Sheriff. I told him a single gunshot would be the signal. Open the door, ma'am! (MARY *exits left.*)

ANNIE (*To* NELSON; *coldly*): Right now, while you're standing here so smug, there are ten trains full of passengers bound for freedom!

NELSON (*Sneering*): But this is one that got derailed! (MARY *leads* SHERIFF HARDCASTLE *on left.*) It's about time!

SHERIFF (*Unmoved*): So you found them, Nelson.

OLD NED (*Hugging* BIRDIE, *who is crying*): Don't worry, Birdie. I won't let them take you.

TEDDY (*Terrified*): Grandpa . . . I don't want anything to happen to you!

OLD NED: They'll split us up for sure now . . . and I can't bear that!

NELSON: You should have thought about that before you ran off! Let's go! (*No one moves.*) Now! (*To* SHERIFF) Sheriff, I demand you do your duty!

OLD NED: You're going to have to kill me first, Sheriff. I promised myself I would die a free man, and I'm keeping that promise.

SHERIFF: Now, see here, old man. The law's the law!

JESSIE (*Pleading*): It's a bad law!

LAURA (*Firmly*): You can't take them back!

LEVI (*Nervously*): Girls . . . be quiet!

SHERIFF (*To slaves*): Come along peacefully!

OLD NED: I can't do that, sir.

ANNIE (*Pleading*): Maybe there's someone who can help us, Ned!

NELSON: Move! (*Aims gun at* NED)

OLD NED: Pull the trigger, and I'm free!

BIRDIE (*Terrified*): Grandpa!

TEDDY (*To* NELSON; *frantically*): No, don't, mister!

NELSON (*Nervously*): I'm not going to tell you again, old man!

SHERIFF (*To* NELSON): Put that gun down, you fool! You won't collect a cent if he turns up dead!

NELSON: He's too old to be worth anything. But the others are valuable! Now, let's go! (SHERIFF, *standing behind* NELSON, *grabs ham from hook, hits* NELSON *on head.* NELSON *crumples to floor.*)

MARY: Thank goodness!

SHERIFF (*To* ANNIE): Get them out of here now!

ANNIE: Bless you, Sheriff! Bless you!

SHERIFF: Go quickly, before he revives. (LAURA *and* JESSIE *give blankets to* OLD NED, TEDDY, *and* BIRDIE. TEDDY *picks up pack.*)

MARY (*To* ANNIE): Can you read?

ANNIE: Yes, ma'am!

MARY (*Scribbling on paper*): Here's where you'll find Diggs Malone. Maybe he can take you in his wagon tonight.

LEVI (*Nervously, glancing at* SHERIFF): Mary!

SHERIFF: It's all right, Mr. Campbell. There are those of us in authority who know injustice when we see it.

ANNIE (*Putting paper in her pocket*): Thank you!

MARY: Jessie . . . Laura . . . show our guests out the back way.

LAURA: Yes, Ma.

LEVI (*Behind counter*): Wait! (*He brings out peppermint sticks.*) These will give you some energy. (*Gives candy to* ANNIE, OLD NED, TEDDY, *and* BIRDIE)

BIRDIE: Thanks, sir!

TEDDY (*Licking candy*): Sure tastes good!

OLD NED: Nothing compared to the taste of freedom, Teddy. Nothing!

ANNIE: Let's hurry! Goodbye, and thank you all! (LAURA *leads* ANNIE, BIRDIE, TEDDY, *and* JESSIE *off right*.)

MARY (*As they exit*): You're going to make it! You'll be in Canada before you know it!

SHERIFF: There are stations all along the way. They'll do fine as long as they don't run into the likes of him again. (*Gestures to* NELSON)

LEVI: What are you going to do with him?

SHERIFF (*Wryly*): It's really a shame this ham fell on him accidentally. I hear tell, after a blow to the head, some folks imagine they've seen and heard things that weren't really there.

LEVI: Like fugitive slaves?

SHERIFF (*Shrugging, smiling*): I never saw one.

LEVI (*Smiling*): Neither did we—isn't that right, Mary?

MARY (*Worriedly*): But we'll be watched now.

SHERIFF (*Pointing to* NELSON): Not by this one. He fired his gun inside the city limits, disturbed the peace, and has been a general nuisance. With his record, he'll be very willing to leave the county for good, or be locked up for a long time.

LEVI: I'd hate to think this station had seen its last train arrive.

MARY (*Proudly*): I knew you wouldn't let us down, Levi.

LEVI: Mary, we'll keep that lantern lit as long as we have to— until *all* people are free. (*Curtain*)

THE END

Production Notes

FREEDOM TRAIN

Characters: 5 male; 5 female.

Playing Time: 25 minutes.

Properties: Mugs; spoons; various bundles or satchels of clothes, one wrapped in a patterned shirt; broom; bandages; pan of water with cloth; gun; ham; paper and pencil; peppermint sticks.

Costumes: 1850s period dress for all: long dresses for girls and women (Jessie and Laura also wear aprons or pinafores, Birdie and Annie wear capes). Shirts, pants, suspenders for Levi and Nelson; Levi wears rain slicker and hat when he first enters, Nelson coat and hat. Old coats and pants with patches for Old Ned and Teddy. Dark coat and hat for Sheriff.

Setting: Campbell Grocery and Dry Goods Store. Long counter center has scales, sugar sacks, boxes of thread, bolts of material on it. Flour sacks and a barrel sit in front of it. Hams hang from hooks above counter. Shelves behind counter hold canned goods, plates, blankets, etc. Table and two chairs are down right. Window with shade or curtain that can be closed is left. Lantern hangs on wall, right. Wing entrances are right and left, right leading to rest of house, left to outside.

Lighting: No special effects.

Sound: Knock on door; gunshot.

The Birthday Guests

by Maureen Crane Wartski

The spirit of Lincoln helps Civil War foes find peace . . .

Characters

AMANDA PHELPS, *15*
GRANDMA PHELPS
MRS. PHELPS
JOHNNY PHELPS, *13*
LT. DEAN, *Confederate soldier*
CAPT. CARLIN, *Union soldier*

SCENE 1

TIME: *Toward the end of the Civil War.*
SETTING: *The kitchen-living room of a farmhouse on the Kentucky border. A table with an oil lamp on it stands center, and a stove is behind it. Four chairs are placed around table. At right are two more chairs, a couch, and table with daguerreotype and lamp on it. There is a window in wall up center. Entrances are at right, to outside, and left, to other rooms.*
AT RISE: AMANDA *is setting the table.* MRS. PHELPS *is at stove, left, cooking, with her back to audience.* GRANDMA *is on couch, reading a letter.*
AMANDA (*Upset*): Oh, Mother! I did it again! I set six places for dinner, as if Pa and Ben were still home. I wish they'd never gone off to fight those rebs!

MRS. PHELPS (*Turning*): We all wish that, Amanda. (*Wipes hands on apron*)

AMANDA: I wonder where they are tonight. Read me their letter again, Grandma.

GRANDMA: It says they're fine, that they'll be home as soon as they can. (*She puts letter down.*) Ben writes that Lincoln is the best man this country could have as President. He's doing everything he can to end this terrible war.

AMANDA: There'll be no peace till those rebs are all licked!

MRS. PHELPS: Now you're talking like Johnny. Where is that boy? He should have driven the cow in from pasture by now. (*She goes to the window.*) Heavens, it's misty! How can he see his way home in this?

AMANDA: Don't worry. Johnny knows his way home. He'll smell the dinner cooking!

MRS. PHELPS (*Crossing to stove*): Yes. Still, with Pa and Ben gone. . . . I worry. (*She shakes her head.*) What if something happened? Our nearest neighbor is miles away. . . (*She breaks off.*) I hear something. Is that Johnny?

AMANDA (*Going to window*): Yes, it is, Mother. (JOHNNY *enters, right.*)

JOHNNY: Hello, Ma. (*Crosses to table, center*)

MRS. PHELPS: Johnny! We were worried about you.

JOHNNY (*Upset*): Ma, I . . . I lost the cow.

GRANDMA (*Shocked*): Lost old Bridget!

JOHNNY: I'd left her grazing while I was finishing up the farm chores. When I looked for her, I couldn't see her. It was all foggy and misty. I listened for her cowbell, but I couldn't hear it. I'm sorry, Ma.

MRS. PHELPS: Now, don't you fret. Bridget won't go far. As soon as this mist clears, we'll find her. (*Puts dishes on table*)

AMANDA (*Coming to table*): But, Mother, if Bridget's lost, what will we do for milk? And . . . and cheese, and butter?

GRANDMA: Now, no more fretting. We're going to sit down to dinner and give thanks for the food we have.

AMANDA (*Bitterly*): How can we give thanks when Pa and Ben are far away? When there's a war going on?

GRANDMA: We should try to be more like Ben, and be grateful that we have a President like Abraham Lincoln who's trying to unify our nation. (*She rises and crosses center. All sit around table, hold hands, and bow their heads for a second.*)

JOHNNY: I can't sit here when Pa and my big brother might be . . .

MRS. PHELPS (*Sharply*): Johnny!

JOHNNY: Suppose they never come back from the war? (*Gets up, stalks to window*) I hate the rebs! I hate them all!

GRANDMA (*Firmly*): Johnny, come back to the table. It's Ben's birthday, and we are going to celebrate it just as if he were here.

AMANDA (*Wistfully*): Do you remember the last birthday party we had for Ben before they went away? We had cake and presents and guests.

GRANDMA (*Softly*): Yes. . . guests. It would be nice to have birthday guests again.

JOHNNY (*Suddenly*): Hush! (*He runs to table, seizes the lamp and blows it out. Stage lights dim.*) Be quiet, all of you! Be quiet!

MRS. PHELPS: Whatever is the matter?

JOHNNY (*Frightened*): Someone's coming this way! Listen! (*All freeze. Sound of knock on door is heard.*)

LT. DEAN (*From offstage*): Is anyone home? (*More knocking*) Open this door!

AMANDA: I don't recognize the voice! (*She runs to MRS. PHELPS, who puts her arms around her.*) Mother, I'm frightened!

LT. DEAN (*From offstage*): I hear movement in there! Open this door or I'll break it down!

JOHNNY (*In a hoarse whisper*): You all stay back! (*He goes right, opens door. LT. DEAN enters, in gray Confederate uniform.*) A reb! You're a rebel! (*Others gasp, and rise from chairs, alarmed.*)

LT. DEAN (*Dryly*): I take it that this is a staunch Union house-hold. (*He starts to walk into room.*)

JOHNNY: Don't you come in here! Don't you take another step, or. . . .

MRS. PHELPS: Johnny!

LT. DEAN (*Bowing to* MRS. PHELPS): Good evening, madam. I regret to say I didn't see you before in the darkness. I'm Lieutenant Jeb Dean, of the 87th Battalion. I became separated from my men in this dense fog some hours ago, and wandered for a while in the woods until I was thoroughly lost.

MRS. PHELPS: I am Mrs. Phelps. (*Gestures*) This is my mother, and these are my children, Amanda and Johnny. (*To* AMANDA) Light the lamp, Amanda. (*Pause*) What do you want with us? (AMANDA *lights lamp and the stage grows bright again.*)

LT. DEAN: I need food . . . and a chance to rest. When the fog lifts, I will attempt to find my men.

AMANDA: You can't stay here! We don't want you!

GRANDMA: It's true, Lieutenant. You aren't welcome here.

LT. DEAN: I'm sorry, but I must insist. (*He shrugs back his cloak and puts his hand on the hilt of his sabre.*)

GRANDMA (*Hastily*): How did you find us? We're far back in these woods.

LT. DEAN: A cow brought me here. (*Others exchange surprised glances.*) I heard a cowbell in the fog, and then a cow moo. (*His voice softens.*) It made me think of home.

MRS. PHELPS: Why so, sir?

LT. DEAN: I have a farm like this back home.

AMANDA (*Surprised*): You do?

LT. DEAN (*Smiling*): Yes. We have two cows, three horses, and a goat. My wife and sister tend it while I'm away. (*He sighs, wearily.*) I am very tired. May I sit down?

MRS. PHELPS (*Coldly*): We can't stop you. (LT. DEAN *sits, right.*) Johnny, go put the cow in the barn. (LT. DEAN *moves, as if to object.*) There's no place Johnny can run for help, Lieutenant. You're safe. (JOHNNY *exits, right, looking over his shoulder at* LT. DEAN.) We were sitting down to dinner when you arrived.

LT. DEAN: Please don't let me interrupt you.

MRS. PHELPS (*Ignoring him*): We will eat as soon as Johnny comes in. What food would you like? I will bring it to you here.

LT. DEAN: Don't trouble yourself. I can get up. (*Half rising*)

MRS. PHELPS (*Coldly*): We don't eat with the enemy, Lieutenant.

LT. DEAN (*Sitting again*): I see. Whatever you say, then, madam. (*He wraps his cloak around him and stretches out his legs. His head falls back.* AMANDA, MRS. PHELPS, *and* GRANDMA *back away toward left.*)

AMANDA: He's going to fall asleep. What'll we do?

MRS. PHELPS: Nothing. We'll feed him and wait for the mist to lift.

GRANDMA: He's just a few years older than Ben.

MRS. PHELPS: To think that on my oldest child's birthday we have to entertain an enemy in our house!

AMANDA (*Slowly*): He did bring Bridget back. . . .

MRS. PHELPS: Bridget brought *him*! Don't feel sorry for him, Amanda. (JOHNNY *reenters, right, and stands looking angrily at the sleeping* LT. DEAN.)

GRANDMA: Some birthday guest we are entertaining tonight! (*Curtain*)

* * * * *

SCENE 2

TIME: *Before dawn, the next day.*

SETTING: *Same as Scene 1.*

AT RISE: LT. DEAN *is sitting at the kitchen table. Before him are an old basket, dented pots, a broomstick. He is tying straw into broomstick.*

LT. DEAN (*To broomstick*): There you are—as good as new. A bit of twine in the right place will keep you going for a while.

(*He picks up basket.*) I can re-weave you, too. Otherwise you'll have a big hole in your side. (*As he speaks,* AMANDA *enters.*)

AMANDA: What are you doing?

LT. DEAN: After that good dinner your mother cooked for me, I wanted to repay you for your kindness. So I've mended a few things that were broken.

AMANDA (*Haughtily*): We don't need you to repay us. You forced us to feed you. If we hadn't, you probably would have killed us with that sabre of yours!

LT. DEAN (*Putting hand on hilt of sabre*): My sabre? (*Smiles and pulls out sabre, which is broken off a few inches below the hilt*) Look at this broken old thing. I couldn't harm anyone with it.

AMANDA (*Flustered*): Oh. But we didn't know it was broken!

LT. DEAN: I guess I frightened you. Sorry. When I was separated from my men, I was upset and frightened ... but happy, too.

AMANDA: What did you have to be happy about?

LT. DEAN: This is the first time I've been away from the fighting. I have to go back to it soon, but for now it's wonderful to be in a home again.

AMANDA: Tell me about your family ... and farm.

LT. DEAN (*Standing with back to window*): We have a farmstead in Virginia—the most beautiful land you've set eyes on. There are mountains in the background, and a river winds through our farm. (*Dreamily*) I met my wife not far from where we live. We were married just before I left for the war.

AMANDA: How hard it must be for her!

LT. DEAN: She's very spunky, and strong-willed. She can take care of herself and the farm until I get back. (*Pause*) If I get back.

AMANDA (*Strongly*): You will! (*He smiles at her.*) I mean it.

LT. DEAN: Thanks, Miss Amanda. I hope your brother and father come home safely, too. (*They smile at one another. Suddenly,* LT. DEAN *looks out window.*) What's that sound? Someone's coming!

AMANDA (*Alarmed*): Who is it? (*She runs to window.*) It's a man! On a horse! Is that one of your men?

LT. DEAN: I can't tell. (*Sound of knocking is heard from off-stage.*)

AMANDA (*Calling*): Who's there?

CAPT. CARLIN (*From offstage*): My name is Captain Carlin, of the 6th Brigade.

LT. DEAN (*Whispering*): A Yankee!

CAPT. CARLIN (*From offstage*): I was on my way back to my lines when I became lost in this fog. By accident I saw your homestead. I need shelter till the fog lifts.

AMANDA (*Calling*): Yes, of course, Captain. One minute. (*To LT. DEAN, in whisper*) You must hide!

LT. DEAN: Miss Amanda, thanks for the kind thought, but I couldn't hide! An officer of the Confederacy doesn't hide from the enemy.

AMANDA: Oh, bother your pride! If that captain sees you, he'll take you prisoner!

LT. DEAN: He'd have to subdue me first. (MRS. PHELPS, GRANDMA *and* JOHNNY *enter left.*)

JOHNNY: What's going on? I heard knocking.

AMANDA: Johnny, don't open that door!

JOHNNY: Why? Are there more rebs outside?

AMANDA: No . . . it's a Union officer!

JOHNNY: Hooray! (*He hurries right.* AMANDA *stops him.*) Get out of my way, Amanda!

AMANDA (*Urgently*): Don't let that man in, Johnny, or he and Lieutenant Dean will have a fight right here in this house! Captain Carlin will take Lieutenant Dean prisoner!

JOHNNY: Good for Captain Carlin! I'll help him! (MRS. PHELPS *goes to table, picks up basket* LT. DEAN *has repaired, and looks at it curiously.*)

MRS. PHELPS: Who fixed this basket?

AMANDA: Lieutenant Dean. He wanted to pay us back for the food we gave him, and for taking him in.

MRS. PHELPS (*Turning the basket over*): Your father made this for me, before he went to war. (*Knocking is repeated.*)

JOHNNY: Amanda, I'm going to open that door!

MRS. PHELPS: No, Johnny. Wait! Amanda's right. We want no violence here. Lieutenant Dean, children, Grandma . . . I want your word that you'll all do as I say.

JOHNNY: But, Mother!

MRS. PHELPS: Give me your word! (*All nod.*)

JOHNNY (*Sulkily*): All right, Mother. (MRS. PHELPS *goes right, opens door.*)

MRS. PHELPS: Come in, Captain. (CAPT. CARLIN *enters, right.*)

CAPT. CARLIN: Thanks, ma'am. (*He sees* LT. DEAN.) What's this? I've blundered into a nest of Confederates!

GRANDMA: How dare you, sonny! This is a Union household!

JOHNNY: My father and older brother are fighting for the Union side!

CAPT. CARLIN: What is this man doing here? (*He points to* LT. DEAN.)

MRS. PHELPS: Lieutenant Dean was lost in the fog, as you were. He is a guest in my home.

CAPT. CARLIN (*In disbelief*): A guest! It's my duty to take this rebel prisoner!

LT. DEAN (*With hand on hilt of sabre*): I'd like to see you try it, Captain!

MRS. PHELPS (*Stepping between them*): Stop! Gentlemen, you are both lost and far from your lines. (*Pleading*) Can't you just call a truce? (*She turns to* AMANDA.) Set six places at the table, Amanda.

AMANDA (*Shocked*): What, Mother?

MRS. PHELPS: I said, set six places. Johnny, help her. We'll have an early breakfast. Put cheese and bread and milk and ham on the table.

JOHNNY: Ma, what's the matter with you?

GRANDMA (*Sharply*): Don't talk to your mama like that, young

man! You get busy and do as she told you! (JOHNNY *and*
AMANDA *quickly set table.*)

LT. DEAN: Well, Captain Carlin, shall we put aside our differences?

CAPT. CARLIN (*Reluctantly*): This is the lady's home, and we
are guests. But when we leave this place, we have unfinished business.

LT. DEAN (*Haughtily*): I will be at your service! (*Curtain*)

* * * * *

SCENE 3

BEFORE RISE: *Sounds of family and guests talking and laughing, clink of knives and china, are heard. Curtain opens.*

* * *

TIME: *An hour later.*

SETTING: *The same as Scene 1.*

AT RISE: AMANDA, GRANDMA, MRS. PHELPS, JOHNNY,
CAPT. CARLIN, *and* LT. DEAN *are at the table, laughing and
chatting.* CAPT. CARLIN *and* LT. DEAN *are sitting next to
one another. The meal is almost over.*

MRS. PHELPS: So, all in all, we owe Lieutenant Dean our
thanks. If he hadn't found Bridget, she'd never have been able
to give us this milk.

CAPT. CARLIN: I can forgive a man much for this milk, ma'am.
I haven't tasted any as sweet since I left home.

LT. DEAN: The butter is wonderful. My own mother couldn't
have made better.

CAPT. CARLIN (*Shocked*): Your mother makes the butter? Why
not your slaves?

LT. DEAN: We don't have any. I never believed in slavery.

CAPT. CARLIN: Well, I'll be!

GRANDMA: No politics tonight. Have some more jam, Captain
Carlin. (*Passes jar*)

CAPT. CARLIN: This jam reminds me of home. I have an apple orchard outside of Boston.

LT. DEAN (*Smiling*): I visited Boston before I began at the University of Virginia.

CAPT. CARLIN: Virginia! I have been to Virginia, too. Beautiful countryside. I hear there is good fishing in the streams of Virginia.

JOHNNY (*Interested*): Fishing? Do you catch trout and bass?

LT. DEAN: They actually leap into my net, they're so eager to be caught!

JOHNNY: Go on with you! You're joshing me!

CAPT. CARLIN: If it's fish you want, you must come to Boston, Johnny. There, we hunt for whales!

JOHNNY (*Impressed*): Whales!

AMANDA: Now, the Captain's joshing you, Johnny!

CAPT. CARLIN: No, on my honor! Whaling schooners leave Boston every day. When I was a lad, I wanted to be a whaler. But I married, and settled down to apple raising.

GRANDMA: You look homesick, Captain. I'll bet you miss your wife.

CAPT. CARLIN: I do. I was married only a little while before I left.

LT. DEAN (*Quietly*): So was I.

CAPT. CARLIN (*Surprised*): You were?

LT. DEAN (*Smiling*): We rebels get married, too.

CAPT. CARLIN (*Apologetically*): I'm sorry. I wasn't thinking. Do you have children? (LT DEAN *shakes his head.*) Nor I. But someday, when this war is over (*Breaks off*) . . .

MRS. PHELPS (*Softly*): Yes, Captain?

CAPT. CARLIN: I did not mean to talk about the war. I had forgotten it, for a short time. (*Pause*) This gathering has seemed not enemy with enemy, but a meal with friends.

MRS. PHELPS: Lieutenant Dean, Captain Carlin, before you came I was feeling very sad and bitter. I kept wondering, why can't we have peace? Then, suddenly, when I saw the basket

Lieutenant Dean mended for me, I realized we'll never have peace until we make it in our own hearts.

AMANDA (*Nodding*): If we called each other friend, there would be no need to fight each other.

MRS. PHELPS: Ben tells us that he prays each night for peace. He would be glad to know that although his birthday guests were enemies when they sat down at this table, now they are friends.

LT. DEAN (*Slowly*): We are still on different sides. We have different ideas. I must go back to my men.

CAPT. CARLIN: So must I.

MRS. PHELPS: You talked of "unfinished business" before you sat at the table. Do not part enemies, gentlemen. Let peace begin in our hearts.

JOHNNY (*Going to window*): The mist is lifting! I can see the woods!

LT. DEAN (*Rising*): It's time to go.

CAPT. CARLIN (*Also rising*): Yes. (*They look at each other, and then* CAPT. CARLIN *extends his hand.*) Godspeed back to your men, Lieutenant Dean.

LT. DEAN (*Slowly taking outstretched hand*): I wish you the same, Captain Carlin. (*He turns to the others.*) I will never forget that here, for a few hours, we were all at peace. (CAPT. CARLIN *and* LT. DEAN *put on cloaks. They salute, then exit right.*)

JOHNNY (*At the window*): They're saluting each other. Now, they're going in separate directions. They're waving to us.

GRANDMA: Don't you have any manners, boy? Wave back! (*As* JOHNNY *waves, the stage lightens.*)

AMANDA: The sun is rising, Mother . . . it's a new day. Do you think it will be a bright day?

MRS. PHELPS (*Smiling*): Yes, Amanda. A bright, *bright* day. (*Curtain*)

THE END

Production Notes

THE BIRTHDAY GUESTS

Characters: 3 male; 3 female.

Playing Time: 25 minutes.

Costumes: Mrs. Phelps, Grandma, Amanda wear long skirts or dresses, aprons. Johnny wears shirt and dark trousers tucked into work boots. Lt. Dean wears gray uniform and a gray cloak, boots. Captain Carlin wears blue uniform, blue cloak, and boots.

Properties: Letter. Two sabres, one broken. Plates, cups, cutlery, etc., and food, for supper and breakfast.

Setting: Kitchen-livingroom of a farmhouse on Kentucky border. A large table with an oil lamp on it stands center, and cooking stove is behind it. Four chairs are placed around table. At right are two more chairs, a couch, and table with daguerreotype and lamp on it. There is a window in wall up center. Entrances are at right, to outside, and left, to other rooms. In Scene 2, there are old basket, dented pots, and broomstick on large table.

Lighting: Lights come up, as indicated in text.

Sound: Knock on door.

Bind Up the Nation's Wounds

by *Graham DuBois*

Abraham Lincoln's efforts to hold war-torn Union together . . .

Characters

ABRAHAM LINCOLN
MARY TODD LINCOLN, *his wife*
LAMON, *in charge of Lincoln's bodyguard*
ANN PRESTON, *one of Lincoln's New Salem friends*
JOHN PRESTON, *Ann's son*
EDNA MARTIN, *John's fiancée*
BELLE BOYD, *Confederate spy*

TIME: *Afternoon of April 14, 1865.*
SETTING: *Lincoln's study in the White House. A small table used as a desk stands down center. On it are inkstand, paper, pens, etc. There are chairs on each side of desk, and one before the window in left wall. Exit to bedroom is left; to rest of White House, right.*
AT RISE: MARY TODD LINCOLN *sits staring out window.*
LINCOLN (*Entering*): Still at the window, Mary? (*Crosses to* MARY) You have been sitting there all afternoon. (*Puts hand on her shoulder*) Why do you spend hours just staring into the street?
MARY: I'm not staring into the street. . . . In which direction is Springfield?

LINCOLN (*Pointing left*): Over there, to the west. Why do you ask?

MARY (*Pathetically*): Our son lies in Springfield. He was too young to die.

LINCOLN (*Sighing; kindly*): You must get a hold of yourself. In the months since Willie left us I have seldom seen you smile.

MARY (*Impatiently*): How can I smile? It pained me yesterday to hear you spinning yarns with members of the cabinet and laughing boisterously.

LINCOLN (*Walking to table*): There have been times, I reckon, when laughter has saved my reason. (*Sits behind table*)

MARY (*Suddenly gentle*): I understand, my dear. This dreadful war has exhausted you. You paced the floor all night. There's something on your mind.

LINCOLN: There's always something on my mind, Mary. That's one of the penalties of being President. And yesterday was a trying day. There were many problems that kept me awake last night.

MARY: Was Belle Boyd one of them?

LINCOLN (*Chuckling*): You're not jealous of Belle, are you?

MARY (*Indignantly*): Of course not! My only regret is that three years ago you didn't deal with her properly, when you had her in Old Capitol Prison. Secretary Stanton recommended the severest measures, but did you listen to him? Oh, no—not you! You saw to it that she was one of two hundred prisoners exchanged and sent to Richmond.

LINCOLN (*Wearily*): What would you have had me do?

MARY (*Firmly*): You treated her as a prisoner of war, but she was a spy, wasn't she? She could have been shot like other spies and we would never have heard of her again.

LINCOLN (*Quietly*): It has not been my policy to make war on women, Mary.

MARY (*Bitterly*): She has made war on you, hasn't she? If you ever capture her again, I hope you have learned your lesson.

LINCOLN: We have captured her.

MARY (*Surprised*): You have?

LINCOLN: Yes—early last week.

MARY: Good! I hope you deal properly with her this time.

LINCOLN (*Shaking his head*): I can't—she has escaped.

MARY (*Incredulous*): Escaped? Such inefficiency.

LINCOLN (*Seriously*): I'm not worried about Belle, Mary. Now that this dreadful war is over, she can't do much damage. I'm worried about the man in the case.

MARY: I didn't know there was a man in the case.

LINCOLN (*Smiling*): Isn't there always when the Cleopatra of the Confederacy is concerned? Belle has a way with the men, you know.

MARY: Do you know who the man is?

LINCOLN: Yes, a certain Captain John Preston.

MARY (*Amazed*): Not that handsome boy who was stationed here for a while in charge of your bodyguard?

LINCOLN: The very same.

MARY: I would have trusted him anywhere. Why, your very life may be at stake. Suppose Belle persuades him to join that secessionist group in Washington that has been plotting to kill you? He knows your daily habits; he is almost as familiar with the White House as you are. Are you afraid they won't find him?

LINCOLN: No, Mary; I'm worried because they have. He is under arrest right here in Washington.

MARY (*Impatiently*): I don't understand you! Why are you worried because they have this disloyal man in custody?

LINCOLN: Because, in the first place, his record doesn't indicate any disloyalty. Though there are suspicious circumstances, I reckon he was young and weak enough to fall victim to the wiles of a very clever and attractive woman. He probably didn't know she was an enemy agent. (*Sighs*) But the worst part is that he is Ann Preston's son.

MARY (*Surprised*): Ann Preston, your old friend from New Salem?

LINCOLN: That's right. She is coming here this morning with

the girl John plans to marry, and I debated all night what to say to them.

MARY (*Angrily*): Abe, sometimes you try my patience. (*Rising*) You never seem to realize the danger you are in.

LINCOLN (*Patiently*): My dear, I have lived with danger ever since I came to the White House. Hatred hangs about me like a fog. There are dozens of men in Washington who would gladly sacrifice their lives to take mine.

MARY: These discussions always give me a headache. (*Walks to door*) I'd better go to my room and lie down.

LINCOLN (*Gently*): That might be wise, my dear. (MARY *exits left, as* LAMON *enters right.*)

LAMON: Good afternoon, Mr. President.

LINCOLN (*Heartily*): Good afternoon, Lamon. I'm glad to see you. Do you bring me any news?

LAMON: I do indeed, sir. We have Belle Boyd.

LINCOLN (*Surprised*): You have? Where? Maryland? Virginia?

LAMON: Right here at the White House door.

LINCOLN: You amaze me! What was she doing—hiding in the shrubbery?

LAMON: No, sir. She came boldly to the front entrance and asked to see you. She said she had important news in the Preston case.

LINCOLN (*Indignantly*): What does she want to do? Put that boy before a firing squad?

LAMON: I don't know, sir. She will tell us nothing; says she will talk only with you. (*Hesitantly*) If you care to see her, we will send her in.

LINCOLN (*Smiling*): I do want to see the incomparable Belle. Ask her to wait downstairs.

LAMON: Very well, sir. (*He exits.* LINCOLN *shakes his head. A knock at door right is heard.*)

LINCOLN (*Calling*): Come in! (ANN *and* EDNA *enter.*)

ANN: Abe Lincoln! You haven't changed a bit. I would have known you anywhere.

LINCOLN (*Rising and advancing to* ANN, *both hands out-*

stretched): Ann Preston! It has been a lifetime since I saw you last. (*To* EDNA) And this must be Edna, John's fiancée. (*Takes her hand*)

EDNA: It's an honor to meet you, Mr. President.

LINCOLN (*To* EDNA): John and I used to have long talks about you, young lady. (*To both women*) Please, sit down. (ANN *and* EDNA *sit in chairs at each side of table;* LINCOLN *leans against table.*) Before we get down to more serious business, Ann, tell me about my friends in New Salem. (*Sighs*) I'll never get that place out of my mind and heart. How is dear old Granny Spears? Still reading the future, I suppose?

ANN: Yes, Abe. She sent you a message.

LINCOLN: She did? Bless her heart!

ANN (*Seriously*): She told me to tell you to keep away from public places, avoid crowds.

LINCOLN (*Chuckling*): That's just like her—always warning me that I would be killed. (*More seriously*) Well, there are dozens of others who give me the same warning, and some in the form of threats. I guess they are having their effect on me, for last night I dreamed that I was lying dead in the White House. But enough of these gloomy thoughts!

ANN (*Worriedly*): I do hope you take care to protect yourself, Abe.

LINCOLN (*With dismissive gesture*): I try not to think of it. (*Pauses*) I know that Hannah Armstrong is still alive. She came to see me not long ago. We talked about old times for an hour. . . . Sometimes at night, when the day has been hard and I can't sleep, I call the roll of old friends to myself, and somehow it gives me strength. (*Looks at* EDNA, *who is fidgeting nervously*) But I see that our little friend is concerned about more immediate matters.

EDNA (*Anxiously*): Yes, Mr. President. I—I do want to know about John. Do—do things look serious for him?

LINCOLN (*Soberly*): I won't deceive you, my dear. (*Sighs and shakes his head*) John is suspected of having been in the company of the spy Belle Boyd. She was arrested and soon escaped. John was picked up by the authorities. His pistol was missing.

EDNA (*Indignantly*): But what of that? Many things can happen to a pistol.

LINCOLN (*With understanding*): Yes, my dear, that is true. But the question is, what did happen to it?

EDNA (*Emphatically*): John couldn't be guilty of treason. I know it.

LINCOLN (*Gently*): You know it, John's mother knows it, and I believe it; but when you go before a military court you have to have more than belief in the accused man's innocence. You have to have facts.

ANN (*Anxiously*): If—if things should go against John, would the penalty be severe?

LINCOLN (*Very seriously*): I'm afraid it would, Ann.

ANN: Even death?

LINCOLN (*Solemnly*): Even death. (ANN *covers her face with her hands.*)

EDNA: But that isn't just, Mr. President. The war is over.

LINCOLN: Unfortunately, my child, it wasn't over when this incident occurred—about ten days ago. (EDNA *takes out her handkerchief and dabs her eyes.*) But let us not take such a gloomy view of things. Nothing has been proved.

LAMON (*Entering*): Excuse me, Mr. President. (*Crosses to table*) I have something here that may interest you. (*Hands him a pistol in a holster*)

LINCOLN: It belongs to—?

LAMON: Captain John Preston.

ANN: Thank heaven it has been found.

LINCOLN: Who had it?

LAMON: Belle Boyd.

EDNA (*Sobbing*): Oh, I can't believe it!

LINCOLN: Was it found on her?

LAMON: No, sir, that is the most surprising part of it. She handed it over to us without our even asking for it. (*Walks to door*) There's a little document in the holster. (*Exits*)

LINCOLN (*Taking pistol from holster*): What an amazing woman Belle is! (*Lays pistol on table, and examines holster*) Absolutely unpredictable! (*Draws piece of paper from holster*) Ah, here's the document Lamon spoke of. (*Glances at paper*) It seems to be a letter. (*Reads*) "My Most Beautiful Flower in a Garden of Girls." Well, that's eloquent enough. (*Hands paper to* EDNA) Is that John's handwriting?

EDNA (*Scrutinizing paper*): It certainly is. I would recognize it anywhere. (*Glances over paper*) What romantic language! (*Reads*) "The days since last I saw you have seemed an eternity." (*Looking at* LINCOLN) Why—why, what does that mean?

LINCOLN (*Shaking his head sadly*): I'm afraid it may mean too much.

ANN: Why, Abe, you can't think that John would—

EDNA (*Reading*): "I am counting the moments until I see you again."

LINCOLN (*Seriously*): It looks as if John had been meeting Belle regularly.

EDNA (*Tossing letter on table, and jumping up*): I am through with him! Innocent or guilty, I don't want to see him again.

LINCOLN (*Calmly*): Don't be too hasty. John is being held right here in Washington. I shall send for him. (*Calling*) Lamon!

LAMON (*Appearing at door*): Yes, Mr. President.

LINCOLN: Show Belle Boyd in. (ANN *rises quickly.*) And have Captain Preston brought to the White House. (LAMON *exits.*)

ANN: We must be going, Abe. We can't—

EDNA (*Bitterly*): We don't want to see the woman who has ruined our lives.

LINCOLN (*Putting his hand on* ANN's *arm*): Please stay. I want very much to have you hear everything. Perhaps Belle may clear up this whole matter.

EDNA: She may make matters even worse!

LINCOLN (*Persuasively*): Please stay. For the sake of old times, Ann. (ANN *looks at* EDNA, *nods, and the women sit.*)

LAMON (*At door*): Belle Boyd, Mr. President. (*Ushers* BELLE *in, then exits*)

LINCOLN (*Rising and extending his hand*): I am very happy to see you, Miss Boyd.

BELLE (*Amazed*): You—you would shake hands with me?

LINCOLN: Of course I would. Why not? (BELLE *shakes his hand.*) The war is over. We are fellow Americans now. It was your great leader, General Lee, who said, "Bring your children up to know no North, no South. Bring them up to be Americans." Don't you agree with that?

BELLE (*Uncertainly*): I—I think I do.

LINCOLN (*Suddenly aware of* ANN *and* EDNA): Oh, pardon me. (*Pointing*) Miss Boyd, this is Mrs. Preston and Miss Martin. (ANN *and* EDNA *nod coldly.*) Please have a seat, Miss Boyd. (BELLE *sits.*) Now, what can you tell us about the unfortunate Captain Preston?

BELLE: Not a great deal to tell, except that he is innocent.

ANN: Thank God!

EDNA: I knew he was!

LINCOLN: But what about that pistol? How did it come into your possession?

BELLE: It was in a crowded little restaurant. When I entered, there was an army overcoat on one chair and on the table, in front of the chair, was that pistol. (*Points to pistol*) I took it and left.

LINCOLN: But of what use was a pistol to you?

BELLE: I didn't want the pistol; I took it for the holster.

LINCOLN (*Surprised*): For the holster?

BELLE: You probably don't know, Mr. President, that we have found some valuable information tucked away in the holsters of officers' pistols.

LINCOLN: Then I take it you have had little contact with Captain Preston?

BELLE: None at all. I have never met him. I didn't even know his name until I saw it in the newspapers.

LINCOLN: So your visit to Washington was made in the hope that you might get a chance to kill me?

BELLE (*Amazed*): Why, no, Mr. President, not at all. I came here to clear an innocent man. But the guards seized me before I had a chance to explain. (*Pauses*) I did have another reason for coming, however.

LINCOLN: And what was that?

BELLE: I owed you a debt for freeing me from that horrid Capitol Prison instead of turning me over to a firing squad. Since my release, I know that I have made life miserable for you, but lately I have come to respect you.

LINCOLN (*Puzzled*): You amaze me. I was sure you thought of me only as a half-educated baboon. (*Smiles*) That's how I've often been described in the North and the South. You mean you never called me that?

BELLE (*Embarrassed*): Often at first, Mr. President, when I was confined in Capitol Prison. I used to draw pictures of you on the wall, sometimes as a boa constrictor strangling the life out of the South, sometimes as a monkey or a baboon chattering insults at us.

LINCOLN (*Puzzled*): What about the guards? Didn't they try to stop you?

BELLE: Most of them enjoyed it, sir. They used to gather outside my cell and encourage me. A couple of them even made suggestions.

LINCOLN (*Chuckling*): They had a nice sense of humor, didn't they?

BELLE: One of them protested.

LINCOLN: Good for him! What did he say?

BELLE: He said it wasn't fair to the animals.

LINCOLN (*Laughing heartily*): Now there's a fellow with a fine sense of justice. If I knew his name, I'd promote him. But, tell me, Belle—you said you made those beautiful comparisons at first. Does that mean your attitude has changed?

BELLE: It certainly has, sir.

LINCOLN: Can you tell me when?

BELLE: It was during your Inaugural Address a few weeks ago. I was in the crowd. You looked so sad and lonely, your shoulders bowed beneath a burden too heavy for any man to bear. I told myself that though you were my enemy, though you hated me, you were as sincere in your convictions as I was in mine.

LINCOLN: I can truthfully say that in my whole life I have never hated anybody.

BELLE (*Thoughtfully*): I reckon that's another reason I'm here. I have come to believe that you are the best friend—perhaps the only friend—the South has in the North.

LINCOLN: There are those North and South who would be happy to see me dead.

BELLE (*Strongly*): Nobody could strike a greater blow against the South than to kill you. If you were to die, our best hope would be gone. We would be treated as conquered territory, our property confiscated, our leaders thrown into prison.

LINCOLN (*Sadly*): I regret to say that there are many who would adopt such a policy. They were the ones I tried to appeal to in my Inaugural Address.

BELLE: You appealed to everybody, sir. There were parts of it that made me weep. "With malice toward none; with charity for all." Who in the South or anywhere can forget those words? They brought reassurance to countless thousands. Now, if only we could be rid of the fire-eaters of the North who thirst for vengeance. . . .

LINCOLN (*Vehemently*): These little men shall not prevail so long as I live. (*Brings down his hand emphatically upon table*) If four more years of life are granted me, I shall devote them to molding a nation from all sections of this Union. I have committed myself to binding up the nation's wounds. To that cause I shall devote the rest of my life; for that cause I would gladly die. (BELLE *rises.* ANN *and* EDNA *rise.* ANN *advances to* BELLE *and extends her hand.* LINCOLN *writes on a slip of paper.*)

ANN: I can never thank you enough for what you have done for my son.

BELLE (*Taking* ANN's *hand*): I couldn't let an innocent man die.

EDNA (*Extending her hand to* BELLE): Miss Boyd, I, too, thank you—and you have made me feel differently toward the South. I hope that some day we can be friends.

BELLE (*Taking* EDNA's *hand*): Why, you're my friend already, honey—even if you are a Yankee.

LINCOLN (*Walking to* BELLE): Give this to Lamon as you leave, Belle. (*Hands her the slip of paper*)

BELLE: Of course, Mr. President. (*Reads slip aloud*) "Please release Miss Belle Boyd so that she may return home." (*Looking up in amazement*) You mean, Mr. President, that—that you won't hold me for trial?

LINCOLN: Why, no, Belle. Why should I hold one who could, I believe, be instrumental in bringing about a better understanding between North and South—to help build the new union of which I dream?

BELLE: Then I'm not even to go to prison?

LINCOLN (*Chuckling*): Why throw into prison a person who would escape anyhow?

BELLE (*Laughing merrily*): I have been rather successful in that, haven't I? (*Suddenly serious*) Bless you, Mr. Lincoln! (*Shakes his hand, and then, impulsively, kisses his check*)

LINCOLN (*Much moved, taking off his spectacles and wiping them with his handkerchief*): Ask Lamon to send in Captain Preston, would you, Miss Boyd? (BELLE *nods, exits.*)

ANN: I wish you could come home, Abe.

LINCOLN: You will never know how I would love to go back. Just as soon as my second term is finished, I shall return to Springfield, practice a little law, and run down to New Salem as often as I can. I think of New Salem as the place in which my life really began, where my first lasting friendships were formed, where I first ran for public office, and where some of the most cherished memories of my life had their origin.

(JOHN PRESTON *enters.* LINCOLN *rises.*) Ah, John! (*Shakes* JOHN*'s hand*) It's good to see you.

ANN (*Rushing to* JOHN *and embracing him*): Oh, my boy, thank goodness you're safe.

EDNA (*Tearfully*): For a while, John, I thought I had lost you in more ways than one.

JOHN (*Embracing her*): There is no way in which you could ever lose me, Edna.

EDNA: But what about that letter in the holster, John?

JOHN: I'll tell you all about that just as soon as I have explained the pistol to President Lincoln. (*To* LINCOLN) You see, sir, after I had finished my meal in a restaurant, I sat at the table writing a letter. Before I completed it, it was time to go on duty, and so I tucked it into the holster of my pistol. As I was doing so, a friend across the room signaled that he wanted to see me, and I carelessly left the pistol on the table for a few moments. When I returned, it was gone.

LINCOLN (*Wryly*): It is always dangerous to leave pistols lying around.

EDNA (*Persistently*): But what of that letter, John! How—

LINCOLN (*Rising; to* ANN): Ann, there's a little room right across the corridor. You and I can finish our chat there. (*Leads* ANN *to door*) The little drama that's about to be enacted in this room should only have two characters. (*Exits with* ANN)

EDNA: Now you can speak freely, John. I don't understand that letter.

JOHN (*A bit testily*): It is clear enough.

EDNA: Maybe it's too clear. "My most beautiful flower in a garden of girls." Oh, I admit that Belle is beautiful.

JOHN (*Emphatically*): I have never seen Belle in my life.

EDNA: Just how many flowers have you in your garden of girls?

JOHN: You know there is only one.

EDNA (*Convinced but teasing him*): Rather unusual, isn't it, to devote a whole garden to just one girl?

JOHN: Not when the girl is as unusual as mine.

EDNA (*Quoting*): "The days since last I saw you have seemed an eternity." What a sweet conception of time!

JOHN (*Seriously*): Let me explain, Edna. It's all very simple. I can show you—

EDNA (*Quoting*): "I am counting the moments until I see you again." How long does it take to count to an eternity of moments?

JOHN: Edna, you are deliberately misinterpreting me. Don't you see? Every word was intended for you.

EDNA: And to make sure that I would get them, you tucked them into a pistol holster—and forgot all about them.

JOHN: I didn't forget. I hadn't finished that letter, and so I put it into the holster until I could add something.

EDNA (*In mock surprise*): Add something? Add something to eternity? Put another flower into your garden of girls?

JOHN: You are teasing me! And I know just how to stop it. (*Embraces* EDNA, *as* ANN *and* LINCOLN *enter*)

LINCOLN (*To* ANN): We are just in time to witness the climax of the little drama. And it's ending just as I knew it would. (*To* JOHN) John, your mother tells me that she and Edna must take a train to New Salem soon. I appoint you their military escort to the station.

JOHN: You couldn't give me a more delightful assignment, Mr. President.

LINCOLN (*Opening door and calling off to* LAMON): Lamon, you will release Captain Preston at once. I am sending him on a special mission. I'll make out the proper papers a little later. (*Closes door and turns to* ANN)

ANN (*Seizing* LINCOLN's *hand in both her own*): Oh, Abe, I'll be grateful to you for the rest of my life.

LINCOLN: Nonsense, Ann! A visit from an old New Salem friend is balm to my weary soul. (*Pats her shoulder, turns to* EDNA) I congratulate you and John. I'll attend the wedding— provided that I am invited.

EDNA (*With a broad smile*): I'll see that you get a special invitation. (*Seizing* LINCOLN's *hand and pressing it to her lips*) We can never repay you for what you have done.

ANN: You look so tired, Abe. You ought to have more relaxation.

LINCOLN: I'm going to have some tonight. Mary has arranged for us to see a play.

ANN: Oh, do be careful, Abe. Remember what Granny Spears said about avoiding crowds and public places.

LINCOLN: Pay no attention to dear old Granny. I couldn't be safer anywhere than I'll be this evening at the theater. I will be surrounded by my bodyguards and a loyal audience. As you speed along on that train to New Salem, think of me sitting in Ford's Theater laughing at the antics of Miss Laura Keene and her company in "Our American Cousin." (*Opens door.* ANN, EDNA, *and* JOHN *exit.* LINCOLN *closes door, takes off spectacles, wipes them with his handkerchief, and walks slowly toward table as curtain falls.*)

THE END

Production Notes

BIND UP THE NATION'S WOUNDS

Characters: 3 male; 4 female

Playing Time: 30 minutes.

Costumes: Everyday dress of the period for all characters except John, who wears Army uniform. Lincoln wears spectacles, has handkerchief in pocket. Edna also carries handkerchief.

Properties: Holster containing pistol and piece of paper.

Setting: Lincoln's study in the White House. A small table, which Lincoln uses as desk, stands down center. On the desk are an inkstand, paper, pens, etc. There are chairs on each side of the desk, and one before the window in the left wall. Exit left leads to bedroom; exit right leads to rest of White House.

Lighting: No special effects.

Once Upon a Dream

by Claire Boiko

The journey of three young immigrants . . .

Characters

OLD-COUNTRY WOMAN
BEN MOSCOWITZ
GRANDFATHER MOSCOWITZ
GRANDMOTHER MOSCOWITZ
ANNA SWENSON
INGRID
COUNTESS, *offstage voice*
MARCO ROSSELLI
LUIGI ROSSELLI
IMMIGRANT FAMILIES, *chorus*
THREE SAILORS
THIEF
TWO IMMIGRATION INSPECTORS
MEDICAL EXAMINER
NORWEGIAN MOTHER

SCENE 1

TIME: *1910.*
BEFORE RISE: IMMIGRANT FAMILIES *are seated before curtain, dressed in costumes of various European countries.* OLD-COUNTRY WOMAN, *in long dress and apron, enters, addresses audience thoughtfully.*

160

OLD-COUNTRY WOMAN (*Shaking head ruefully*): Here it is, the year 1910. The first decade of the twentieth century, on the continent of Europe. We work hard. We struggle. And what for? It might as well be the Dark Ages.

FAMILIES (*Somberly*):
Too many people. Not enough land.
Not enough food. Not enough hope.

OLD-COUNTRY WOMAN: That's the worst thing about our lives. There's no hope. (*She crosses down center, sits on apron, burying head in hands. BEN MOSCOWITZ, in Russian costume and carrying worn suitcase, enters right. He takes small English-language book from pocket and reads aloud from it.*)

BEN: Good morning. How are you? May I have some breakfast, please? (GRANDFATHER *and* GRANDMOTHER MOSCOWITZ *hurry in left.* GRANDMOTHER *waves small package wrapped in kerchief.*)

GRANDMOTHER: Ben, wait! You forgot the bread. You won't get bread like this in America!

BEN (*To* GRANDMOTHER): Thank you, Grandmother. (*Takes package*)

GRANDFATHER: We really came to say goodbye again, even though we've said it a hundred times.

BEN (*Pleading*): Grandfather, please let me stay here in Russia with you.

GRANDFATHER: No, no, Ben. You must go to your uncle in New York. The Russian Cossacks are rounding up young men. If you stay here, they'll take you away from us and put you in the army.

BEN: But I'm too young for the army.

GRANDMOTHER: Nobody is too young for them. They took a boy of eight last week to fetch and carry for the soldiers.

GRANDFATHER: And there's no future for you here in Russia. You have such a good mind, Ben. You speak English already. What could you do here? Sell pots and pans from town to town? You want to study for the law. (*Sound of train whistle is heard.*) That's your train. We must hurry to the station.

GRANDMOTHER: Come. We'll walk with you to the depot.

BEN: But I don't want to leave you here alone. I'll worry about you. Please, let me stay.

GRANDFATHER: No, Ben! Don't worry. We'll be just fine. And when you have enough money, you'll send for us, right?

BEN: I will. Oh, I will, Grandfather.

GRANDMOTHER (*Pointing to sky*): Look up there, Ben. That's the evening star. When you see that star in America, remember us.

GRANDFATHER: You keep your head high. America is a wonderful place. No one will take your land or hurt your family in America. Here in Russia, dreams are like soap bubbles— they burst into nothing. But in America, dreams come true. (*Sound of train whistle grows louder.*)

GRANDMOTHER (*Taking* BEN *by the arm*): Come on, Benjamin Moscowitz—don't keep America waiting! (*They exit left. ANNA SWENSON, dressed in long skirt, blouse, and worn cloak, and carrying battered suitcase, enters center, through curtain. She crosses down left, sets her suitcase down with a thump, then folds her arms and stamps her foot.*)

ANNA (*Defiantly*): I won't! I won't! I *won't*! I won't stay in Stockholm one more minute. I don't care if I have to walk across the whole Atlantic Ocean. I'm going to America. I am! I am! I am! (INGRID, *in uniform, runs on through curtain.*)

INGRID: Anna! Come quickly. The Countess is screaming for you. Oh, Anna, you are in such trouble.

ANNA: I don't care. I'm going away forever.

INGRID (*Shocked*): But where?

ANNA: To America. There are no countesses in America, because every girl is a countess. I have packed my suitcase. I have five kroner.

INGRID: Five kroner? But that won't even take you to the middle of Stockholm.

ANNA: Then, I'll—I'll walk to America. Oh, Ingrid, I'm so tired of being a servant girl.

INGRID (*Sighing heavily*): So am I. Maybe it wouldn't be so bad

if we worked for a reasonable person. But the Countess is
so difficult!

ANNA (*In imitation, shrieking unpleasantly*): Anna! Ingrid!
Come here this instant. My tea is cold. Go down and bring me
fresh tea. Do you hear me? (*In her own voice*) What a dragon!

INGRID: Oh, Anna, don't go to America. If you stay, in a few
years you could be a first parlormaid.

ANNA: I don't want to be any kind of maid. Why, I can read
and write. A person who can read and write can do almost
anything in America.

INGRID: But you can't speak English.

ANNA: Yes, I can. I listen at the keyhole when the Countess
has her English lesson. And I bought this little book. (*Takes
from pocket same language book* BEN *has*) Listen: Good morning. How are you? May I have some breakfast, please?

COUNTESS (*Shouting offstage*): Anna! Ingrid!

INGRID (*Shuddering*): Oh-h, she makes my head ache. Anna,
where would you go in America?

ANNA: I wrote to my Uncle Nils and Aunt Christina in Minnesota. I begged them to let me come to their farm. I said I would
do anything. Even milk cows. But I haven't heard from them.

INGRID (*Suddenly*): Minnesota? Oh! I almost forgot. (*Reaches
into pocket*) A letter came for you this morning. It's from Minnesota! (*Hands letter to* ANNA, *who opens it quickly*)

ANNA (*Reading letter to herself, her face registering incredulity
and joy*): Oh! It's a miracle! (*She hugs* INGRID, *dances around
with her.*) My American miracle, just in time.

INGRID (*Puzzled*): What is in that letter? A million kroner?

ANNA: Better than that. (*Holds up slip of paper*) A steamship
ticket to America. From Aunt Christina and Uncle Nils. And
a railroad ticket to Minnesota. Beautiful, beautiful Minnesota!

COUNTESS (*Offstage*): Anna! Ingrid! Come here at once.

ANNA (*Shaking her head; smiling*): Not today, Countess. Not
ever again.

INGRID (*Despondently*): I'll miss you so much, Anna. Promise
you'll write to me.

ANNA: I promise.

INGRID: Go—quickly. Let me be the one to tell the Countess.
(ANNA *picks up suitcase and exits center.* INGRID *calls off,
triumphantly.*) Oh, Countess! Anna cannot come at once.
Anna cannot come at all. Anna has gone to Minnesota. Beautiful, beautiful Minnesota! (*She exits joyously.* MARCO ROS-
SELLI *enters, carrying worn suitcase and reading from same
language book as* BEN *and* ANNA.)

MARCO: Good morning. How are you? May I have some breakfast, please? (*He strikes a pose, flourishing the book, and begins to sing the words as if they were an operatic aria.*) Good
morn-ing! How are *you*-oo-oo! May I have some *break*-fast,
please. . . . (LUIGI ROSSELLI *enters, watches* MARCO *and
shakes his head in disbelief.*)

LUIGI (*Pretending awe*): No. It can't be. It's the famous opera
singer, Marco Rosselli, in his first American engagement. Oh-
h-h, how exciting it is!

MARCO: Don't laugh, little brother. Anything can happen in
America. The streets are lined with gold, and Italian tenors
sing for the President. Best of all, there's room enough for
everybody.

LUIGI: Dream on, Marco. But when you're shining shoes on
those streets lined with gold, remember me. I'm coming to
America next year—if you earn enough money for my steamship passage.

MARCO (*Airily*): Of course I'll earn enough. How many shoeshine boys sing opera while they buff your toes? I'll earn
enough to bring the rest of Italy to America. And I'll tell you
what. When you get there, I'll even give you a free shoeshine.

LUIGI (*Sarcastically*): A free shoeshine. I've been waiting all
my life for a free shoeshine. Now—when you get to America,
which one of our brothers is meeting you?

MARCO: They're *all* meeting me. All seven. And our sisters.
And Mama. And Papa. They're having a big party for me.

LUIGI (*Sighing*): Oh, Marco, tell the truth for once.

MARCO (*Crestfallen*): Well . . . just Anthony. Everybody else is too busy. Now, listen, Luigi. You be a good boy, hear? Mind Cousin Giuseppi, *o-kay?*

LUIGI: What is that—"*o-kay*"?

MARCO: It's what everybody says in America. You'd be surprised how much English I learned carrying luggage for the tourists. *O-kay?*

LUIGI: *O-kay.* (*Sound of boat whistle is heard.*)

MARCO: That's the boat to America. (*Hesitating*) Well . . .

LUIGI (*Looking at his feet*): Well . . .

MARCO: Time to go, Luigi. Oh—(*Takes battered opera score from his pocket*) This is for you.

LUIGI (*Awed, taking score*): But this is your music, Marco. The score to *Rigoletto.*

MARCO: You keep it. I know it by heart. Besides, I've heard you sing.

LUIGI: You have?

MARCO (*Offhandedly*): You're pretty good. (*Mussing* LUIGI's *hair*) You're almost as good as I am.

LUIGI (*Happily*): Thanks, Marco! (*Sound of boat whistle is heard again.* MARCO *picks up suitcase, crosses left, pauses, turns and waves to* LUIGI.)

MARCO: *Arrivederci,* little brother. Until we meet in America. (*He exits left.*)

LUIGI: *Arrivederci,* big brother. I'll see you in the White House. (*He exits left.* OLD-COUNTRY WOMAN *raises her head.*)

OLD-COUNTRY WOMAN: Did I say there was no hope? But there *is* hope. There is a place for us. (*She stands.*) America.

FAMILIES:
Plenty of land. Plenty of food.
And plenty of hope. America!

1ST SOLO: In America, nobody is "Your Majesty." Everybody is "mister." Even the President!

2ND SOLO: In America, you can say what you think. Even

when what you think is not what the government thinks you should think.

3RD SOLO: In America, everyone has the same rights. Even the street sweepers. It's written down for everyone to see, in the Declaration of Independence.

FAMILIES (*In unison*): "We hold these truths to be self-evident: That all men are created equal, that they are endowed by their Creator with certain unalienable rights, that among these are life, liberty, and the pursuit of happiness. . . . "

OLD-COUNTRY WOMAN: Where is this place? On the moon? Over the rainbow? Is it a dream?

4TH SOLO: America is a real place.

5TH SOLO: America has a real sky.

6TH SOLO: Real mountains.

7TH SOLO: Real forests.

8TH SOLO: And good rich earth.

OLD-COUNTRY WOMAN: Then why are we waiting? We're coming, America! (*Exits center*)

FAMILIES (*In unison*): We're coming, America.

1ST, 2ND, 3RD, and 4TH SOLOS (*In unison*): By the hundreds . . .

5TH, 6TH, 7TH, and 8TH SOLOS (*In unison*): By the thousands . . .

FAMILIES (*In unison*): By the millions! We're coming to America! (*All sing first verse of "America, the Beautiful." When they finish,* IMMIGRANT FAMILIES *exit behind curtain as musical reprise is played.*)

* * * * *

SCENE 2

BEFORE RISE: THREE SAILORS *run through curtain, address audience.*

1ST SAILOR: All aboard!

2ND SAILOR: Steady as you go.

3RD SAILOR: Ship's a-sailing. On the tide.

1ST SAILOR: Steaming west—

2ND SAILOR: West to a star—

3RD SAILOR: West to America. (*Music to "Blow, Ye Winds, Westerly" is heard. SAILORS may sing first verse, if desired. When they finish, they exit as curtain goes up.*)

* * *

SETTING: *Top deck of ship, the bow. Backdrop depicts sea and sky at sunset. Up center are packing cases.*

AT RISE: ANNA, *shivering, her cloak wrapped around her, sits on small packing case, using a larger one as a desk. She writes a letter with pencil. Her purse, holding passport and railroad ticket, lies unguarded at her side. She finishes letter, then strolls down center, reading it aloud. As she does,* THIEF, *in shabby clothing, sneaks around stack of packing cases, opens purse and holds up passport. He scrutinizes it, shakes his head, replaces passport, then removes railroad ticket. He smiles, nods his head and pockets the ticket, putting purse back in its original position. He sneaks off left.*

ANNA (*Reading*): "Dear Ingrid. Here I am aboard the steamship *Olympic*. You can't imagine how crowded it is in steerage. There must be two thousand people all jammed together, speaking fifty different languages. It is so noisy I have to come up on deck, even if it is cold and windy. Everybody seems to have a family but me. Believe me, it is no fun to travel alone. But I shouldn't complain. Things will be much better when I get to America. Your friend, Anna Swenson. . . . " (*She folds letter, puts it in her pocket, and takes out her English book, strolling down right. As she reads aloud,* BEN *enters left, studying his book. He sits up center, on carton, as* MARCO *enters, his nose in his English book, and strolls down left.*)

BEN (*Reading aloud*): Will you direct me to Hester Street, please?

MARCO (*Reading aloud*): What time is it, please?

ANNA (*Looking up at boys*): Are you speaking to me?

BEN (*Hesitantly*): You speak English?

ANNA (*Confidently*): Of course.

MARCO: I speak English, too. (*They run toward each other, meeting down center.*)

BEN: This is wonderful. I haven't spoken to anyone since the boat left Hamburg.

MARCO: I haven't, either. I thought I was losing my voice.

ANNA: But don't you have a family on the ship?

MARCO: No. I'm traveling alone.

BEN: So am I.

ANNA: I'm alone, too. My name is Anna Swenson—from Sweden. (*Puts out her hand. Boys grab it.*)

BEN: Ben Moscowitz. From Russia.

MARCO: Marco Rosselli—your friendly tenor from Italy. (*He looks amused at three-sided handshake.*) Three friends. I read a book about three friends. It's called *The Three Musketeers*.

BEN (*Laughing*): That's who we are. The Three Musketeers. Except the Three Musketeers were all men.

ANNA: In America, I could be a Musketeer. In America, you can be anything you want.

MARCO: Well, then, the Three Musketeers it is. One for all, and all for one.

BEN: Where are you going in America, Anna?

ANNA (*Proudly*): To Minnesota. Beautiful, beautiful Minnesota! I have a railway ticket. Look—I'll show you. (*She goes to pick up purse, rummages in it, then looks up, puzzled.*) Well, my passport's here, but my ticket . . . where's my ticket? (*Turns purse upside down, shaking it*)

MARCO: Oh, no. Somebody's taken it. This morning some of the people below decks were complaining to the steward that their money was gone.

BEN (*Dismayed*): This is a terrible thing. If you don't have a ticket to a destination in America, you could be deported— sent back to Sweden.

ANNA (*Panicky*): What? Well, I won't go! They'll have to drag me. I'll kick! I'll scream!

MARCO: Calm down, Anna. We won't let them send you back.

BEN: No. We'll think of something. (*Sound of bell is heard.*) That's the dinner bell. We'd better go below. (*Thoughtfully*) Hm-m-m. I have an idea. Come with me, Marco. Anna, we'll meet you here on deck after dinner.

ANNA (*Upset*): Thank you for trying to help. I'll meet you here—but I don't believe in miracles anymore. (*Blackout. BEN, MARCO, and ANNA exit down left. Musical reprise of "Blow Ye Winds, Westerly," then lights come up. BEN enters down left, followed by MARCO. They turn and beckon to IM-MIGRANT FAMILIES off left, who enter quickly. Half of group, in shabby clothes, forms audience downstage, facing other group—in colorful costumes—who arrange themselves on cartons upstage. BEN and MARCO stand center. FAMILIES chatter excitedly.*)

BEN (*Loudly*): Sh-h-h! Quiet, please. (*All quiet down.*) Marco, is Anna coming? (*MARCO crosses left, peers offstage.*)

MARCO: She's on her way. (*To others*) Remember what to say when she comes on deck, o-kay?

ALL: *O-kay!* (*As ANNA enters down left, MARCO escorts her center.*)

ANNA (*Puzzled*): What is this? What's going on? (*As MARCO signals, all shout.*)

ALL: Surprise! (*All clap and cheer.*)

MARCO: Tonight, for the first and only time on the high seas, we present a benefit performance for Anna Swenson. Please be seated, Miss Swenson. (*MARCO ceremoniously escorts her center. ANNA sits.*)

BEN (*Bowing*): Good evening. It is my pleasure to present that great Italian singer, the toast of five continents . . . Signor Marco Rosselli! (*Music to "Santa Lucia" is heard, then MARCO sings first verse. All may repeat chorus with MARCO. At end, all clap.*)

MARCO: And now—a song from Ben Moscowitz.

BEN: Well, I'm not the toast of five continents, but if you'll help me, we'll sing together. (*Music to "The Volga Boatman" or another Russian song is heard.* BEN *sings; others may accompany him, if desired.*)

MARCO (*At end of song*): And now, ladies and gentlemen, it is your turn.

BEN: Entertain us, please. (BEN *and* MARCO *sit in audience next to* ANNA, *while those in native costumes sing, dance, or play instruments reflecting national origin.*) If you enjoyed the show, please contribute something for our friend, Anna Swenson. (MARCO *passes hat. All contribute money.* MARCO *presents his hat to* ANNA.)

MARCO: Anna, this is for you.

BEN: Now you can buy a railroad ticket to Minnesota.

ANNA (*Rising*): Thank you. Thank you all. (*To* BEN *and* MARCO) Someday, I'll find a way to help you. I promise. (*Sound of boat whistle is heard.* SAILORS *enter down right. Lights dim. Silhouettes of New York harbor and Statue of Liberty with lighted torch appear on backdrop.*)

1ST SAILOR: Look ahead. There it is. New York harbor. (*All turn to face backdrop.*)

2ND SAILOR: Look ahead. To the future. There's America!

3RD SAILOR: Look ahead. Someone is waiting for you.

SAILORS (*Together*): Lady Liberty.

ANNA: She seems to be speaking to us. What is she saying?

3RD SAILOR: She's welcoming you.

2ND SAILOR: We know her words by heart. . . . (*"The New Colossus" may be spoken or sung.*)

1ST SAILOR:
Give me your tired, your poor,

2ND SAILOR:
Your huddled masses yearning to breathe free,

3RD SAILOR:
The wretched refuse of your teeming shore.

SAILORS (*Together*):
Send these, the homeless, tempest tost to me,

I lift my lamp beside the golden door.
(*Above the torch, a bright star appears.* BEN *points to it, excited*)

BEN: Look! The evening star. Grandmother, Grandfather—I'm in America. America, at last!

ALL (*Lifting hands in salute to Statue of Liberty*): America. America at last! (*Blackout. Quick curtain as musical reprise of "America, the Beautiful" is played.*)

* * * * *

SCENE 3

BEFORE RISE: TWO IMMIGRATION INSPECTORS *enter right.* MEDICAL EXAMINER *enters left.* 1ST INSPECTOR *carries landing card.*

1ST INSPECTOR (*Addressing audience*): People of the world—welcome to Ellis Island. Your journey is almost over.

2ND INSPECTOR: You are in America—almost. But before you enter, America has some questions to ask you.

1ST INSPECTOR: Please form a line. Have your passport in your hand.

MEDICAL EXAMINER: First, you must be examined. Do you have any condition that will prevent you from earning a living? Do you have a communicable disease? It is our job to find out. But please, do not worry. Only two percent of all the people we examine are turned back.

1ST INSPECTOR: Next you must answer a few questions. If you cannot answer in English, we have interpreters to help you.

2ND INSPECTOR: When you complete the examination, this landing card will be issued to you. (*Holds up card*) Attach it to your clothing. It is your ticket of admission to America.

1ST INSPECTOR: When you take the ferry to lower New York, you are on your own.

2ND INSPECTOR: Work hard. Study hard. Be good citizens. America needs you.

MEDICAL EXAMINER: Be happy. Be healthy. We wish you well. (*"America" is heard. Curtain opens.*)

* * *

SETTING: *Registry room. Backdrop shows windows, balcony, and large flag draped above windows. Upstage are wooden benches; down left is a table holding papers and medical instruments, and two chairs. Center right is small desk with ship's manifest. Down right are desk holding inspection forms and cards, and chair.*

AT RISE: MEDICAL EXAMINER *sits at table.* 1ST INSPECTOR *sits at small desk, reading from manifest.* 2ND INSPECTOR *is at desk down right.* SWEEPER, *leaning on broom, stands down right, on apron.* ANNA, MARCO, *and* BEN *enter.* ANNA *wears card with number 40 on it;* BEN *wears 41;* MARCO, *42. As they enter,* BEN *coughs and* MARCO *sneezes into handkerchief.*)

SWEEPER (*To* BEN): Hey, watch where you're coughing.

BEN: Sorry. It's just a little cold.

MARCO (*Sneezing again*): We sang too much last night. That's all.

SWEEPER (*Suspiciously*): A little cold. That's what you say. What's important is—what will *he* say? (*Points to* MEDICAL EXAMINER) He's a stickler, that doctor. Why, I've seen him turn back folks who just had warts on their fingers.

ANNA: Turn back? You mean Ben and Marco could be deported for having colds?

SWEEPER: Maybe. That doctor—he'll turn a simple cold into something deadly like pneumonia. You watch and see.

BEN: But that's awful. (*Coughs, covers his mouth as* MEDICAL EXAMINER *looks around at* IMMIGRANT FAMILIES, *sternly*)

SWEEPER (*Indicating benches*): You'd better sit down and keep quiet before that doctor puts chalk marks on you fellows.

MARCO (*Puzzled*): Chalk marks? Why would he do that?

SWEEPER: A chalk mark means you're sick. So sick you can't even put your foot on American soil.

BEN: Oh, no!

ANNA: You're just trying to scare us.

SWEEPER: I've been the sweeper here for three years. I know what I've seen. (ANNA, BEN, *and* MARCO *cross upstage, sit on wooden bench.*)

BEN (*Fearfully*): Marco—what if they deport us?

MARCO: I don't know, Ben.

ANNA: There must be something we can do.

BEN: What we need is another miracle.

MARCO (*Sneezing*): A miracle cure.

ANNA: A cure . . . (*Thinking*) Hm-m. Well, maybe not a cure, but . . .

1ST INSPECTOR: Numbers 40, 41, and 42. Swenson, Moscowitz, and Roselli. Report to the Medical Examiner, please. (ANNA *leads the way, followed reluctantly by* BEN *and* MARCO, *who suppress coughs and sneezes.*)

MEDICAL EXAMINER (*To* ANNA): Name?

ANNA: Anna Swenson.

MEDICAL EXAMINER: Where are you from?

ANNA: Sweden. Where are you from? (BEN *and* MARCO *giggle.*)

MEDICAL EXAMINER (*Sternly*): I'll ask the questions here. I heard coughing and sneezing. Were you coughing and sneezing?

ANNA (*Faking a cough and sneeze*): Of course. It's dusty in here. You don't know how to keep a place clean. Now, I'm Swedish, and I know how to keep a place clean. Watch! (*She runs to* SWEEPER.)

MEDICAL EXAMINER: Here, come back! (ANNA *grabs* SWEEPER'*s broom and begins to sweep vigorously upstage.*)

SWEEPER: Hey! That's my broom!

MEDICAL EXAMINER: What are you doing?

ANNA: I'm showing you how we sweep floors in Sweden! (*She whirls around stage, sweeping. As she does so,* IMMIGRANT

FAMILIES *cough and sneeze.* ANNA *sweeps down left around* BEN *and* MARCO. MEDICAL EXAMINER, BEN, *and* MARCO *cough and sneeze.*)

MEDICAL EXAMINER: Stop. (*Coughs*) That's enough. Come back here. (ANNA *crosses to* SWEEPER, *handing him the broom, then returns to* MEDICAL EXAMINER. *She smiles triumphantly and curtseys.* EXAMINER *hastily checks* ANNA, BEN, *and* MARCO, *and waves them toward* 2ND IN-SPECTOR.) They're all yours. (ANNA, BEN, *and* MARCO *line up behind* 2ND INSPECTOR's *desk.*)

BEN (*To* ANNA): That was a close call. Thank you, Anna.

MARCO: I'll never forget what you did for us, Anna.

2ND INSPECTOR: Anna Swenson, Swedish? Ben Moscowitz, Russian? Marco Rosselli, from Italy? (*They nod.*) I see from the passenger manifest that you are unaccompanied minors. Have you sponsors in the United States?

BEN: My uncle, Samuel Moscowitz from Hester Street in New York City, is my sponsor.

MARCO: My sponsor is Anthony Rosselli. He's my brother, and he lives on Mulberry Street in New York City.

ANNA: My sponsors are Uncle Nils and Aunt Christina. From beautiful, beautiful Minnesota. May I go to America now, please?

2ND INSPECTOR: Not so fast, young lady. Have you a ticket for the railroad trip to Minnesota?

ANNA: Not yet. But I have twenty-five whole dollars for it. See? (*Opens purse for* INSPECTOR *to see*) Now, may I go?

2ND INSPECTOR: No, I cannot let you travel by yourself all the way to Minnesota. Somebody must escort you. It's the rule.

MARCO (*Upset*): Oh, no. If I had the money for a ticket, I'd take you there, Anna.

BEN: So would I.

2ND INSPECTOR: Well, have you an escort?

ANNA (*Hanging head*): No.

BEN (*To* IMMIGRANT FAMILIES): Please—won't somebody

volunteer to take Anna Swenson to Minnesota? (FAMILIES *look blankly at each other.*)

MARCO: Please. I can vouch for Anna Swenson. She wouldn't be any trouble at all. Well, hardly any.

2ND INSPECTOR: Come, come. I haven't got all day. I have five hundred more people to process. (*Again, all look at each other and shrug shoulders.*)

NORWEGIAN MOTHER (*Standing resolutely*): *Ja,* I will volunteer to look after the young lady. My family and I are from Norway, and we are on our way to North Dakota. We will take good care of her.

ANNA: Thank you. But you are Norwegian. Do you really want to bother with a Swede? You know, Swedes and Norwegians don't always get along.

NORWEGIAN MOTHER (*Crossing down to* ANNA): That is the past. Here in America nobody cares about old quarrels. Here, we are all one big family. Welcome to my family, Anna Swenson. (*All cheer and clap.*)

2ND INSPECTOR: Good. That concludes your legal examination. Here are your landing cards. Ride the ferry to lower New York, and you will take your first steps in the United States of America. (*Each takes card.*)

MEDICAL EXAMINER *and* INSPECTORS: Good luck!

ANNA (*To* BEN *and* MARCO): Goodbye, Ben and Marco. I'll think of you every day in Minnesota.

MARCO: Goodbye, Anna.

BEN (*Taking two slips of paper from his pocket*): Here's my address. Let's write to each other, so we never forget the Three Musketeers. (ANNA *and* MARCO *puts slips of paper into their pockets.*)

ANNA (*Offering* BEN *and* MARCO *her hand*): One for all—

MARCO *and* BEN (*Taking her hand*): And all for one. (*Ferry whistle is heard.*)

ANNA (*Running down to apron*): That's the ferry to New York. We're on our way. (MARCO *and* BEN *join her downstage.*)

BEN: It's a whole new world. A better world.

MARCO: I feel like Christopher Columbus! (*Music to "God Bless America" is heard.* IMMIGRANT FAMILIES, INSPECTORS, *and* SAILORS *join* ANNA, MARCO, *and* BEN *in singing "God Bless America." They may all carry small flags. At end of song, curtain falls.*)

THE END

Production Notes

ONCE UPON A DREAM

Characters: 6 female; 4 male; 7 male or female for Sailors, Thief, Immigration Inspectors, Medical Examiner; as many male and female extras as desired for Immigrant Families.

Playing Time: 40 minutes.

Costumes: Old-Country Woman: shabby dress of the period. Ben: well-worn Russian boy's costume with yarmulka. Grandfather: black suit, white wig, yarmulka. Grandmother: long, dark dress, shawl, white wig, kerchief, high-topped shoes. Anna, skirt, blouse, cloak, high-topped shoes; her hair may be braided in loops. Ingrid: maid's uniform. Marco and Luigi, knickers, suspenders, shirt; Marco also wears coat and cap; Immigrant Families: Performers wear colorful ethnic costumes; others may wear nondescript peasant clothing. Sailors: ordinary sea costumes of the period. Thief: dark trousers, coat, cap pulled over eyes. Immigration Inspectors: semi-military uniforms or dark suits with ties. Medical Examiner: dark suit and tie, stethescope around neck. Norwegian Mother: ethnic costume or dark skirt and blouse.

Properties: Three small books, three suitcases tied with straps or rope, dark bread wrapped in a kerchief, letter with two tickets in envelope, libretto, passports, pencil, letter paper, purse with passport and ticket in it, stage money, medical equipment, numbered cards on strings, landing permits on tags, ship's manifests, inspection forms, handkerchiefs, broom, small flags, if desired.

Setting: Scene 1, there are long benches in front of curtain. Scene 2, top deck of ship. Backdrop depicts sea and sky at sunset. Up center are packing cases. Later, there are silhouettes of Statue of Liberty with lighted torch and New York harbor (these may be cutouts or shadow projections); bright evening star above torch. Scene 3, Ellis Island registry room, with backdrop of windows and a balcony with large American flag draped over it. There are benches upstage; table and chairs down left; desk and chair down center right.

Lighting: Dimming, blackouts, lighted torch and star, as indicated.

Sound: Train whistle; boat whistle; dinner bell; ferry whistle.

Music: "America the Beautiful," "Blow, Ye Winds Westerly," "Santa Lucia," "The Volga Boatman," "America," "God Bless America."

Civilians Stay Put

by Mildred Hark and Noel McQueen

A story of the home front during World War II . . .

Characters

GRANDPA
CAITLIN, *his granddaughter, 18*
ANDY, *Grandpa as a boy, 17*
WALT ⎫
BOB ⎪
PHIL ⎬ *his friends*
SUSIE ⎪
PAT ⎭
JOE, *owner of a soda shop*
THREE SOLDIERS

SCENE 1

SETTING: *Easy chair and ottoman are down left in front of curtain.*

BEFORE RISE: GRANDPA *enters carrying newspaper. He sits in chair, puts his feet up and begins to read paper. After a moment, shouting is heard off. GRANDPA lowers paper and listens. Door slamming is heard. He winces, shakes his head and goes back to paper. A moment later CAITLIN storms on right.*

CAITLIN: There you are, Grandpa. You've got to help me!

GRANDPA (*Lowering paper*): What's the matter, Caitlin?

178

CAITLIN (*Throwing up her hands; exasperated*): Mom and Dad are so unreasonable! (GRANDPA *takes his feet off ottoman and pats it.* CAITLIN *sits.*) Everyone I know is driving to Florida for spring break, and Mom and Dad won't let me go. You've got to talk to them.

GRANDPA: Well, maybe you can go to Florida next year. (CAITLIN *looks at him, appalled.*) Besides, I thought you were going to help your mother at the hospital over vacation.

CAITLIN (*Jumping up; furious*): I should have known you wouldn't understand!

GRANDPA (*Calmly*): Hey, I didn't always get to go where *I* wanted for spring break either, but sometimes you make the best of it.

CAITLIN (*Surprised*): I didn't even know they had spring break when you were my age.

GRANDPA: Of course they did. (CAITLIN *sits again.*)

CAITLIN (*Intrigued*): Did you have beach week?

GRANDPA: Hardly! There was a war going on. World War II. Things were pretty different.

CAITLIN (*Frowning*): Different how?

GRANDPA: Well, there was rationing, for one thing. You couldn't just *drive* to Florida; you needed coupons for gas—that's assuming you were lucky enough to have a car. The country was pulled together, trying to fight a war, and it was hard on civilians as well as the people fighting.

CAITLIN: So where did you want to go for spring break?

GRANDPA (*Sighing*): Home.

CAITLIN (*Incredulous*): Home?

GRANDPA: Yep. (*Looks off wistfully*) I remember one year . . . must have been 1945, the last year of the war . . . (*Curtain opens; characters remain seated watching action onstage.*)

* * *

TIME: *1945.*
SETTING: *Boy's dormitory room. Simple bed is right. Desk with*

chair is left. Period posters are on backdrop. Second chair is center.

AT RISE: ANDY *sits at desk working.* WALT *and* BOB *enter right, laughing.* WALT *carries a baseball.*

WALT: Hi, Andy!

ANDY (*Looking up*): Hey, Walt. Hi, Bob.

BOB (*Flopping on bed*): Are you still struggling with that geometry? Forget it! Don't you know spring vacation is practically here?

ANDY (*Sighing*): Vacation's still a week away, and this is due tomorrow. (WALT *sits in chair and begins tossing ball up and catching it.*)

WALT: So? Do it tonight. Come play ball with us.

ANDY: I can't. I'm working at Joe's tonight.

BOB (*Resolute*): I'm not doing any more work till after vacation. (*Eagerly*) I can hardly wait to get home and see Mom and Dad and all the gang.

ANDY: Yeah, me, too. (*Thinking*) Vacation seems to mean more this time. I mean, it won't be long before I'm eighteen and if I go into the Air Corps—(*Sighs*)

WALT (*Nodding*): Yeah, I'm planning to try for the Marines. This might be the last vacation we get to see everyone for a while.

BOB: Hey, have you fellows heard from your folks yet? I mean about tickets and stuff?

ANDY: No, and I can't understand it. Dad always sends me money way ahead to get my ticket.

WALT (*Concerned*): Tickets might be hard to get now. You know how crowded the trains are these days. (PHIL *enters right, carrying letters.*)

PHIL (*Excitedly*): Mail's here, and we each got something! (*Hands out letters, then sits on bed next to* BOB)

BOB (*As boys eagerly tear into their letters*): What do you bet they've got checks in them? (*Gleefully*) Tickets home!

ANDY (*Disappointed*): My letter hasn't got any check.

OTHERS (*Crestfallen, as they pull out letters; ad lib*): Mine, either. Nothing. No check here. (*Etc. It's quiet for a moment, as each begins reading his letter.*)

ANDY (*Looking up from letter*): Listen to this. (*Reads*) "Your mother and I have decided that you had better not come home for spring vacation—"

BOB (*Reading his letter; incredulous*): That's what my folks say, too.

ANDY (*Reading more*): "Traveling is so difficult these days—"

PHIL: My parents talk about how difficult it is to travel, too.

WALT: Mine, too. But, jeepers, so what? We're tough! We wouldn't mind that!

ANDY: They go on to say how expensive the tickets are and how they've been trying to save all they can.

PHIL: Can you beat it? If you didn't know our parents lived miles apart, you'd think they all got together in a conspiracy.

BOB (*Upset*): Mom and Dad are always as excited about spring vacation as I am. There must be some reason—

WALT (*Seriously*): Do you think—what with buying war bonds and all the higher prices—do you think our folks are really short of money?

BOB (*Suddenly*): I'll bet that's it! And they've been trying to keep it from us.

ANDY (*Sadly*): Gosh, I'll bet you're right.

PHIL (*Sighing*): It's going to be awfully dull spending spring vacation here.

WALT (*Eagerly*): Hey, I've got a swell idea! Let's go home anyway! We've all been earning money at Joe's—

BOB: Yeah! We'll buy our own tickets and surprise our folks!

PHIL (*Excitedly*): Can't you see their faces when we walk in!

ANDY (*Doubtfully*): But I told my dad I was going to use the money I earned to help out with clothes and books.

BOB: So did I—but don't you think they'd rather see us than have us buy new clothes?

ANDY (*Considering*): I guess you're right. Why don't you fellows stop by Joe's tonight? Maybe he can give us all some extra work.

PHIL: Yeah. We'd better put in every minute we can until the time comes.

BOB (*Wistfully*): Home sweet home! (*Rises*) Well, we should let you finish your work, Andy. See you at Joe's later. (PHIL *and* WALT *rise. Boys ad lib goodbyes. They exit. Curtain*)

* * * * *

SCENE 2

BEFORE RISE: *Lights come up on* CAITLIN *and* GRANDPA.

CAITLIN (*Stunned*): Wow. You guys must have wanted to go home really badly if you were willing to spend all your own money. (*Considering*) So you're saying if I don't ask Mom and Dad for any money for the trip, they might let me go.

GRANDPA (*Shaking his head*): No, I'm not saying that at all. I don't think the money is the reason for their reservations.

CAITLIN (*Sharply*): Then I'm not sure I understand your point.

GRANDPA: Money wasn't really at the root of my parents' reservations, either. Sometimes you need to think of things that are bigger than you are. Sometimes there are things that are more important than getting your own way.

CAITLIN (*Confused*): But you ended up getting your own way, right? You just had to pay for it yourself.

GRANDPA: No. Not exactly. We didn't end up going home that year.

CAITLIN: What happened?

GRANDPA: Well, we met at Joe's that night, as we'd planned. (*Chuckles*) Actually, your grandmother was there, too, I remember. She had on a beautiful red sweater. (*Grins*) But that's another story. (*Lights dim on them, as curtain opens.*)

* * *

SETTING: *Joe's Sweet Shoppe. Counter wraps along back and side wall. Some papers are on one end of counter. Four small tables with chairs are up and down stage. War Bond poster, hammer, and tacks are behind counter, as are coffee cups, coffee pot, and sandwiches on plates.*

AT RISE: ANDY, *wearing a white apron, is behind counter.* SUSIE, *wearing a red sweater, and* PAT *are seated at a table finishing sodas.*

ANDY (*Calling to them as he wipes counter*): You girls want another soda?

PAT: Nope. (*Preening*) We have to think of our figures.

SUSIE (*Earnestly*): Andy, I think it's wonderful that you're planning to go home even though your folks didn't send you money for tickets. (ANDY *smiles.*)

PAT: So do I. If I don't hear from my folks I'll do the same thing. I've been saving up to buy a War Bond, but I'll use that money for a train ticket if I have to! (WALT, PHIL, *and* BOB *enter right and ad lib greetings.*)

BOB: Where's Joe? Is he around? (*They pull up chairs and sit at table with girls.*)

ANDY: No. But he ought to be back soon.

BOB: I'm anxious to see if he can give us all some extra work this week.

SUSIE: You know Joe; if you need any kind of help, he's your man. (JOE *enters.*)

JOE (*Looking around*): Well, well, I've got the whole school here.

OTHERS (*Ad lib greeting*): Hello, Joe. Hi, Joe. (*Etc.*)

JOE: Is Andy fixing you boys up with some sodas?

WALT: Not exactly. We're—well, we're a little short of money.

JOE: You know your credit's always good here.

BOB: Not this time, Joe. We're really saving up.

PHIL: In fact, we came to ask you if you might be able to give us some extra hours this week.

JOE: All of you? (*Boys nod.*) Well, I don't see why not. As it turns out, I'm going to be extra busy this week.

ANDY: You are?

JOE: Sure. Don't tell me you haven't heard about the big War Bond drive the city is having?

WALT: That's right. I did hear something.

JOE: I'm kind of in charge of it—got to be in and out of the store a lot.

BOB: Great! We'll be here every minute we can.

JOE: You fellows can start right away. (JOE *goes behind counter, fumbles underneath for a minute, then brings out tacks, a hammer and a big War Bond poster.*) Here, put this up where everyone can see it. (BOB *takes tacks and hammer.* PHIL *takes poster. They look around, then go to rear wall. They tack up poster during next few lines.*) Why the sudden need for money? You boys saving up to buy some of these bonds yourself?

WALT: No, Joe. It's for spring vacation.

PHIL (*As he works with poster*): Our folks didn't send us money for tickets.

BOB: So we've decided to use our own money and go home anyway.

JOE (*Surprised*): I kind of figured you'd all be sticking around here for vacation.

SUSIE: Around here?

ANDY: But, Joe, you know we always go home.

JOE: Sure, but this year, with the trains so crowded, I just figured—

WALT (*Lightly*): We don't mind that. We can squeeze our way on somehow.

JOE: I wasn't thinking of you, exactly. (*Breaking off as he sees they've finished with poster.*) Say—that looks fine! Everyone who comes in will be sure to see it. (PHIL *puts hammer on counter.*) I've got some orders to go over. Can you all hold down the fort if I do some work over here? (*Picks papers up from counter and goes to table upstage, puts papers down*)

BOYS (*Ad lib*): Sure. You can count on us. (*Etc.* JOE *begins working, as* THREE SOLDIERS *enter right, looking tired and discouraged. They wear various insignia.*)

SUSIE (*Nudging PAT*): Pat, look! Soldiers!

PAT (*Impressed*): Look at the decorations on that one.

1ST SOLDIER (*As they walk to counter*): Got any coffee in here, bud?

ANDY: Sure, coming right up!

2ND SOLDIER: How about a sandwich?

3RD SOLDIER (*Wearily*): Any kind. We're not particular.

BOB: I'll give you a hand with the sandwiches, Andy. (*Joins ANDY behind counter; to SOLDIERS*) We'll have something for you to eat in no time at all. (*Periodically JOE looks up and watches conversation.*)

2ND SOLDIER: Good. (*Turning to other SOLDIERS*) Might as well sit, I guess. (*SOLDIERS go to a table and sit.*)

3RD SOLDIER: Sit and wait.

1ST SOLDIER: I can't believe we have to wait till tomorrow to catch a train out of here. (*BOB carries coffees over to SOLDIERS.*)

2ND SOLDIER (*Hitting table with fist in frustration*): What a lousy break! Stuck here in this dump!

BOB (*Putting down coffee cups; defensively*): Excuse me, sir, but this town isn't so bad.

2ND SOLDIER (*Smiling for first time*): Sorry, it's just a figure of speech. I'm sure this is a grand little place, but there's only one town I want to see at the moment and that's my hometown.

ANDY (*From behind counter, still working on sandwiches*): Are you on your way home now? Are you on furlough?

2ND SOLDIER: Yes, my first in a year and maybe my last for some time to come. That goes for my pals, too. Jim here has been across. (*Indicates 3RD SOLDIER*)

WALT (*Turning in his chair and studying SOLDIERS; impressed*): I thought you had, sir, with all those decorations pinned on you.

PHIL: Boy, look at 'em all!

2ND SOLDIER: And we haven't got long either before we have to get back.

3RD SOLDIER: When I think of all the time we're wasting, when we could be getting nearer and nearer home—(*Shakes his head, frustrated;* ANDY *brings three plates of sandwiches, sets them down.*)

ANDY: Did you fellows miss the train or something?

1ST SOLDIER: We didn't miss it, we just couldn't get on it. (*Takes bite of sandwich*)

2ND SOLDIER: We're not the only ones stranded, either.

3RD SOLDIER: No room on that train at all.

WALT: Couldn't you have squeezed on somehow?

3RD SOLDIER (*Smiling*): A mosquito couldn't have squeezed on. People were hanging out the windows.

BOB: I guess there are a lot of soldiers riding them these days.

2ND SOLDIER: Soldiers and civilians, too. Lots of 'em. (*Shakes his head*) Wouldn't you think civilians could stay put unless they just *had* to travel?

3RD SOLDIER (*Shrugging*): You'd think so. (BOB *and* ANDY *exchange glances.*)

1ST SOLDIER: They must not realize or they wouldn't do it. No American would—I'm sure of that. (SOLDIERS *eat sandwiches, as* BOB *and* ANDY *go to their friends' table.*)

ANDY: Are you thinking what I'm thinking?

BOB: I sure am. (*Disappointed*) Gee whiz! (BOYS *all hang their heads.* 1ST SOLDIER *nudges* 2ND, *points to boys.*)

2ND SOLDIER (*Curiously*): Say, what's the matter with you kids all of a sudden?

ANDY: Nothing. It's just—we were planning on going home for spring vacation, even though our folks didn't send us any money for train tickets.

BOB: We were going to earn the money to buy our own tickets, but after what you've just told us, there's no way we can go.

WALT: Of course not. We might be keeping some soldiers like you from getting their furloughs.

PHIL: Sure, and I'll bet that's what our folks meant all along. We just didn't understand.

ANDY (*Wholeheartedly*): We're going to stay right here for spring vacation.

SUSIE: Hooray for you! (*Beams at* ANDY, *who looks down, embarrassed.*)

PAT: I'm not going to take up any space on the trains, either.

2ND SOLDIER (*Smiling broadly*): That's very patriotic of you all.

SUSIE (*Enthusiastically*): I think we ought to get everyone in the school in on this! Let's start a campaign—our slogan can be "Civilians stay put!" (SOLDIERS *chuckle.* JOE *watches, pleased.*)

BOB: Yeah! And with all of us staying put, it won't be dead around here! We can plan things.

ANDY (*Eagerly*): We can help Joe with his War Bond drive.

SUSIE (*Clapping*): And let's plan a dance—a great big one. We'll call it a victory ball.

WALT (*Scowling*): A dance? You girls always want to have a dance or something.

3RD SOLDIER (*Grinning*): Don't let him kid you. Boys like to dance as well as girls. (WALT *looks embarrassed.*) I used to talk like that myself.

ANDY: And with the extra money we earn this week, maybe we can buy a War Bond ourselves.

BOB (*Suddenly serious*): But that's not going to help you fellows get home any faster.

ANDY (*Sadly*): Yeah. Gee, I wish there were some way—

JOE (*Rising*): Wait! There is a way! (*All turn to him, surprised.*) Sorry. I couldn't help eavesdropping. There's a train that leaves Pleasant City tonight. I'll drive you over there.

1ST SOLDIER (*Surprised*): But Pleasant City's forty miles away. What about gas coupons?

JOE: That's all right. I only use my car for emergencies—and this is sure as guns an emergency, getting you boys home as quickly as possible.

3RD SOLDIER (*Stunned*): But you don't even know us!

JOE: I guess I know you all right. You fellows are fighting for us all, aren't you?

1ST SOLDIER (*Grinning*): I don't know what to say.

ANDY (*Eagerly*): Say you'll do it!

JOE (*Laughing*): See? These kids won't be happy unless you soldiers get to that train. Ready to go?

1ST SOLDIER (*Jumping up*): Yes, sir! (*Other* SOLDIERS *rise, too.*)

2ND SOLDIER: Well, so long, kids. (*Salutes them*) You're the greatest.

BOYS and GIRLS (*Ad lib*): Goodbye! So long! Good luck. (*Etc.*)

1ST SOLDIER: If we had to be stranded, I don't know where I'd rather have been than here.

3RD SOLDIER: You kids have restored my confidence tonight. Young America's all right. And when I leave again—well, I'll feel mighty good leaving my country in hands like yours. (*He salutes and goes out with the others. The young people are all quiet for a minute, looking after them.*)

BOB: Did you hear what he said?

OTHERS (*Ad lib; in awe*): Yeah ... Wasn't that something? ... (*Etc.*)

ANDY (*Letting out a deep breath*): Boy, we've got to try to live up to that! (*Curtain. Lights come up slowly on* CAITLIN *and* GRANDPA.)

* * *

CAITLIN (*After a moment; thoughtfully*): Things really were different for you. (*Confused*) But why were the trains so crowded?

GRANDPA (*Shrugging*): It was really the only way to travel. You wouldn't take a car trip, because it was so tough to get gasoline. And there wasn't much air travel in those days.

CAITLIN (*Curiously*): Did you have that dance, Grandpa? That victory ball?

GRANDPA (*Smiling*): Yes, we did. (*Wistfully*) I remember I danced nearly every dance with your Grandma that night. And we had a "Civilians Stay Put" rally. And we sold lots of War Bonds. (*Chuckles*) I suppose we worked harder that week than we would have if we'd been in school!

CAITLIN: But you had fun, didn't you?

GRANDPA: We had a grand time, because we were so proud of what we were doing. We believed in our cause.

CAITLIN (*Hesitating*): If I can't go away on break, maybe I can find something to do around here that I could feel really proud of.

GRANDPA (*Nodding*): Good idea. Maybe helping your mother with the hospital work?

CAITLIN (*Nodding; considering*): Yeah. Maybe. (*Slyly*) How do you think Mom and Dad would feel about my doing hospital work in Florida? (GRANDPA *hits her over the head with the newspaper playfully.* CAITLIN *squeals and runs offstage.* GRANDPA *picks up paper and chases her off.*)

THE END

Production Notes

CIVILIANS STAY PUT: A STORY FROM WORLD WAR II

Characters: 9 male; 3 female.

Playing Time: 25 minutes.

Costumes: Grandpa and Caitlin wear modern, everday clothes. Other characters wear 1940s-era clothes. Susie wears red sweater. In Scene 2, Andy wears white apron. Soldiers wear uniforms adorned with various medals.

Properties: Newspaper, baseball, papers, War Bond poster, hammer, and tacks, three coffee cups, coffee pot, three sandwiches on plates.

Setting: Easy chair and ottoman are down left in front of curtain. Scene 1: dorm room. Simple bed is right. Desk, with notebooks and pencils on it, and chair are left. Second chair is center. Period posters are on backdrop. Scene 2: Joe's Sweet Shoppe. Counter wraps along back and side wall. Four small tables with chairs are up and down stage.

Lighting: Lights dim and come up on Before Rise action, as indicated in text.

Sound: Slamming door.

I Have a Dream

by *Aileen Fisher*

Martin Luther King's struggle for racial equality . . .

Characters

JEFF
SUSAN
GRANDFATHER
SAMUEL
OTHER AUDIENCE MEMBERS
M.C.
BUS DRIVER
MRS. ROSA PARKS
BUS PASSENGERS
POLICE OFFICER
MARTIN LUTHER KING
BLACK MEN AND WOMEN
DALTON
COREY
CHORUS, *6 or more male and female*
STAGEHANDS
MARCHERS
LOUDSPEAKER VOICE

BEFORE RISE: *Music of "We Shall Overcome" is played in background as several audience members enter from back of auditorium and go to front rows to take seats. JEFF and SUSAN enter, carrying on conversation.*

JEFF: Until we studied about Martin Luther King in school, I never realized what a difference he made to this country.

SUSAN (*Nodding*): He was a great man. I'm glad the school is honoring his birthday with this program. (*Looks around for seats*) Jeff, here are two good seats together. (*They sit. GRANDFATHER and SAMUEL enter at back of auditorium, start walking toward front.*)

SAMUEL: Where do you want to sit, Grandpa?

GRANDFATHER: Thanks to Martin Luther King, Samuel, we can sit any place we please. We black folks couldn't always do that.

SAMUEL: I know. We were considered second-class citizens, weren't we? When I hear you and Grandma talk about it, I wonder why it was like that.

GRANDFATHER: That's what Martin Luther King was always wondering—and asking. And he did something about it— something that changed the whole country. He reminded everyone that people in the United States should all have the same chance. That's what the Constitution says—"with liberty and justice for all."

SAMUEL (*Pointing to two seats*): Let's sit right here, Grandpa. (*Lights dim.*) The program's about to begin.

* * *

SETTING: *Stage is bare. M.C.'s stand is at one side of stage. At the other side are two rows of chairs, angled so that they face the audience. A large sign reading* RESERVED FOR WHITES *is placed near the chairs in front. Chairs at the back have sign reading* COLORED SECTION. *A single chair for Bus Driver is placed in front of the two rows.On the backdrop is a large picture of Martin Luther King. If available, slides of Martin Luther King and activities in which he was engaged may be flashed on the backdrop from a projector throughout the play.*

AT RISE: *Spotlight goes up on M.C.'s stand. M.C. enters and addresses audience.*

M.C.: We are gathered here today to celebrate the birthday of a great American—Martin Luther King—who made a lasting impression on our history in his short life of 39 years. Actually, his career as a leader in the freedom movement didn't begin until he was 26 years old. Before that his life ran smoothly enough. He went to college, received a doctorate in theology, married, and became pastor of a Baptist church in Montgomery, Alabama. But on a December night in 1955, something happened that changed the direction of his life. Picture a crowded bus in the city of Montgomery, carrying passengers home after a busy day (BUS DRIVER *enters, sits in single chair. BUS PASSENGERS enter and sit in chairs— white passengers in front section, blacks in back section. Spotlight goes up on chairs. BUS DRIVER pantomimes driving for a few moments, then stops. More PASSENGERS enter, pay fare to DRIVER, and take seats. MRS. ROSA PARKS, a black woman carrying heavy bags, enters, pays fare to DRIVER, then looks wearily at the chairs—mostly filled except for one in front section. She sits there.)*

PASSENGER (*Angrily; to* ROSA): You'll have to move to the back of the bus, lady. (ROSA *doesn't move.*) Can't you read? (*Points to* RESERVED FOR WHITES *sign*) These seats are for whites only. (DRIVER *looks around, gets up, and goes over to* ROSA.)

DRIVER: Lady, these seats are reserved. Go to the back of the bus where you belong. (ROSA *doesn't move or speak.*)

OTHER WHITE PASSENGERS (*Ad lib*): She won't move! Doesn't she know she can't sit in the front of the bus? (*Etc.*)

DRIVER (*Angrily*): All right, lady. You asked for it. (*Steps to center stage, calls off*) Officer! Officer, would you come here, please? (OFFICER *enters.*)

OFFICER: What seems to be the problem?

DRIVER (*Pointing to* ROSA): This lady is the problem. She won't move to the back of the bus.

OFFICER (*To* ROSA): You won't move, eh? (*Grabs her arm, pulls her out of chair*) Then you're under arrest. (*He drags*

ROSA *off. Light goes out on chairs.* DRIVER *and* PASSEN-
GERS *exit;* STAGEHANDS *remove chairs and signs. Spotlight
goes up on* M.C.)

M.C.: For years black people in Alabama and other southern
states had been treated as if they had no rights. If they com-
plained, they were put in jail. White people made the rules,
and black people were expected to follow them. But the arrest
of Mrs. Parks aroused the black community in Montgomery
to join together and do something. They turned to their pastor,
Martin Luther King, for help. (MARTIN LUTHER KING,
COREY, DALTON, *and several* BLACK MEN *and* WOMEN
enter, stand center stage.)

1ST MAN: Reverend King, we have to fight against this injustice.

1ST WOMAN: What happened to Rosa Parks is a disgrace.
We've all suffered enough from white people's laws.

COREY: Let's take action—now! Not next week or next year!

OTHERS (*Ad lib; angrily*): Yes, that's right! Let's fight! (*Etc.*)

KING (*Holding up hand for silence*): I agree the time has come
to act. But we must do it peacefully, not with meanness and
violence. Excited talk blocks common sense, and the only way
for us to fight unjust laws is to unite against them. We have
to fight injustice with words and nonviolent action instead of
clubs or guns.

DALTON: Reverend King, I have an idea. What if we all boycott
the buses—walk to our jobs and have our children walk to
school, instead of riding in the back of the bus.

2ND WOMAN: But my job is five miles away! I can't walk that
far twice a day!

KING: Dalton has a good idea. (*To* 2ND WOMAN) You could
find a ride with someone who has a car. Anything but ride
the bus. If we all unite to boycott the buses, then maybe the
white men who make the laws will change those laws!

OTHERS (*Ad lib*): Maybe a boycott could work! Yes, let's try
it. (*Etc.*)

KING: But always remember the boycott must be orderly, and

peaceful. No threats, no fighting, no violence. We're not doing this out of hatred of the white men, but to make them see that our cause is just.

COREY: That's right, Reverend King. We're tired of being mistreated, tired of being kicked about. It's time to act, but in a peaceful way! When will the boycott start?

KING: Tomorrow morning! Let's spread the news to our brothers and sisters, and remember to impress upon them the importance of nonviolence. "He who lives by the sword shall perish by the sword." (KING *and others exit. Spotlight goes up on* M.C.)

M.C.: The very next day, December 5, 1955, the boycott began. Bus after bus clattered down the street with no black passengers. Bus after bus, day after day, for months—until finally, the law was changed and blacks could sit anywhere on a bus, not only in Montgomery, Alabama, but in other cities and states as well. (MARTIN LUTHER KING *enters and crosses to center stage. Spotlight comes up on him.*)

KING: At last the words of our Declaration of Independence are beginning to have some meaning! "We hold these truths to be self-evident—that all men are created equal; that they are endowed by their Creator with certain inalienable rights; that among these are life, liberty, and the pursuit of happiness."

M.C.: Other words, bold words, mighty words, were written into the preamble to the Constitution of the United States.

KING: "We the people of the United States, in order to form a more perfect Union, establish justice, insure domestic tranquillity, provide for the common defense, promote the general welfare, and secure the blessings of liberty to ourselves and our posterity. . . ." (KING *exits. Spot up on* M.C.)

M.C.: Martin Luther King's work for liberty had just begun. In many states, white children and black children were not permitted to go to the same school; black children could not play in public parks. Many restaurants had signs in their windows: COLORED NOT WELCOME. One by one, Martin Luther King tackled the issues, driven on by his dreams of justice, and more and more black people looked to him for leadership. Meanwhile, Reverend King was put in jail again and again for his uncompromising stand on equality. His house was bombed. Still, his faith never wavered. (CHORUS *crosses backstage, singing first stanza of "We Shall Overcome.")*

CHORUS: We shall overcome

We shall overcome

We shall overcome some day.

Oh, deep in my heart

I do believe

We shall overcome some day.

M.C.: Then came August, 1963, one hundred years after Abraham Lincoln issued his Emancipation Proclamation freeing the slaves. With the blessing of Martin Luther King, more than 200,000 people, black and white, took part in a "march for jobs and freedom" and gathered at the Lincoln Memorial in Washington, D.C., where Dr. King gave his famous "I Have a Dream" speech. It was carried in newspapers all over the country. (KING *enters, crosses center. Spotlight goes up on him.)*

KING: I have a dream that my four little children will one day live in a nation where they will not be judged by the color of their skin but by the content of their character.

I have a dream today.

I have a dream that one day the state of Alabama will be transformed into a situation where little black boys and black girls will be able to join hands with little white boys and white girls and walk together as sisters and brothers.

I have a dream today. . . .

And if America is to be a great nation this must become true. So let freedom ring from the prodigious hilltops of New Hampshire! . . .

Let freedom ring from every hill and mole hill of Mississippi. From every mountainside, let freedom ring.

When we let freedom ring, when we let it ring from every village and every hamlet, from every state and every city, we will be able to speed up that day when all of God's children, black men and white men, Jews and Gentiles, Protestants and Catholics, will be able to join hands and sing that old Negro spiritual, "Free at last! Free at last! Thank God almighty, we are free at last!" (*Exits*)

M.C.: Martin Luther King's success in promoting nonviolence as a solution to racial problems was recognized by the world in 1964, when he received the Nobel Peace Prize. He was only 35 years old, the youngest person ever to receive the prize. All over the world people watched on television as he accepted the award of $54,000. He donated it all to the civil rights movement. (KING *enters; spotlight goes up on him.*)

KING: On behalf of all men who love peace and brotherhood, I accept this award . . . with an abiding faith in America and an audacious faith in the future of mankind . . . and a profound recognition that nonviolence is the answer to the crucial political and moral question of our time. Though 22 million of our black brothers and sisters in the United States are still fighting for full freedom and justice in nonviolent ways, I have faith that eventually they will achieve their goal, and that the long night of racial injustice will be over. I still believe that we shall overcome. (*Exits;* CHORUS *sings offstage*)

CHORUS: We'll walk hand in hand
We'll walk hand in hand
We'll walk hand in hand some day.
Oh, deep in my heart
I do believe
We'll walk hand in hand some day.

M.C.: The climax of Martin Luther King's career came in the spring of 1965, with the 54-mile march from Selma, Alabama, to Montgomery, the state's capital. It was a march to dramatize the "right to vote" problem. Although the 15th Amendment, ratified almost 100 years before the Selma march, gave blacks in this country the right to vote, blacks in some states still couldn't vote, because they were not allowed to register.

This was an injustice that Martin Luther King was determined to fight. He faced bitter opposition in Alabama.

Hundreds of marchers, of every faith and race, started on the walk from Selma under a sweltering spring sun. But they had gone only a few blocks when they were met at a bridge by a living blockade of state troopers wearing helmets and swinging billy clubs. They carried canisters of tear gas. The marchers knelt down before the troopers, who pressed ahead swinging their clubs with abandon and spraying the air with gas. Dr. King saw that there was nothing to do but to retreat.

Two weeks later he tried again, this time leading 8,000 black and white supporters on the long march to the state capital. Meanwhile, a federal court order was issued to protect the marchers, and National Guard troops were on hand in case of trouble. Five days later the long march ended at the capitol building in Montgomery, where 25,000 people had gathered to welcome Reverend King and his fellow marchers. (MARTIN LUTHER KING *and* MARCHERS *enter, gather at center.*)

KING: We are on the move! And we are not about to go back. We will go on, with faith in nonviolent action, for our cause is humane and just. It will not take long, because the arm of the universe bends toward justice. . . .

MARCHERS (*Ad lib*): We will go on! (*Etc.*)

M.C.: As a champion of peace, Martin Luther King opposed the war in Vietnam. He spoke out against it with anxiety and sorrow.

KING: We must work for peace by peaceful means. War is madness, and this madness must cease. Those who love peace must organize as effectively as those who love war. (*Exits with* MARCHERS)

M.C.: For his outspoken views on this and many other national problems, Martin Luther King was continually in danger for his life. His family, too, suffered from threats, and several times the King home was bombed. In April, 1968, he went to Memphis to address striking sanitation workers. As usual his message was for peace, justice, and equality. No one was prepared for the violence that erupted. While Dr. King was speaking to a friend from the balcony of his motel, a shot rang out. Dr. King slumped to the floor. . . .

LOUDSPEAKER: Special news bulletin from Memphis, Tennessee! Martin Luther King has just been assassinated! Who the assassin is, no one knows at this point. We will supply more details as they come in. . . .

M.C.: Martin Luther King died just an hour after the shooting, a martyr to the cause of equality and peace. He was not yet forty years old. (*Music of "We Shall Overcome" is heard softly offstage.*) Yes, Martin Luther King had a dream, a dream for the future that will bring hope to the oppressed wherever they are, a dream to overcome injustice with fairness and equality. For as Reverend King said, the arm of the universe bends toward justice. (*Music of "We Shall Overcome" swells as curtain falls.*)

THE END

Production Notes

I HAVE A DREAM

Characters: 7 male; 2 female; 1 male or female for M.C.; male and female extras for all other characters.

Playing Time: 20 minutes.

Costumes: Jeff, Susan, Grandfather, Samuel, Other Audience Members and M.C. wear modern, everyday dress. All other characters wear clothes appropriate for the 1950s and early 1960s.

Properties: Shopping bags for Rosa Parks.

Setting: Stage is bare. M.C.'s stand is at one side of stage. At other side are two rows of chairs, angled so that they face the audience. Large sign reading RESERVED FOR WHITES is near chairs in front. Chairs at the back have sign reading COLORED SECTION. Single chair for Bus Driver is in front of the two rows. On the backdrop is a large picture of Martin Luther King. If available, slides of Martin Luther King and activities in which he was engaged may be flashed on backdrop from a projector throughout the play.

Lighting: Spotlights, as indicated.

Music: "We Shall Overcome."

An American Story

by Arlene J. Morris

Pageant highlights great moments in America's history . . .

Characters

UNCLE SAM
CHORUS
TOWN CRIER
FOUR COLONISTS
THOMAS JEFFERSON
BEN FRANKLIN
JOHN ADAMS
GEORGE WASHINGTON
REPORTER
TWENTY NARRATORS
DANCERS
WILLIAM LLOYD GARRISON
FREDERICK DOUGLASS
SLAVE
ABRAHAM LINCOLN
STROLLING COUPLE
BARBERSHOP QUARTET
ELIZABETH CADY STANTON
APPLE SELLER
TWO MEN
STUDENTS
MARTIN LUTHER KING

BEFORE RISE: UNCLE SAM *enters in front of curtain.*
CHORUS *may be seated in front of cutain to one side of stage.*
UNCLE SAM (*To audience*): Well, well, well, so I'm over two
hundred years old! It seems like only yesterday that I was
born. (*Points to child in audience*) You're whispering, young
man. (*Pauses as if listening*) Oh, I see. You think I'm an old
man. Why, son, I've only just begun to live. My future is
crammed full of promises. And why not? Think of all those
noble pledges I've made and kept these past two hundred
years! Once a mere child of mother country England, I grew
so that now I am a power in my own right. I am . . . perhaps
not all that I wish to be yet; mighty powerful today, ah, but
tomorrow, the perfect union for all the people of this giant
land. (*Points to another child in audience*) What's that? What
have I done to deserve the right to exist this long? Son, the
tales I could tell you if I had the time! This United States, its
heroes and heroines, its glorious deeds, its fearless pioneers
. . . Oh, yes, I remember it all so well. (UNCLE SAM *exits.*
Curtain opens.)

* * *

SETTING: *At four angles of stage are four flats, each depicting*
two figures in costumes representative of successive American
fashions from 1775 to present. Backdrop is projection screen
for slides (optional).
AT RISE: TOWN CRIER *enters, carrying placard reading,* 1775.
He moves across stage, ringing bell as he walks. As CRIER
exits, FOUR COLONISTS *enter, crossing to center. They ges-*
ture angrily.
1ST COLONIST: The English have no right to tax us!
2ND COLONIST: England is our mother country. The King
knows what's best for us.
3RD COLONIST: No man, not even the great King George, has
the right to tax without representation.
4TH COLONIST: I say that we should oppose his decree. The

tea shall be sipped only by the fish in the sea. (COLONISTS *exit, still gesturing angrily.* TOWN CRIER *reenters carrying placard reading,* 1776. *He rings bell as he crosses stage. As* CRIER *exits,* THOMAS JEFFERSON, BENJAMIN FRANKLIN, *and* JOHN ADAMS *enter.* JEFFERSON *holds unrolled parchment. Other men read over his shoulder.*)

FRANKLIN: Mr. Jefferson, are you prepared to read us your statement, this declaration we are going to send to King George?

JEFFERSON: I most certainly am.

ADAMS: Mr. Franklin, what shall we call this piece of writing Mr. Jefferson has composed?

FRANKLIN: There is no better name, Mr. Adams, than the one which best states our aim. We shall call this noble scroll the Declaration of Independence.

ALL (*Ad lib*): Excellent. Fine. Yes, that's perfect. (*Etc.* JEFFERSON *exits, holding paper before him, as if reading, and others follow him off.*)

VOICE (*Offstage*): "We hold these truths to be self-evident, that all men are created equal, that they are endowed by their Creator with certain unalienable Rights, that among these are Life, Liberty and the pursuit of Happiness." (TOWN CRIER *enters, ringing bell, carrying placard reading,* VALLEY FORGE. *As* TOWN CRIER *exits,* GEORGE WASHINGTON *enters, holding and reading large roll of parchment. He appears worried, and paces.* REPORTER *enters, carrying quill pen and piece of parchment.*)

REPORTER: General Washington, sir, about this war. What are our chances? Can we defeat the British?

WASHINGTON: Sir, we have no choice. Lest there be those who do not feel the desire to govern themselves; lest there be those who wish to remain fledglings till eternity, then we must do battle. Freedom, sir, is our right. We will be free men in a free land or we will die.

REPORTER: Good luck, sir. (*He shakes hands with* WASHINGTON *and exits.* WASHINGTON *resumes his pacing. Curtain closes. If* CHORUS *is not seated onstage, they enter at this point and exit after song. They enter and exit in similar fashion for remainder of play.*)

CHORUS (*Singing "Johnny Has Gone for a Soldier"*):
  Here I sit on Buttermilk Hill,
  Who could blame me, cry my fill?
  And every tear would turn a mill,
  Johnny has gone for a soldier.
  (*When song is completed,* 1ST NARRATOR *enters before curtain.*)

1ST NARRATOR: The war was fought.
  The American Revolution.
  A sad and grueling war.
  A dream, a victory, freedom.
  The chains of a colonial past were broken.
  We were a nation on our own.
  The Constitution was born.
  Strength, goals, ideals,
  They abounded in this new land.
  America had grown
  From a helpless infant to an adult.

1ST NARRATOR *exits. Curtain opens. If desired,* DANCERS *may enter and perform minuet to appropriate music of Revolutionary period. At conclusion of dance,* DANCERS *exit.* 2ND NARRATOR *enters.*)

2ND NARRATOR: It was 1812. The United States was reaching out to define itself as a nation. It was the time of the Industrial Revolution, bringing many new inventions. Robert Fulton had built his steamboat. Eli Whitney's cotton gin was being used with increasing popularity. We were planning how to use our natural resources. The Erie Canal opened. Cargo shipping would be easier and faster now. The United States was becoming recognized as an independent country. It was time to explore our frontier lands. Pioneers were moving into the Northwest Territory. They were settling the land. Brave people, Lewis and Clark, Daniel Boone, and Sacajawea, and others dared to search for trails that few had traveled. (*Stage lights go out.* 2ND NARRATOR *exits. Slides of steamboat, Robert Fulton, Daniel Boone, and/or Lewis and Clark, are flashed on backdrop. Stage lights come on. Curtain closes.*)

CHORUS (*Singing "Erie Canal"*):

I've got a mule, her name is Sal,

Fifteen years on the Erie Canal. . . .

(*At conclusion of song,* 3RD NARRATOR *enters in front of curtain.*)

3RD NARRATOR: Our country was growing

In knowledge and size.

But a burning question

Pierced the heart

Of this country.

Slavery . . .

Passions, fears, hatred, distrust . . .

It was the issue

That almost destroyed

The nation founded on

Equality for all.

(*Curtain opens, revealing* WILLIAM LLOYD GARRISON, FREDERICK DOUGLASS, *and* SLAVE, *with backs to audience.*)

GARRISON (*Turning toward audience, holding out placard reading,* abolish slavery): I am William Lloyd Garrison. I am an abolitionist.

DOUGLASS (*Turning to audience; holding placard reading,* DOWN WITH SLAVERY): I am Frederick Douglass, a former slave who escaped from a plantation to Massachusetts. I work as an abolitionist because I believe slavery is inhuman. (SLAVE, *with head bent, plods across stage, while* 3RD NARRATOR *recites following dialogue.*)

3RD NARRATOR: My pen cannot

remain idle, nor my voice be suppressed,

My heart cannot cease to bleed

While two million of my fellow beings

Wear the chains of slavery.
(3RD NARRATOR *exits. Stage lights go out.* 4TH NARRATOR *enters and speaks as slides of gold miners and pioneers in wagons are flashed on backdrop.*)
4TH NARRATOR: The United States expanded.
Our territories were stretching from coast to coast.
"Remember the Alamo," they cried in Texas.
"We must be free of Mexico."
"Gold," they cried in California.
The Oregon Trail, the Santa Fe Trail, "Pike's Peak or Bust."
This was our Manifest Destiny,
To control from Atlantic to Pacific.
(4TH NARRATOR *exits.* 5TH NARRATOR *enters.*)
5TH NARRATOR: But still the
     bitterness hung over.
We were a nation united,
But divided.
The North proposed freedom
For all men.
The South cried,
"We will secede from the Union."
Could this country survive?
A divided nation
Was like a man
Without a soul.
(5TH NARRATOR *exits. Stage lights come up.* DANCERS *enter and perform dance to* "My Old Kentucky Home" *or other music. At conclusion,* DANCERS *exit.* 6TH NARRATOR *enters.*)
6TH NARRATOR: But the Court ruled a slave
Was a slave. He was at his master's mercy.
The abolitionists denounced that claim,
But only a few listened.
Then the South took its stand.
There would be no more union.
Abe Lincoln, the President then,

Refused to accept that decision.
A war was fought—
The Civil War.
Brother against brother,
A life for a life.
It was a shameful blot
On a past filled with so much glory.
(LINCOLN *enters.*)
LINCOLN: "Fourscore and seven years ago our fathers brought
forth on this continent a new nation conceived in liberty and
dedicated to the proposition that all men are created equal."
(LINCOLN *freezes in position and curtain closes.* 6TH NAR-
RATOR *exits.*)
CHORUS (*Singing "Battle Hymn of the Republic"*):
"Mine eyes have seen the glory of the coming of the Lord. . . . "
(7TH NARRATOR *enters.*)
7TH NARRATOR: By 1865 the Civil War was over.
The South remained a part of the Union.
The slaves were now free.
And . . . Abraham Lincoln was dead,
Killed by an assassin's bullet.
(*Curtain opens. Stage lights go off. Slide of Abraham Lincoln
flashes on screen for several moments, then is removed.* 7TH
NARRATOR *exits. "Home on the Range" is heard off.* 8TH
NARRATOR *enters. Stage lights go up.*)
8TH NARRATOR: It was 1865. The
United States was growing up.
It was a time for movement.
But sometimes dreams are
Not for everyone.
The Indian people
Bore the pain
Of America's westward calling.
They were moved to reservation towns.
Cowboys, miners, farmers
Yearned for the open spaces

And the gold.
But how,
How could the United States
Connect its eastern settlers
With its western pioneers?
The Union Pacific, the railroads
Solved this country's problems.
And so the West was settled.
CHORUS (*Singing "I've Been Working on the Railroad"*):
"I've been working on the railroad
All the live-long day. . . . "
(*Stage lights go off at conclusion of song, and* 8TH NARRA-
TOR *exits.* 9TH NARRATOR *enters in spotlight downstage.*)
9TH NARRATOR: What is America?
Literature, art, music?
Mark Twain, Stephen Foster?
A pioneer spirit, a determination, an inventive mind?
Thomas Edison, Alexander Graham Bell,
The Wright Brothers, Henry Ford.
These were just a few. It was a new type of living in America.
It was industry's turn now.
(*Slides of Model T and first airplane flash on screen.* 9TH
NARRATOR *exits. Stage lights come up.* 10TH NARRATOR
enters.)
10TH NARRATOR: America was
over a hundred years old.
She was no longer an agricultural land.
Factories were booming.
Big money names screamed through the land.
Pittsburgh's Andrew Carnegie and his steel mills;
Henry Clay Frick and his coke ovens;
John D. Rockefeller, the oil tycoon.
Ida M. Tarbell, the journalist, writing, trying to keep a big
    business honest—
This was America at the turn of the century.
Oh, yes, those were the times.

Factories meant pollution, strikes, slums, child labor.
But they meant jobs and money for all,
Especially those people coming to America from Europe,
The immigrants.
(10TH NARRATOR *exits.* DANCERS *enter and perform appropriate folk dance, then exit.* 11TH NARRATOR *enters.*)
11TH NARRATOR: It was an exciting time for America.
The immigrants came to their new home,
Tired and poor.
But they believed in a dream, freedom from
Terror and want.
An American ethnic parade, the old and the new.
A melting pot, they called it.
There were hard times, and sad times, and moments of regret.
But they tried to succeed; they wouldn't give up.
Life here was busy.
There were moments of fun,
Strolls through the park.
Ice cream parlor dates.
And the singing songs of those barbershop quartets.
(STROLLING COUPLE *enters, arm in arm, and crosses to side of stage, where they freeze in position.* BARBERSHOP QUARTET *enters, stands center. They sing "Down By the Old Mill Stream," or other typical selection. At end of song, curtain closes.* 11TH NARRATOR *exits.* 12TH NARRATOR *enters.*)
12TH NARRATOR: It was 1917 . . .
Europe was fighting a war, to save democracy.
We in the United States wouldn't sit back
And watch our friends die.
"Never," said Woodrow Wilson.
And so it was.
Our boys went over.
Their strength and spirit helped win World War I.
But our nation had learned a lesson.
Let us make a commitment
For World Peace.

And the League of Nations was begun
To prevent any more bloodshed.
(12TH NARRATOR *exits*. CHORUS *sings "Over There."* 13TH
NARRATOR *enters*.)
13TH NARRATOR: Americans were becoming world famous.
Lindbergh made air history
In a flight across the Atlantic.
There were fights for women's rights.
Elizabeth Cady Stanton, Susan B. Anthony
Led those daring women,
The Suffragists.
(*Curtain opens*. ELIZABETH CADY STANTON *stands on
box*.)
STANTON (*Gesturing*): It is time we women take a stand. We
must no longer be denied the right to vote. We will battle
until victory is achieved. (*Freezes in position*)
13TH NARRATOR: And it was. In 1920 the nineteenth amend-
ment was passed. Women were a part of the democratic proc-
ess. (*Curtain closes*. 13TH NARRATOR *exits*. 14TH
NARRATOR *enters*.)
14TH NARRATOR: But for most,
It was a time
To pursue fun.
Movies with sound,
"Talkies" became the rage.
Dancing The Charleston
Was the nation's pastime.
Flappers and curls . . .
Oldsmobile rides . . .
"The Roaring Twenties."
(14TH NARRATOR *exits*. DANCERS *enter and perform the
Charleston to appropriate music*. DANCERS *exit*. 15TH NAR-
RATOR *enters*.)
15TH NARRATOR: The twenties ended.
A decade of peace had passed.
Depression set in. Americans faced a test.

There were no jobs, no money.
Men selling apples on street corners
Were the common sight now.
(APPLE SELLER *enters slowly, carrying bushel basket. From
the other side of stage* TWO MEN *enter, heads down, moving
slowly. The three figures meet, center.* APPLE SELLER *panto-
mimes peddling apples.* 1ST MAN *refuses;* 2ND MAN *panto-
mimes buying apple.* APPLE SELLER *exits, and* TWO MEN
resume walking. During this scene, CHORUS *sings "Brother,
Can You Spare A Dime?")*
It took a great leader to soothe the nation's fears.
Don't worry, folks. Franklin Delano Roosevelt is here.
(*Curtain opens. Lights go out. Slide of Roosevelt flashes on.
"Happy Days Are Here Again" is heard. Music plays during
following dialogue.*)
Franklin Delano Roosevelt, a man who was strong,
Helped guide this unhappy nation.
Work programs, jobs, a sense of pride—
FDR tried to solve our nation's woes.
Slowly, with work, we recovered,
And FDR became the people's hero.
(*Music stops.* 15TH NARRATOR *exits.* 16TH NARRATOR
enters.)
16TH NARRATOR: But another crisis was on hand. In Europe,
another war, another threat to democracy. We sat back for a
while, sadly watching Europe crumble, until—(*Sound of three
loud tom-tom beats is heard.*) December 7, 1941. Pearl Harbor,
a U.S. naval base in the Hawaiian Islands, was attacked by
Japan. Many died. It was war. FDR wouldn't allow anyone to
destroy this nation's honor. We entered a war with Japan and
joined Europe's battle. Finally, it was 1945. The war was over
in Europe. Our troops were coming home. A few months later
it would be over in the Pacific, but not before America had
uncovered a terrifying new weapon, the atomic bomb.
(DANCERS *enter and perform the Lindy. They exit.* 16TH

NARRATOR *exits.* *Curtain closes.* 17TH NARRATOR *enters before curtain.*)

17TH NARRATOR: Post World War II. . . . It was our job now to maintain peace. The United Nations was formed to help the world keep a permanent peace. And we began a new type of expansion. We began to explore space. This would be our new frontier. Explorer I soared through space, searching. . . .

(17TH NARRATOR *exits.* 18TH NARRATOR *enters.*)

18TH NARRATOR: The fifties . . .

It was a new way of life.

TV was tops.

"It's Howdy Doody time."

"M-I-C-K-E-Y—M-O-U-S-E."

But there were other noises:

"Hey, man, like, cool, Daddy."

Skirts and sweaters, slicked-back duck-tail hair. . . .

"You Ain't Nothin' But a Hound Dog."

The teenager became an American symbol.

It was 1956.

Elvis Presley introduced the world to rock and roll.

(*Curtain opens. A slide of Elvis Presley flashes on screen. Lights come up. Music to "Jailhouse Rock" is heard. DANCERS enter, perform jitterbug, then exit. 18TH NARRATOR exits. 19TH NARRATOR enters. CHORUS sings a few bars of "Camelot."*)

19TH NARRATOR: 1960 . . .

John F. Kennedy, President.

Camelot is a beautiful place where nothing is ever wrong.

Ah, yes, the sixties began as Camelot,

And ended . . . with the nation torn apart.

John F. Kennedy was assassinated.

Then Martin Luther King.

Unrest in the United States had begun.

"All men are created equal. . . . "

This slogan stood for Civil Rights.

"We are a part of America too"—

This was the sound of women's lib.
Yes, those were the events. . . .
So were rioting in the ghettos,
Bloodshed on the campuses.
"Peace," cried the young.
It became an obsession.
And yet, perhaps it was time to settle the score.
Black men and women led on by King
Dared to dream dreams they had never dreamed.
(STUDENTS *enter, carrying signs reading,* PEACE, WOMEN'S
LIB, GET OUT OF VIETNAM, BLACK RIGHTS. MARTIN LUTHER
KING, JR. *enters opposite side.*)
KING: I have a dream. I have a dream that all God's chil-
dren. . . . (KING *and* STUDENTS *meet center. In pantomime*
KING *addresses* STUDENTS *while they motion angrily. Then
in background* CHORUS *sings, "We Shall Overcome." All
freeze until song finishes. Curtain slowly closes.* 19TH NAR-
RATOR *exits.* 20TH NARRATOR *enters.*)
20TH NARRATOR: But, we had made great strides.
Apollo II landed on the moon.
It was one large step for mankind.
And we were cleaning our own house.
We were working together toward
Making all men and women equal.
We were a vibrant nation once again.
The years passed.
It was the seventies.
The American nation revisited its past. . . .
The Bicentennial year 1976.
The heroes of old came to life.
America looked back and smiled.
For with every minute of pain
There was an hour of glory.
America . . . born from a seed,
Grown to a giant oak.

(20TH NARRATOR *exits.* CHORUS *sings, "This Land Is Your Land." UNCLE SAM enters through curtain, center.)*

UNCLE SAM (*To audience*): Over two hundred years old, am I? Why, I feel like a newborn baby. I couldn't think of retirement. There's too much left undone. Disease to conquer, poverty to eliminate, health care for all. Those are my challenges. And there's more. How can we conserve our natural resources? How can we, our mighty nation, help the world realize all people must be treated with dignity? We will find those answers as the century closes, just the way we solved other problems. (*Points to child in audience*) What did you say? No, I'm not going to do it myself. Who's left? Who's able enough? Who can make America the more perfect Union? Why, the solution is simple. Uncle Sam needs you! (*Points into audience, then crosses to side of stage. Lights go off. Curtain opens. "America the Beautiful" is heard. Six slides representing moments in American history flash on screen, then go off. Entire cast marches on and sings "America the Beautiful." At conclusion, performers bow in unison. Curtain closes.)*

THE END

Production Notes

AN AMERICAN STORY

Characters: 12 male; 2 female; 40 or more male or female for Narrators, Town Crier, Colonists, Reporter, Slave, Barbershop Quartet, Apple Seller, Students, Chorus, and Dancers.

Playing Time: 35 minutes.

Costumes: Narrators wear modern dress. Uncle Sam, red, white, and blue suit, and traditional top hat. Town Crier, Colonists, Franklin, Jefferson, Adams, Washington, and Reporter wear stockings, knickers, white shirts, and tri-cornered hats. Abolitionists wear Victorian period costumes. Slave wears torn, cut-off pants, torn shirt, and kerchief. Abraham Lincoln wears top hat and black suit. Barbershop Quartet wears striped jackets and straw hats. Strolling Couple: male is in suit, female in long dress and gloves. Elizabeth Cady Stanton wears long skirt and blouse. Apple Seller and Depression Era Men wear old sports jackets and worn pants and shirts. Martin Luther King, suit and tie. Students, street clothes.

Properties: Bell; parchment; quill pen; box; bushel basket; placards reading, 1775, 1776, VALLEY FORGE, ABOLISH SLAVERY, DOWN WITH SLAVERY, PEACE, WOMEN'S LIB, GET OUT OF VIETNAM, AND BLACK RIGHTS.

Setting: Placed on four angles of stage are four flats—wooden frames covered with muslin, each depicting two figures in costumes representing different successive eras in American fashion, e.g., Colonial, Civil War, Victorian, etc. There is a backdrop which is the projection screen for slides (optional).

Lighting: Lights on and off; optional slides.

Sound: Various musical selections representative of American song and dance through various periods. Recorded music may be substituted for Chorus.

Appendix

The Constitution of the United States

Preamble

WE, the people of the United States, in order to form a more perfect Union, establish justice, insure domestic tranquility, provide for the common defense, promote the general welfare, and secure the blessings of liberty to ourselves and our posterity, do ordain and establish this Constitution for the United States of America.

The Original 7 Articles

ARTICLE I
Section 1. Legislative powers; in whom vested
All legislative powers herein granted shall be vested in a Congress of the United States, which shall consist of a Senate and House of Representatives.

Section 2. House of Representatives, how and by whom chosen Qualifications of a Representative. Representatives and direct taxes, how apportioned. Enumeration. Vacancies to be filled. Power of choosing officers, and of impeachment.
1. The House of Representatives shall be composed of members chosen every second year by the people of the several States, and the elector in each State shall have the qualifications requisite for electors of the most numerous branch of the State Legislature.
2. No person shall be a Representative who shall not have attained the age of twenty-five years, and been seven years a citizen of the United States, and who shall not,

215

when elected, be an inhabitant of that State in which he shall be chosen.

3. Representatives [and direct taxes] {Altered by 16th Amendment} shall be apportioned among the several States which may be included within this Union, according to their respective numbers, [which shall be determined by adding the whole number of free persons, including those bound to service for a term of years, and excluding Indians not taxed, three-fifths of all other persons.] {Altered by 14th Amendment} The actual enumeration shall be made within three years after the first meeting of the Congress of the United States, and within every subsequent term of ten years, in such manner as they shall by law direct. The number of Representatives shall not exceed one for every thirty thousand, but each State shall have at least one Representative; and until such enumeration shall be made, the State of New Hampshire shall be entitled to choose three, Massachusetts eight, Rhode Island and Providence Plantations one, Connecticut five, New York six, New Jersey four, Pennsylvania eight, Delaware one, Maryland six, Virginia ten, North Carolina five, South Carolina five, and Georgia three.

4. When vacancies happen in the representation from any State, the Executive Authority thereof shall issue writs of election to fill such vacancies.

5. The House of Representatives shall choose their Speaker and other officers; and shall have the sole power of impeachment.

Section 3. Senators, how and by whom chosen. How classified. State Executive, when to make temporary appointments, in case, etc. Qualifications of a Senator. President of the Senate, his right to vote. President pro tem., and other officers of the Senate, how chosen. Power to try impeachments. When President is tried, Chief Justice to preside. Sentence.

1. The Senate of the United States shall be composed of two Senators from each State, [chosen by the Legislature thereof,] {Altered by 17th Amendment} for six years; and each Senator shall have one vote.

2. Immediately after they shall be assembled in consequence of the first election, they shall be divided as equally as may be into three classes. The seats of the Senators of the first class shall be vacated at the expiration of the second year, of the second class at the expira-

tion of the fourth year, and of the third class at the expiration of the sixth year, so that one-third may be chosen every second year; [and if vacancies happen by resignation, or otherwise, during the recess of the Legislature of any State, the Executive thereof may make temporary appointments until the next meeting of the Legislature, which shall then fill such vacancies.] {Altered by 17th Amendment}

3. No person shall be a Senator who shall not have attained to the age of thirty years, and been nine years a citizen of the United States, and who shall not, when elected, be an inhabitant of that State for which he shall be chosen.

4. The Vice-President of the United States shall be President of the Senate, but shall have no vote, unless they be equally divided.

5. The Senate shall choose their other officers, and also a President pro tempore, in the absence of the Vice President, or when he shall exercise the office of the President of the United States.

6. The Senate shall have the sole power to try all impeachments. When sitting for that purpose, they shall be on oath or affirmation. When the President of the United States is tried, the Chief Justice shall preside: and no person shall be convicted without the concurrence of two-thirds of the members present.

7. Judgement in cases of impeachment shall not extend further than to removal from office, and disqualification to hold and enjoy any office of honor, trust, or profit under the United States: but the party convicted shall nevertheless be liable and subject to indictment, trial, judgement and punishment, according to law.

Section 4. Times, etc., of holding elections, how prescribed. One session in each year.

1. The times, places and manner of holding elections for Senators and Representatives, shall be prescribed in each State by the Legislature thereof; but the Congress may at any time by law make or alter such regulations, except as to the places of choosing Senators.

2. The Congress shall assemble at least once in every year, and such meeting shall be [on the first Monday in December,] {Altered by 20th Amendment} unless they by law appoint a different day.

Section 5. Membership, Quorum, Adjournments, Rules, Power to punish or expel. Journal. Time of adjournments, how limited, etc.

1. Each House shall be the judge of the elections, returns and qualifications of its own members, and a majority of each shall constitute a quorum to do business; but a smaller number may adjourn from day to day, and may be authorized to compel the attendance of absent members, in such manner, and under such penalties as each House may provide.

2. Each House may determine the rules of its proceedings, punish its members for disorderly behavior, and, with the concurrence of two-thirds, expel a member.

3. Each House shall keep a journal of its proceedings, and from time to time publish the same, excepting such parts as may in their judgement require secrecy; and the yeas and nays of the members of either House on any question shall, at the desire of one-fifth of those present, be entered on the journal.

4. Neither House, during the session of Congress, shall, without the consent of the other, adjourn for more than three days, nor to any other place than that in which the two Houses shall be sitting.

Section 6. Compensation, Privileges, Disqualification in certain cases.

1. The Senators and Representatives shall receive a compensation for their services, to be ascertained by law, and paid out of the Treasury of the United States. They shall in all cases, except treason, felony and breach of the peace, be privileged from arrest during their attendance at the session of their respective Houses, and in going to and returning from the same; and for any speech or debate in either House, they shall not be questioned in any other place.

2. No Senator or Representative shall, during the time for which he was elected, be appointed to any civil office under the authority of the United States, which shall have increased during such time; and no person holding any office under the United States, shall be a member of either House during his continuance in office.

Section 7. House to originate all revenue bills. Veto. Bill may be passed by two-thirds of each House, notwithstanding, etc. Bill, not returned in ten days to become a law. Provisions as to orders, concurrent resolutions, etc.

1. All bills for raising revenue shall originate in the House of Representatives; but the Senate may propose or concur with amendments as on other bills.

2. Every bill which shall have passed the House of Representatives and the Senate, shall, before it become a law, be presented to the president of the United States; if he approve, he shall sign it, but if not, he shall return it, with his objections, to that house in which it shall have originated, who shall enter the objections at large on their journal, and proceed to reconsider it. If after such reconsideration, two thirds of that house shall agree to pass the bill, it shall be sent, together with the objections, to the other house, by which it shall likewise be reconsidered, and if approved by two-thirds of that house, it shall become a law. But in all such cases the votes of both houses shall be determined by yeas and nays, and the names of the persons voting for and against the bill shall be entered on the journal of each house respectively. If any bill shall not be returned by the president within ten days (Sundays excepted) after it shall have been presented to him, the same shall be a law, in like manner as if he had signed it, unless the Congress by their adjournment prevent its return, in which case it shall not be a law.

3. Every order, resolution, or vote to which the concurrence of the Senate and House of Representatives may be necessary (except on a question of adjournment) shall be presented to the president of the United States; and before the same shall take effect, shall be approved by him, or, being disapproved by him, shall be re-passed by two-thirds of the Senate and House of Representatives, according to the rules and limitations prescribed in the case of a bill.

Section 8. Powers of Congress

The Congress shall have the power

1. To lay and collect taxes, duties, imposts and excises, to pay the debts and provide for the common defence and general welfare of the United States; but all duties, imposts and excises shall be uniform throughout the United States;

2. To borrow money on the credit of the United States;

3. To regulate commerce with foreign nations, and among the several States, and with the Indian tribes;

4. To establish an uniform rule of naturalization, and uniform laws on the subject of bankruptcies throughout the United States;

5. To coin money, regulate the value thereof, and of foreign coin, and fix the standard of weights and measures;

6. To provide for the punishment of counterfeiting the securities and current coin of the United States;

7. To establish post-offices and post-roads;

8. To promote the progress of science and useful arts, by securing for limited times to authors and inventors the exclusive right to their respective writings and discoveries;

9. To constitute tribunals inferior to the supreme court;

10. To define and punish piracies and felonies committed on the high seas, and offences against the law of nations;

11. To declare war, grant letters of marque and reprisal, and make rules concerning captures on land and water;

12. To raise and support armies, but no appropriation of money to that use shall be for a longer term than two years;

13. To provide and maintain a navy;

14. To make rules for the government and regulation of the land and naval forces;

15. To provide for calling forth the militia to execute the laws of the union, suppress insurrections and repel invasions;

16. To provide for organizing, arming and disciplining the militia, and for governing such part of them as may be employed in the service of the United States, reserving to the States respectively, the appointment of the officers, and the authority of training the militia according to the discipline prescribed by Congress;

17. To exercise exclusive legislation in all cases whatsoever, over such district (not exceeding ten miles square) as may, by cession of particular States, and the acceptance of Congress, become the seat of the government of the United States, and to exercise like authority over all places purchased by the consent of the legislature of the State in which the same shall be, for the erection of forts, magazines, arsenals, dock-yards, and other needful buildings;—And,

18. To make all laws which shall be necessary and proper for carrying into execution the foregoing powers, and all other powers vested by this constitution in the

government of the United States, or in any department or officer thereof.

Section 9. Provision as to migration or importation of certain persons. Habeas Corpus, Bills of attainder, etc. Taxes, how apportioned. No export duty. No commercial preference. Money, how drawn from Treasury, etc. No titular nobility. Officers not to receive presents, etc.

1. The migration or importation of such persons as any of the States now existing shall think proper to admit, shall not be prohibited by the Congress prior to the year 1808, but a tax or duty may be imposed on such importations, not exceeding 10 dollars for each person.

2. The privilege of the writ of habeas corpus shall not be suspended, unless when in cases of rebellion or invasion the public safety may require it.

3. No bill of attainder or ex post facto law shall be passed.

4. [No capitation, or other direct tax shall be laid unless in proportion to the census or enumeration herein before directed to be taken.] {Altered by 16th Amendment}

5. No tax or duty shall be laid on articles exported from any State.

6. No preference shall be given by any regulation of commerce or revenue to the ports of one State over those of another: nor shall vessels bound to, or from one State, be obliged to enter, clear, or pay duties in another.

7. No money shall be drawn from the treasury but in consequence of appropriations made by law; and a regular Statement and account of the receipts and expenditures of all public money shall be published from time to time.

8. No title of nobility shall be granted by the United States: And no person holding any office or profit or trust under them, shall, without the consent of the Congress, accept of any present, emolument, office, or title, of any kind whatever, from any king, prince, or foreign State.

Section 10. States prohibited from the exercise of certain powers.

1. No State shall enter into any treaty, alliance, or confederation; grant letters of marque and reprisal; coin money; emit bills of credit; make anything but gold and silver coin a tender in payment of debts; pass any bill of attainder, ex post facto law, or law impairing the obligation of contracts, or grant any title of nobility.

2. No State shall, without the consent of the Congress, lay any imposts or duties on imports or exports, except what may be absolutely necessary for executing its inspection laws; and the net produce of all duties and imposts, laid by any State on imports or exports, shall be for the use of the treasury of the United States; and all such laws shall be subject to the revision and control of the Congress.

3. No State shall, without the consent of Congress, lay any duty of tonnage, keep troops, or ships of war in time of peace, enter into any agreement or compact with another State, or with a foreign power, or engage in a war, unless actually invaded, or in such imminent danger as will not admit of delay.

ARTICLE II

Section 1. President: his term of office. Electors of President; number and how appointed. Electors to vote on same day. Qualification of President. On whom his duties devolve in case of his removal, death, etc. President's compensation. His oath of office.

1. The Executive power shall be vested in a President of the United States of America. He shall hold office during the term of four years, and together with the Vice President, chosen for the same term, be elected as follows

2. [Each State] {Altered by 23rd Amendment} shall appoint, in such manner as the Legislature may direct, a number of electors, equal to the whole number of Senators and Representatives to which the State may be entitled in the Congress: but no Senator or Representative, or person holding an office of trust or profit under the United States, shall be appointed an elector

[The electors shall meet in their respective States, and vote by ballot for two persons, of whom one at least shall not be an inhabitant of the same State with themselves. And they shall make a list of all the persons voted for each; which list they shall sign and certify, and transmit sealed to the seat of Government of the United States, directed to the President of the Senate. The President of the Senate shall, in the presence of the Senate and House of Representatives, open all the certificates, and the votes shall then be counted. The person having the greatest number of votes shall be the President, if such number be a majority of the whole number of electors appointed; and if there be more than one who have such majority, and have an equal number of votes, then the House of Representatives shall immediately choose by ballot one of them for President; and if no person have a majority, then from the five highest on the list the said House shall in like manner choose the President. But in choosing the President, the votes shall be taken by States, the representation from each State having one vote; a quorum for this purpose shall consist of a member or members from two-thirds of the States, and a majority of all the States shall be necessary to a choice. In every case, after the choice of the President, the person having the greatest number of votes of the electors shall be the Vice President. But if there should remain two or more who have equal votes, the Senate shall choose from them by ballot the Vice President.] {Altered by 12th Amendment}

3. The Congress may determine the time of choosing the electors, and the day on which they shall give their votes; which day shall be the same throughout the United States.

4. No person except a natural born citizen, or a citizen of the United States, at the time of the adoption of this Constitution, shall be eligible to the office of President; neither shall any person be eligible to that office who shall not have attained to the age of thirty-five years, and been fourteen years a resident within the United States.

5. [In case of the removal of the President from office, or of his death, resignation, or inability to discharge the powers and duties of the said office, the same shall devolve on the Vice President, and the Congress may by law provide for the case of removal, death, resignation, or inability, both of the President and Vice President, declaring what officer shall then act as President, and such officer shall act accordingly, until the disability be removed, or a President shall be elected.] {Altered by 25th Amendment}

6. The President shall, at Stated times, receive for his services, a compensation, which shall neither be increased nor diminished during the period for which he shall have been elected, and he shall not receive within that period any other emolument from the United States, or any of them.

7. Before he enter on the execution of his office, he shall take the following oath or affirmation:

"I do solemnly swear (or affirm) that I will faithfully execute the office of the President of the United States, and will to the best of my ability, preserve, protect and defend the Constitution of the United States."

Section 2. President to be Commander-in-Chief.
He may require power. Nomination of certain officers. When President may fill vacancies.

1. The President shall be Commander-in-Chief of the
Army and Navy of the United States, and of the militia
of the several States, when called into the actual service
of the United States; he may require the opinion, in writing, of the principal officer in each of the executive departments, upon any subject relating to the duties of their
respective offices, and he shall have power to grant re-
prieves and pardons for offenses against against the
United States, except in cases of impeachment.

2. He shall have power, by and with the advice and
consent of the Senate, to make treaties, provided two-
thirds of the Senators present concur; and he shall nomi-
nate, and by and with the advice and consent of the Senate, shall appoint ambassadors, other public ministers
and consuls, judges of the Supreme Court, and all other
officers of the United States, whose appointments are not
herein otherwise provided for, and which shall be established by law: but the Congress may by law vest the appointment of such inferior officers, as they think proper,
in the President alone, in the courts of law, or in the heads
of departments.

3. The President shall have the power to fill up all vacancies that may may happen during the recess of the
Senate, by granting commissions, which shall expire at
the end of their next session.

Section 3. President shall communicate to Congress. He may convene and adjourn Congress, in
case of disagreement, etc. Shall receive ambassadors, execute laws, and commission officers.

He shall from time to time give to the Congress information of the State of the Union, and recommend to their
consideration such measures as he shall judge necessary
and expedient; he may, on extraordinary occasions, convene both Houses, or either of them, and in case of disagreement between them, with respect to the time of
adjournment, he may adjourn them to such time as he
shall think proper; he may receive ambassadors, and
other public ministers; he shall take care that the laws
be faithfully executed, and shall commission all the officers of the United States.

Section 4. All civil offices forfeited for certain
crimes.

The President, Vice President, and all civil officers of the United States, shall be removed from office on impeachment for, and conviction of, treason, bribery, or other high crimes and misdemeanors.

ARTICLE III

Section 1. Judicial powers. Tenure. Compensation.

The judicial power of the United States, shall be vested in one supreme court, and in such inferior courts as the Congress may, from time to time, ordain and establish. The judges, both of the supreme and inferior courts, shall hold their offices during good behaviour, and shall, at Stated times, receive for their services a compensation, which shall not be diminished during their continuance in office.

Section 2. Judicial power; to what cases it extends. Original jurisdiction of Supreme Court Appellate. Trial by Jury, etc. Trial, where.

1. The judicial power shall extend to all cases, in law and equity, arising under this constitution, the laws of the United States, and treaties made, or which shall be made under their authority; to all cases affecting ambassadors, other public ministers and consuls; to all cases of admiralty and maritime jurisdiction; to controversies to which the United States shall be a party; [to controversies between two or more States, between a State and citizens of another State, between citizens of different States, between citizens of the same State, claiming lands under grants of different States, and between a State, or the citizens thereof, and foreign States, citizens or subjects.] {Altered by 11th Amendment}

2. In all cases affecting ambassadors, other public ministers and consuls, and those in which a State shall be a party, the supreme court shall have original jurisdiction. In all the other cases before-mentioned, the supreme court shall have appellate jurisdiction, both as to law and fact, with such exceptions, and under such regulations as the Congress shall make.

3. The trial of all crimes, except in cases of impeachment, shall be by jury; and such trial shall be held in the State where the said crimes shall have been committed; but when not committed within any State, the trial shall

be at such place or places as the Congress may by law have directed.

Section 3. Treason defined. Proof of. Punishment

1. Treason against the United States shall consist only in levying war against them, or in adhering to their enemies, giving them aid and comfort. No person shall be convicted of treason unless on the testimony of two witnesses to the same overt act, or on confession in open court.

2. The Congress shall have power to declare the punishment of treason, but no attainder of treason shall work corruption of blood, or forfeiture, except during the life of the person attainted.

ARTICLE IV

Section 1. Each State to give credit to the public acts, etc., of every other State.

Full faith and credit shall be given in each State to the public acts, records and judicial proceedings of every other State. And the Congress may by general laws prescribe the manner in which such acts, records and proceedings shall be proved, and the effect thereof.

Section 2. Privileges of citizens of each State. Fugitives from Justice to be delivered up. Persons held to service having escaped, to be delivered up.

1. The citizens of each State shall be entitled to all privileges and immunities of citizens in the several States. {See the 14th Amendment}

2. A person charged in any State with treason, felony, or other crime, who shall flee justice, and be found in another State, shall, on demand of the executive authority of the State from which he fled, be delivered up, to be removed to the State having jurisdiction of the crime.

3. [No person held to service or labour in one State, under the laws thereof, escaping into another, shall, in consequence of any law or regulation therein, be discharged from such service or labour, but shall be delivered up on claim of the party to whom such service or labour may be due.] {Altered by 13th Amendment}

Section 3. Admission of new States. Power of Congress over territory and other property.

1. New States may be admitted by the Congress into this union; but no new State shall be formed or erected within the jurisdiction of any other State, nor any State be formed by the junction of two or more States, without the consent of the legislatures of the States concerned, as well as of the Congress.

2. The Congress shall have power to dispose of and make all needful rules and regulations respecting the territory or other property belonging to the United States; and nothing in this constitution shall be so construed as to prejudice any claims of the United States, or of any particular State.

Section 4. Republican form of government guaranteed. Each State to be protected.

The United States shall guarantee to every State in this union, a republican form of government, and shall protect each of them against invasion; and on application of the legislature, or of the executive (when the legislature cannot be convened), against domestic violence.

ARTICLE V

Constitution: how amended; proviso.

The Congress, whenever two-thirds of both houses shall deem it necessary, shall propose amendments to this constitution, or on the application of the legislatures of two-thirds of the several States, shall call a convention for proposing amendments, which, in either case, shall be valid to all intents and purposes, as part of this constitution, when ratified by the legislatures of three-fourths of the several States, or by conventions in three-fourths thereof, as the one or the other mode of ratification may be proposed by the Congress: Provided, that no amendment which may be made prior to the year 1808, shall in any manner affect the first and fourth clauses in the ninth section of the first article; and that no State, without its consent, shall be deprived of its equal suffrage in the Senate.

ARTICLE VI

Certain debts, etc., declared valid. Supremacy of Constitution, treaties, and laws of the United States. Oath to support Constitution, by whom taken. No religious tests.

1. All debts contracted and engagements entered into, before the adoption of this constitution, shall be as valid against the United States under this constitution, as under the confederation.

2. This constitution, and the laws of the United States which shall be made in pursuance thereof; and all treaties made, or which shall be made, under the authority of the United States shall be the supreme law of the land; and the judges in every State shall be bound thereby, any thing in the constitution or laws of any State to the contrary notwithstanding.

3. The senators and representatives before-mentioned, and the members of the several State legislatures, and all executive and judicial officers, both of the United States and of the several States, shall be bound by oath or affirmation, to support this constitution; but no religious test shall ever be required as a qualification to any office or public trust under the United States.

ARTICLE VII

The ratification of the conventions of nine States, shall be sufficient for the establishment of this constitution between the States so ratifying the same.

Done in convention by the unanimous consent of the States present the Seventeenth day of September in the year of our Lord one thousand seven hundred and eighty seven, and of the independence of the United States of America the Twelfth. In witness whereof we have hereunto subscribed our names.

George Washington, President and deputy from Virginia.

New Hampshire—John Langdon, Nicholas Gilman.

Massachusetts—Nathaniel Gorham, Rufus King.

Connecticut—Wm. Saml. Johnson, Roger Sherman.

New York—Alexander Hamilton.

New Jersey—Wil: Livingston, David Brearley, Wm. Paterson, Jona: Dayton.

Pennsylvania—B. Franklin, Thomas Mifflin, Robt. Morris, Geo. Clymer, Thos, FitzSimons, Jared Ingersoll, James Wilson, Gouv. Morris.

Delaware—Geo: Read, Gunning Bedford Jun., John Dickinson, Richard Bassett, Jaco: Broom.

Maryland—James McHenry, Daniel of Saint Thomas' Jenifer, Danl. Carroll.

Virginia—John Blair, James Madison Jr.

North Carolina—Wm. Blount, Rich'd. Dobbs Spaight, Hugh Williamson.

South Carolina—J. Rutledge, Charles Cotesworth Pinckney, Charles Pinckney, Pierce Butler.

Georgia—William Few, Abr. Baldwin.

Attest: William Jackson, Secretary.

The Ten Original Amendments: The Bill of Rights

Passed by Congress September 25, 1789.
Ratified December 15, 1791.

AMENDMENT I

Religious establishment prohibited. Freedom of speech, of the press, and right to petition.

Congress shall make no law respecting an establishment of religion, or prohibiting the free exercise thereof; or abridging the freedom of speech, or of the press; or the right of the people peaceably to assemble, and to petition the Government for a redress of grievances.

AMENDMENT II

Right to keep and bear arms.

A well-regulated militia, being necessary to the security of a free State, the right of the people to keep and bear arms, shall not be infringed.

AMENDMENT III

Conditions for soldiers.

No soldier shall, in time of peace be quartered in any house, without the consent of the owner, nor in time of war, but in a manner to be prescribed by law.

AMENDMENT IV

Right of search and seizure regulated.

The right of the people to be secure in their persons, houses, papers, and effects, against unreasonable searches and seizures, shall not be violated, and no warrants shall issue, but upon probable cause, supported by oath or affirmation, and particularly describing the place to be searched, and the persons or things to be seized.

AMENDMENT V

Provisions concerning prosecution. Trial and punishment—private property not to be taken for public use without compensation.

No person shall be held to answer for a capital, or otherwise infamous crime, unless on a presentment or indictment of a Grand Jury, except in cases arising in the land or naval forces, or in the militia, when in actual service in time of war or public danger; nor shall any person be subject for the same offense to be twice put in jeopardy of life or limb; nor shall be compelled in any criminal case to be a witness against himself, nor be deprived of life, liberty, or property, without due process of law; nor shall private property be taken for public use without just compensation.

AMENDMENT VI
Right to speedy trial, witnesses, etc.

In all criminal prosecutions, the accused shall enjoy the right to a speedy and public trial, by an impartial jury of the State and district wherein the crime shall have been committed, which district shall have been previously ascertained by law, and to be informed of the nature and cause of the accusation; to be confronted with the witnesses against him; to have compulsory process for obtaining witnesses in his favor, and to have the assistance of counsel for his defense.

AMENDMENT VII
Right of trial by jury

In suits at common law, where the value in controversy shall exceed twenty dollars, the right of trial by jury shall be preserved, and no fact tried by a jury shall be otherwise reexamined in any court of the United States, than according to the rules of the common law.

AMENDMENT VIII
Excessive bail or fines and cruel punishment prohibited.

Excessive bail shall not be required, nor excessive fines imposed, nor cruel and unusual punishments inflicted.

AMENDMENT IX
Rule of construction of Constitution.

The enumeration in the Constitution, of certain rights, shall not be construed to deny or disparage others retained by the people.

AMENDMENT X
Rights of States under Constitution

The powers not delegated to the United States by the Constitution, nor prohibited by it to the States, are reserved to the States respectively, or to the people.